W9-CDB-594

Computer Supported Cooperative Work

Springer

*London
Berlin
Heidelberg
New York
Barcelona
Hong Kong
Milan
Paris
Singapore
Tokyo*

Reza Hazemi and Stephen Hailes (Eds)

The Digital University – Building a Learning Community

With 29 Figures

 Springer

BOWLING GREEN STATE
UNIVERSITY LIBRARIES

Reza Hazemi, BEng, MSc, PhD
reza.hazemi@rhc.demon.co.uk

Stephen Hailes, MA, PhD
Department of Computer Science, University College London,
Gower Street, London, WC1E 6BT

Series Editors

Dan Diaper, PhD, MBCS
Head, Department of Computing, School of Design, Engineering and Computing,
Bournemouth University, Talbot Campus, Fern Barrow, Poole, Dorset BH12 5BB, UK

Colston Sanger
Shottersley Research Limited, Little Shottersley, Farnham Lane
Haslemere, Surrey GU27 1HA, UK

British Library Cataloguing in Publication Data
Hazemi, Reza, 1966-
    The digital university : building a learning community. –
    (Computer supported cooperative work)
    1. Computer-assisted instruction 2. Universities and colleges
    - Data processing 3. Education, higher – Data processing
    4. Education, higher – Computer network resources
    5. Universities and colleges – Computer network resources
    I. Title II. Hailes, Stephen, 1965-
    378'.00285
    ISBN 1852334789

Library of Congress Cataloging-in-Publication Data
A catalog record for this book is available from the Library of Congress

Apart from any fair dealing for the purposes of research or private study, or criticism or review, as permitted under the Copyright, Designs and Patents Act 1988, this publication may only be reproduced, stored or transmitted, in any form or by any means, with the prior permission in writing of the publishers, or in the case of reprographic reproduction in accordance with the terms of licences issued by the Copyright Licensing Agency. Enquiries concerning reproduction outside those terms should be sent to the publishers.

ISBN 1-85233-478-9 Springer-Verlag London Berlin Heidelberg
a member of BertelsmannSpringer Science+Business Media GmbH
http://www.springer.co.uk

© Springer-Verlag London Limited 2002
Printed in Great Britain

The use of registered names, trademarks etc. in this publication does not imply, even in the absence of a specific statement, that such names are exempt from the relevant laws and regulations and therefore free for general use.

The publisher makes no representation, express or implied, with regard to the accuracy of the information contained in this book and cannot accept any legal responsibility or liability for any errors or omissions that may be made.

Typesetting: Camera ready by editors
Printed and bound at the Athenæum Press Ltd., Gateshead Tyne & Wear
34/3830-543210 Printed on acid-free paper SPIN 10834354

Contents

The Contributors

Gregory D. Abowd

Associate Professor, College of Computing & GVU Center, Georgia Institute of Technology, Atlanta, GA, 30332-0280, USA.

abowd@cc.gatech.edu

Susan Armitage

Learning Technology Development Officer, Higher Education Development Centre, Information Systems Services, Lancaster University, Lancs., LA1 4YW, UK.

s.armitage@lancaster.ac.uk

Jason A. Brotherton

College of Computing & GVU Center, Georgia Institute of Technology, Atlanta, GA, 30332-0280, USA.

brothert@cc.gatech.edu

Mark Bryson

Collaborative Learning Technology Support Officer, Higher Education Development Centre, Lancaster University, Lancs., LA1 4YW, UK.

m.bryson@notes.lancs.ac.uk

Mark D'Cruz

City University Business School, Frobisher Crescent, Barbican Centre, London, EC2Y 8HB, UK.

s/313@city.ac.uk

Kristina Edström

KTH Learning Lab, SE-100 44 Stockholm, Sweden

kristina@it.kth.se

Graham R. Gibbs

Department of Behavioural Sciences, University of Huddersfield, Queensgate, Huddersfield, HD1 3DH, UK.

G.R.Gibbs@hud.ac.uk

Stephen Hailes

Department of Computer Science, University College London, Gower Street, London, WC1E 6BT, UK.

S.Hailes@cs.ucl.ac.uk

Christopher Harris

Department of Computer Science, University College London, Gower Street, London, WC1E 6BT, UK.

christopher.harris@bigfoot.com

Reza Hazemi

reza.hazemi@rhc.demon.co.uk

Clive Holtham

Faculty of Management, City University Business School, Frobisher Crescent, Barbican Centre, London, EC2Y 8HB, UK.

C.W.Holtham@city.ac.uk

Ismail Ismail

Serco Usability Services, 22 Hand Court, London, WC1V 6JF, UK.

ismail.ismail@usability.serco.com

Lisa Kimball

Executive Producer, Group Jazz, 5335 Wisconsin Ave. NW, Suite 440, Washington, DC 20015, USA.

lisa@groupjazz.com

J. Kirakowski

Human Factors Research Group, University College, Cork, Ireland.

jzk@ucc.ie

Brian R. Mitchell

Director, Management Systems Division, University College London, Gower Street, London, WC1E 6BT, UK.

B.Mitchell@ucl.ac.uk

Peter Monthienvichienchai

Department of Computer Science, University College London, Gower Street, London, WC1E 6BT, UK.

P.Monthienvichienchai@cs.ucl.ac.uk

Kent Norman

Department of Psychology, University of Maryland, College Park, MD 20742-4411, USA.

Kent_Norman@lap.umd.edu

Martina Angela Sasse

Department of Computer Science, University College London, Gower Street, London, WC1E 6BT, UK.

A.Sasse@cs.ucl.ac.uk

Ben Shneiderman

Founding Director, Human-Computer Interaction Laboratory, Department of Computer Science, University of Maryland, College Park, MD 20742, USA.

ben@cs.umd.edu

Jacqueline Taylor

School of Design, Engineering & Computing, Bournemouth University, Talbot Campus, Fern Barrow, Poole, BH12 5BB, UK.

jtaylor@bournemouth.ac.uk

Ashok Tiwari

Department of Computing, Faculty of Engineering and Information Sciences, University of Hertfordshire, Hatfield Campus, College Lane, Hatfield, Herts, AL10 9AB, UK.

A.Tiwari@herts.ac.uk

Philip Uys

PO Box 220, Waikanae, New Zealand

philip.uys@globe-online.com

Claude Viéville

Laboratoire Trigone - Equipe NOCE, Université des Sciences et Technologies de Lille 1, Bâtiment B6 - Cite scientifique, 59655 Villeneuve d'Ascq CEDEX - France

Claude.Vieville@univ-lille1.fr

Richard Wheeldon

Department of Computer Science, University College London, Gower Street, London, WC1E 6BT, UK.
r.wheeldon@cs.ucl.ac.uk

Foreword

Ben Shneiderman

The turbulence generated by the integration of information technology into higher education provokes more conversations than the weather. The hot winds of hyperpromises and the cold front of angry skeptics are clouding the judgment of administrators, faculty members, and national planners. A clear forecast is not likely to appear until implementations are in place and thoughtful evaluations are conducted.

This edited collection points the way towards more clear thinking by presenting detailed reports about promising projects and a hint of the thoughtful evaluations that will be so important in the coming years. Multi-level evaluations will be necessary for developers to refine their user interfaces, for professors to adjust their teaching, and for administrators to understand how university life is being changed. The changes implied by the digital university are nicely categorized by the Dearing Report's four areas of activity: teaching, research, systems support, and administration. First generation collaborative software tools are already being applied in all four areas, and they are likely to become more sophisticated, integrated, and ubiquitous. Evaluating the impact of these tools in each area will be a prime occupation for several decades.

Evaluating teaching technologies has always been a challenge because adequate theories were lacking, appropriate controls were difficult to ensure, and reliable metrics were hard to identify. Furthermore, the introduction of new teaching technologies has usually resulted in changes to the curriculum, or at least the actual outcomes, thereby invalidating the existing student assessment tools. For example, the introduction of collaborative methods in software engineering courses shifts the emphasis on to teamwork and communication skills, which are rarely measured by solitary programming tasks on tests. Secondly, collaborative methods often increase student retention, making comparisons with other courses that have high drop-out rates difficult.

Still the benefits of evaluation can be enormous for individual projects as well as for rapid progress in this field. Anecdotes and case studies from developers of new tools are a natural starting point, but these tend to focus on self-serving success stories. Outside evaluators and subjective evaluations questionnaire results from students and faculty are a natural next step, which some of the authors in this volume have done. Logging usage and interviewing students, to understand which features get used and where users run into error messages, are simple low cost steps that provide valuable insights for refinement. We've often been surprised that features we as developers thought were terrific turned out to be useless or too complex. Formal assessments based on a theory-driven hypothesis-testing approach can produce important controlled empirical studies. These require more substantial resources but the payoffs are generalizable insights and publishable results that could influence many developers and theorists.

Each course, informal assessment, or quantitative evaluation requires a re-evaluation of the purpose of education. As the answers swing from information accumulation to process-oriented capabilities, the metrics for success change. Educators increasingly talk about learning to learn, critical thinking skills, self-awareness, and capacity to participate in work environments, neighborhood (or online) communities, and democratic processes. Students need to be able to identify problems, understand existing solutions, explore creative possibilities, consult with peers and mentors, and then implement and disseminate results. This active-learning inquiry-based approach fits well with collaborative methods and service-orientation, but educators are still struggling to assess collaboration.

Like several of the authors in this volume, I promote team projects to accomplish ambitious goals, and add the requirement that the projects be done for someone outside the classroom. This Relate-Create-Donate philosophy [Relate-Create-Donate: An educational philosophy for the cyber-generation, *Computers & Education* 31, 1 (1998), 25-39] has been useful to me in shaping undergraduate and graduate courses, and effective for others with younger and older students.

I believe in the concept of Open Projects in which student work is on the web and students get a grade for how thoughtful they are in suggesting improvements to their colleagues. Then there is a 72 hours revision period before I do my grading. Projects are published on the Web for everyone to see (you can see my students' projects of the past 8 years on the Web by starting at http://www.otal.umd.edu/SHORE2001/ and my summary is at http://www.cs.umd.edu/hcil/relate_create_donate/).

Assessments can then include the intended audience for class projects, as well as the project participants who can contribute peer reviews. Such multi-level evaluations offer richer feedback to guide teachers and students. Questionnaires and interviews with teachers and students can include process improvement questions. Online logging gives useful feedback about the utilization of email, listservs, web sites, and specialized educational software.

Documenting the benefits of these novel teaching/learning methods will help to refine them and overcome the resistance to change in many teachers and students. Some of that resistance is appropriate, and sometimes live lectures are an excellent form of education. Rigorous evaluations of collaborative methods will help promoters of digital universities to get past their wishful thinking, develop more successful strategies, and help calm the turbulence.

Prof. Ben Shneiderman,

July 23, 2001

Chapter 1

Introduction

Reza Hazemi and Stephen Hailes

1.1 The Need

A recent report by Lord Ron Dearing[1] and the National Committee of Inquiry into Higher Education published recently includes recommendations on how the purposes, shape, structure and funding of higher education should develop to meet the needs of the United Kingdom over the next 20 years. While this review is aimed specifically at UK higher education, there is nothing particularly special about the UK system in respect of the need continually to increase efficiency. As a result, many of the report's conclusions are applicable in an international context.

In his report, Sir Ron notes that:

"A sustained effort to improve the effective and efficient use of resources by institutions is required to secure the long term future of an expanding higher education system."

He goes on to note the importance of adopting suitable national and local Communications and Information Technology (C&IT) strategies as a major factor in achieving this aim. At the time of the Dearing report, C&IT spending was estimated as being of the order of £1 billion (or 10% of the total higher education turnover). Since then, further short-term money has been made available, partly for use in enhancing C&IT infrastructure. This perhaps is a reflection of the fact that "the full potential of C&IT in managing institutions has also yet to be realized" but that, when it is, "There are likely to be significant cost benefits from its increased use."

As can be seen from current expenditure, institutions are already recognizing the importance of C&IT. Indeed, of 50 institutions responding to a survey conducted by the Universities and Colleges Information Systems Association (UCISA), over

---

[1] http://www.leeds.ac.uk/educol/ncihe

75% already have in place an integrated C&IT system in each of the areas of personnel management, finance and accounting, and student registration. However, only 26% of the same institutions use such systems in the management of research and consultancy and the collection of institutional statistics, amongst other important functions. They admit that they are severely underutilizing system capacity, even in areas where utilization is highest, leading to Sir Ron's conclusion that universities are "not near to" exploiting the potential of C&IT systems.

As a result of the above considerations it is clear that not only will the absolute levels of investment in C&IT have to remain high, but that what there will have to be spent ever more intelligently. Part of this will come through top-down leadership, the setting of national and institutional goals, but these will have to be realized through the development of appropriate strategies, including the training of higher and middle management in using and developing the potential of C&IT, and consideration of open standards.

1.2   The Solution

In this book, we consider one of the major ways in which the efficiency of higher education institutions can be increased from a number of different perspectives. Specifically, we choose to address the issue of collaboration, using what are known technically as *asynchronous* collaborative techniques. In plain English, these techniques are simply those used within a C&IT setting to allow some number of people to perform some task jointly, without the requirement that those people work in parallel[2]. In its simplest form, this involves the exchange of electronic mail where one person hands over a partly completed task to another.

So, why have we chosen to look at the collaborative aspects of C&IT policy and why, specifically, have we chosen to look at asynchronous collaboration? Firstly, as Sir Ron Dearing notes:

"Collaboration matters. It may, in some cases, make the difference between institutional success and failure. But it needs to apply throughout institutions, from individuals to management teams."

Many of the tasks which universities perform are inherently collaborative: the teaching and learning process involves at least two parties - the lecturer and the student; research normally involves several people, possibly split across different institutions, maybe internationally; and administration inherently involves the administrator and the subject of the administration. Thus, in seeking to increase the efficiency of institutions, it is vital that we consider the potential for, and costs of, different collaborative mechanisms. In fact, we believe that the greatest scope for increase in efficiency specifically lies with asynchronous collaboration. The reason for this belief is that many of the synchronous activities within higher education

---

[2] In contrast, *synchronous collaboration* is typified by video conferencing-type applications, where several people must simultaneously work on the same task for it to have any meaning.

institutions are currently conducted face-to-face without great difficulty, in view of the proximity of those involved. With the widening of the student base and the consequent need for distance learning, and with the increasing inter-institutional cooperation required by Dearing, this may change, though the numbers involved in such activities will remain small compared to those still engaged in face-to-face meetings. On the other hand, most of the significant and increasing administrative load borne throughout universities, for example, is inherently asynchronous in nature, with different subtasks being performed in a linear fashion by those with the necessary information and expertise.

We aim to show throughout this book that there is a significant role for asynchronous collaboration within higher education institutions, that its current limited exploitation can usefully be expanded, and that there are exciting technical developments which promise the potential to increase both cost-effectiveness and the quality of the student experience well into the future. Although this book is (intentionally) rather forward-looking, we recognize that in order for the full potential of any form of C&IT collaborative techniques to be realized, both money and political will within HEI management, the funding bodies, and government will be required. Again, the Dearing report tends to support our view:

"There needs to be more encouragement within institutions, for example to support faculty teams to develop their ideas and evaluate the costs and potential of collaboration, and incentives to staff. At institutional level too, governing bodies should include a review of collaboration in the review of performance recommended in the Dearing Report (Chapter 15). At national level, there is scope for more imaginative funding arrangements which would help institutions to get over the initial costs that can sometimes arise from collaboration before the longer term economies arise. We think that the Funding Bodies might usefully consider bringing forward part of institutions' allocations and offsetting this against future funding, where institutions make strongly-founded proposals with clear educational and financial benefits that cannot otherwise be realized. It will also be important that the new quality assurance arrangements to be developed by the Quality Assurance Agency do not discourage collaboration between institutions where this would lead to improvements in learning and teaching."

The extent to which these laudable aims are realized will largely determine the actual, rather than potential, benefits given by collaboration, and the C&IT techniques which are used to support them.

1.3   The Structure of the Book

In this book we have concentrated on asynchronous collaboration in a learning environment. We look into the future, at the challenges faced by universities and how the technology can be used to meet these challenges.

We have tried to cover policies, market and management of asynchronous collaboration and the technical section covers four main topics of principles, experiences, evaluation and benefits of asynchronous collaboration but there is an overlap between various sections.

Chapter 2 is a tutorial chapter. It examines the functions of a university, which include teaching, research, support and administration, and examines how these functions could be performed more efficiently. The changes in performance of these functions could result in what we term reinventing the academy. The Dearing report which forms the basis of policies made by universities for the next few years has been highly influential in writing this chapter, which also contains some reflections on progress made since its publication.

Chapters 3, 4 and 5 look at managing distance learning and the challenges faced by the universities. Kimball argues that teaching style and strategies impact the quality of learning in distance learning more than the technology itself. She argues that there is a need and a challenge to change the process of teaching and learning in distance education. Norman argues that in order to support quality education, principled models of interaction, user interface design guidelines, and policies for management of interaction and collaboration have to be used. He then presents a model and a metaphor for this purpose, and describes how the interaction between students and teachers could be managed. Uys introduces networked education and networked education management. He discusses networking, student focus, globalization, flexibility, boundary orientation and the information base of networked educational management.

Chapters 6 and 7 describe distance learning systems. Brotherton and Abowd describe eClass, a system for capturing live lectures for later use by students and lecturers. They discuss the motivation behind the design of eClass and describe its structure. Gibbs describes a web-based object oriented tool called coMentor which supports private group-work areas, role-playing, annotation and threaded discussion, concept mapping and synchronous chat. He looks at both synchronous and asynchronous support in a text-based virtual environment.

In Chapter 8, Holtham et al. review the support of asynchronous teams utilizing intranet-based mini-case study publication with web-based conferencing. They report on this exercise from both pedagogic and groupware perspectives.

Chapters 9 to 12 are about support for authoring. Taylor describes the use of CMC systems to support e-seminars and introduces best practice guidelines for authoring e-seminars. Chapter 10 presents TACO a tool used for distributed authoring and management of computer-based coursework developed by Sasse et al. TACO uses a form-based tool which enables lecturers to create web-based self-learning exercises and assessed coursework. Armitage and Bryson illustrate, through the use of case descriptions, how Lotus Notes software is being used to support authoring and research. Kirakowski looks at the application of ISO standards to multimedia learning systems in Chapter 12. He also looks into quality of use, practical considerations and usability guidelines in the development of multimedia learning systems.

In Chapter 13, Edström looks at how the design of courses can connect with student motivations and presents a checklist used to create flexible courses to keep students motivated.

Chapters 14 and 15 look into educational metadata schema and the draft Learning Object Metadata (LOM). They highlight incompatibilities and weak points of the standards. Monthienvichienchai *et al.* present a case study where they investigate the usability of educational metadata schemas for the MALTED (Multimedia Authoring for Language Teachers and Educational Developers) project. Viéville describes the implementation of LOM for the "Le Campus Virtuel" platform and describes the way the system supports learning activities.

Finally, in Chapter 16, Mitchell looks at the relevance of collaborative working to the management of universities. He argues that a formal development of collaborative working practices, supported by appropriate technology, can make a substantial contribution to the effective running of a modern university.

Chapter 2

Universities, Dearing, and the Future

Stephen Hailes and Reza Hazemi

This chapter provides an overview of the ways in which asynchronous collaboration is potentially able to benefit universities. In order to do this, we first examine the functions of a university, then look at the basic tools and techniques of asynchronous collaboration before bringing these together to show which functions of a university are susceptible to support using asynchronous systems.

The importance of this activity cannot be underestimated. In the UK, the 1997 government-commissioned report of Sir Ron (now Lord) Dearing's Committee of Enquiry into Higher Education placed an emphasis on the development of a standard approach to the acquisition and delivery of electronic information, including everything from the management of the teaching and assessment processes through to the delivery of teaching material and the student admission process. Given the unique nature and importance of this report, we present some of its main recommendations.

It is clear from many of the chapters in this book that the development of collaborative technologies for use in higher education has been proceeding apace. It is also clear from the Dearing report, and from the development of institutions such as the Jones International University, a range of Korean virtual university programmes, and many other such activities, that the practical deployment of computer aided techniques for the delivery and management of degree courses will play a very important part in the future of university education worldwide. However, it is less clear that such technologies have been widely adopted amongst traditional universities and the remainder of the chapter will be dedicated to a consideration of some of the practical constraints that tend to oppose their introduction in universities in the UK.

2.1   Collaborative Tasks

There are essentially four different areas of activity within a university: teaching, research, systems support and administration. The first two of these are very high profile, and are assessed externally through TQA and the RAE activities in the UK, the results of which can have a significant impact on the standing and income of a university. However, the ability to perform these key tasks well is affected significantly by the availability and efficiency of support and administrative services. We will, therefore, analyze all four areas independently.

2.1.1 Teaching

Teaching is undoubtedly the activity for which universities are best known. Traditionally, teaching has involved a mixture of lectures, practicals, and tutorials of various types and this is still the predominant public perception of what happens. However, this is overly simplistic. Even from a traditional point of view, there are at least 6 different activities, which could reasonably be considered as constituting part of the teaching "interface" between a university and its students:

1.   *The production of primary teaching material.* This involves the production of slides, notes, videotapes and, increasingly, multimedia material, and affords the primary mechanism through which students will be informed about the course content. In many cases, this material is produced jointly between multiple lecturers and it often relies on prerequisite material in earlier courses or must be complementary to material in other, related, courses.

2.   *The delivery of course material.* This can be done both through synchronous communication, if the teacher is lecturing a class, or can be used to present either primary material (Open University type courses) or supporting material in an asynchronous manner [2].

3.   *Small group teaching.* Almost all courses run activities when small groups of people from a course are involved at any one time. Examples of such activities are tutorials and project supervision. Often, the agenda of such meetings is defined rather more loosely than for the delivery of primary material, if at all.

4.   *The setting and marking of exams and coursework.* As part of the mechanism of obtaining a degree, there is an obvious need to assess the aptitude and progress of students. This can be done in the form of unassessed self-testing to determine what course material has not been understood clearly and hence should be revised, or in the form of formal assessed coursework or examinations.

5.   *Staff student contact.* In addition to the requirements of formal teaching, there are a number of different forms of rather more *ad hoc* student contacts:

   a)   *Ad hoc course queries.*

   b)   *Regulatory and disciplinary matters.* Students must be informed of their rights and responsibilities, and of the rules and regulations which will apply to them in taking particular courses. If they transgress then the disciplinary action taken against them and the grounds for taking it must be made clear and recorded.

   c)   *Complaints.* Occasionally, students have complaints against members of staff, the way in which courses have been taught, or the ways in which they have been examined. In such cases, details of the student complaints must be logged together with any action taken.

6.   *Peer support for students.* In many instances, students learn well when allowed to discuss matters amongst themselves. These interactions can be structured, in the form of activities like supplemental instruction (SI), or can be rather more *ad hoc*, in the form of small online virtual communities. Online discussions can relate to focused activities, such as group projects, or can be wider-ranging discussions on the wider issues within a course.

This view is rather traditional, and would have been recognizable to students of several centuries ago. There are several drivers that are causing it to change:

1.   There is a move away from a rather elitist vision of higher education. Formerly, a small proportion of the populus were competitively selected for higher education. The main political parties in the UK now subscribe to a view in which anything up to 50% of the population should attend university at age 18. Furthermore, the UK government is now offering incentives for universities admitting those from disadvantaged backgrounds.

2.   The government is actively promoting the concept of *lifelong learning.* The withdrawal of student grants in the UK means that most mature students are now unable to attend university in the traditional way.

3.   A pedagogical move away from the concept of "teaching" and towards a concept of more student-centred "learning" and even student-directed learning.

4.   The level of funding in the UK has changed significantly. Over the past 10 years, there has been a drop in the funding levels per student of up to 50%.

5.   There has been pressure to engage with the business community at a number of different levels:

- professional accreditation of (science and engineering) courses now often involves a test of vocational relevance;

- new Masters Training Programmes (MTPs) receive funding on the basis of solid industrial involvement and the ability to become self-sustaining;

- Integrated Graduate Development Programme (IGDP) courses and the like offer more flexible modes of delivery to enable attendance from industry;

- EngD programmes provide PhD-like qualifications for those in industry unable to concentrate research in a single area for three years.

- revenue generating short courses, directly addressing the training needs of industry in a competitive market place.

These points indicate a move towards service provision for industry; fulfilling training needs and allowing participating companies to claim that they have continuing professional development courses for their staff in order to enhance recruitment and retention prospects.

6.   An increase in the number of degrees or parts of degrees accredited by well-known HEIs but usually franchised to lesser-known or lower-grade institutions, sometimes globally.

7.   Further to this, education is now becoming increasingly global. Distance learning is a reality; many famous US universities now offer distance learning courses that carry their imprimatur and consequent kudos. Also, true virtual universities are beginning to appear. Competition for high-grade students is therefore increasingly intense, in particular for those high-revenue-generating students from business or from overseas.

All of these points are leading to an increase in the heterogeneity of students obtaining qualifications from universities and an increase in the diversity (and more vocal expression) of their expectations for what their learning experience should be. At the same time, cost cutting is becoming essential as many UK universities slip into substantial deficit and competition increases globally for the best and most lucrative students.

Clearly, there are many areas within this process of evolution that could benefit from the introduction of technology. The Dearing report foresaw many of these and we discuss some of the main conclusions in Section 2.3. However, there are drivers that are making it hard to implement the necessary changes and we address these as well.

2.1.2 Research

Like teaching, research is not a single unified activity but rather involves both the direct performance of the task, together with a series of monitoring and support activities. In short, there are a number of aspects:

1. *Contact between researchers.* Typically, such researchers will be involved in the same project, but there are sometimes instances of collaborative activity between projects as competitive or complementary work is discovered. In the grant-giving process at present, considerable weight is put on cross disciplinary and inter-departmental work. This is especially true for large proposals (*e.g.,* EC projects), which usually involve consortia containing 5-10 different partners. Simply keeping everyone informed of everyone else's activities is a major source of time and expense in such cases.

2. *Generation of grant proposals.* Very little happens in the way of research without the generation of grant proposals, saying what work is to be carried out and how. Again, these proposals can and often do involve multiple partners, from a mixture of different departments within the same academic institution, a mixture of different academic institutions, and a range of industrial and commercial concerns. Although a proposal is usually a relatively short document, compared to deliverables produced during a project, it must be produced by people who are currently employed on some other activity and the process of negotiatin between potential collaborators must be approached with sensitivity and in full possession of the facts.

3. *Project management.* Once a project has been approved, staff are hired to carry out the work. Not only must those staff be kept in contact at a technical level, but it must be possible to manage them effectively. The day-to-day management of staff is usually done at the sites at which those staff reside. Even in this case there is often more than one academic involved in the management of the project and all of the so-called principal investigators need at least to be informed of the current areas of activity and the progress being made, in order to have meaningful meetings. The problem is compounded where one has a consortium in which there are several institutions involved, each of which has several people involved. Simply finding out who is doing what, never mind managing it, involves a significant amount of effort at present.

4. *Research support activities.* There are some specific activities which must be performed by those undertaking research. For example, researchers should (even if they do not) log details of those publications they have read, together with short reviews or abstracts of them. In an ideal world, where several people working in the same area would potentially be interested in such reviews, this annotated bibliography could be held in a common format online, accessible to those who need it.

5. *Reviewing papers and proposals.* All academics are asked, at one time or another, to review material destined for books, journals, conferences, workshops, *etc.* or to review the technical and organizational content of research proposals. These reviews are often submitted by post or fax, rather than electronically, and those contributing or reviewing often need to be chased (repeatedly!), making the organization and collation of information rather more tedious than it need otherwise be.

In view of the pressures of activities like teaching, many academics cannot be as actively involved in research as they would like, and often confine their activities to the supervision of work, writing up research for publication, applying for grants and managing projects. Those who perform the day-to-day activities are usually employed specially for that purpose, and are relieved to some extent of the need to see the bigger picture. In order to achieve the best results from the money invested, it is essential that there be fast and accurate communication between research management and those performing the tasks, as well as across management teams and between researchers.

2.1.3 Support

Academics and researchers only make up a proportion of those employed in universities. Others are employed to support their activities and to manage the finances of the university as a whole. There are two particular areas in which academics and those who want access to them interface with support staff:

1. *Meeting/diary management.* Contrary to popular mythology, today's academics are extremely busy people, and finding slots in which several of them can meet is almost always difficult since, to do it efficiently, it relies on the simultaneous availability of the participants so that they can consult their respective diaries. Arranging meetings by successive exchanges of email is painful, if more than two people are involved. Automated diary management systems can help in this task, since they can be consulted in the absence of the people to whom they refer.

2. *System support.* Within departments, there is often a need to request technical support (*e.g.*,please install Windows 2000 on my machine), or to indicate that something is broken (the roof leaks), or to schedule activities that can be conducted offline (*e.g.*,requesting NMR runs for particular samples). In the current financial climate, technical services often suffer cutbacks first, and the staff who run them are frequently hard to obtain synchronously. As a result, there is little alternative but to use asynchronous techniques.

    As the nature of students changes in line with the drivers described in Section 2.1.1 and increasing numbers have computers that they use remotely, the nature of support will change. No longer do system administrators have complete control over the physical and logical configuration of all the machines used for teaching. This gives rise not only to a security problem, but also to a more general maintenance problem as the number and type of software and hardware environments explodes.

2.1.4 Administration

Administration is awarded a section of its own because it is an activity that underlies an academic's ability to perform any task. There is a considerable range of administrative activity, from that performed by individual academics to the interaction with central administrative authorities:

1. *Financial issues.* The most important administrative activity in universities is that which concerns money. Money in universities comes from several different sources. Much of a university's income is given directly by the government, based on the number of students in each department. Thus it is imperative that accurate records be kept, since individual departments receive funding based on the number of FTEs they teach, and some of these may be from other departments, so the university as a whole needs to know what its numbers are in each particular area. Other monies come from research funding councils, charities and industry. Clearly, all of these need to be accounted for and managed both at a departmental and college level. Furthermore, it is necessary that the principal investigators on any given grant be able to monitor precisely what has been spent, and under what budget headings. In terms of expenditure, the college has wages to pay, buildings to heat and keep in good repair, *etc.* At a more mundane level, expenses claims by academics and researchers need to be authorized then processed, requisitions need to be authorized, then forwarded to whoever acts as the purchasing manager, then monitored until delivery is made, invoices are processed, and the money is deducted from the appropriate account.

2. *Personnel issues.* Academics and researchers have a career structure, which involves a sliding scale of wages, several levels of possible promotion, and all the standard personnel-type information, which must be exchanged (preferably securely) between department heads and the central college authorities.

3. *Student admissions.* Offers must be made to prospective students, usually conditional on obtaining a given set of "A" level grades. This information must be recorded at UCAS. Once the "A" level results are produced they need to be retrieved and matched against these offers. Problems need to be highlighted and dealt with. The same is true of postgraduate courses, though, in that case, there is no central authority with which one can deal.

4. *Student management issues.* There is a growing need to maintain precise records about students, including which courses they attended, their

attendance records, their marks, medical evidence which could affect the final grade awarded to them, any disciplinary matters, and so forth.

5.   *Creating and holding student references.* Every student, when applying for a job, requires references from their university. Often these requests go directly to lecturers who know the students particularly well (*e.g.*,their project supervisors). If these lecturers leave, then it can be hard to generate references for students.

6.   *Careers advice.* Students require advice and counselling regarding potential careers. Likewise, they need access both to traditionally advertised jobs and the large number of non-advertised direct approaches that careers officers receive both at college and departmental level.

7.   *Student occupations.* Universities are required to keep details of the first destinations of students after they have graduated. Where possible, these are kept up to date as students inform universities of their movements.

8.   *Training.* All research students and research assistants who assist lecturers must be appropriately trained. Records must be kept of which courses they have attended.

Administration is often viewed as a necessary evil; however, there is a considerable amount of it in a university since there are a large number of employees, and thousands of students to be dealt with. Accurate record keeping is essential, but administration is not an end in itself; it is there to support the primary aims of a university - teaching and research. As such, it needs to be done as cheaply and with as little effort as is consistent with achieving the desired accuracy. There is a lack of coherence in the automated systems in a university (where they are actually used), and it is often the case that data is transferred on paper only to be re-entered elsewhere in a different form. Clearly, this is not consistent with obtaining the greatest efficiency possible, and funds which would otherwise go to support teaching, releasing effort for research, are being devoted to servicing this inefficiency.

2.1.5 Comment

Academics are required to perform a very wide range of tasks today and, further, to do them relatively efficiently. As university funding is squeezed, the increase in efficiency required to maintain services means that there is less time which is unaccounted for both for academics and those that support them. This is double-edged, since it means that communication between students, academics, researchers, and those that support them is extremely hard to schedule synchronously. Thus the choice lies either in delaying the communication to some future point, which can be difficult to fix in time without proper diary support, or, alternatively, in using some form of asynchronous communication. Typically this is done using email (if the department has ready access to computers and is computer literate) or paper if it is not. Both are some considerable way from being ideal.

There are numerous sources of inefficiency in a university, as in any large organization. Furthermore, there is now more teaching, research, and administration required than a few years ago, so waste due to inefficiency has a greater impact. Crudely put, inefficiency absorbs funds which could better be used elsewhere. While it used to be the case that inefficiencies which took academics' time were effectively free, since academics receive the same salary regardless of what they do, academics are now reaching saturation point, and this is no longer the case; either teaching or research standards will slip, affecting the standing of the university, or more staff will need to be employed to cover the shortfall.

As a result, we need to look at solutions which will enable academics to do what they are best at - teaching and research - and either reduce the amount of time they spend in related activities, or make it more productive. As Dearing [1] says:

15.31   "Over the next 20 years, C&IT will provide increasing opportunities to improve institutional effectiveness and efficiency. A continuing challenge to institutional managers will be to realize the potential and to ensure that the systems they introduce are used to full effect. Furthermore, there will be new and essential tasks that institutions will be unable to perform without significantly enhanced usage of their hardware and software. Some of the other developments advocated in our report will depend on institutions securing fuller benefits from C&IT in their management. For example:

● institutions and those that fund their teaching are likely to want to know more about patterns of student participation and achievement;

● tracking student progress through one institution, or several, and throughout lifelong learning, will assume a greater significance;

● the single "learner record" which we advocated in Chapter 8 will require better exploitation of the common language capacity of C&IT across institutions, within and outside the higher education sector;

● the use of online registration of students and the use of "smart cards" to secure access to facilities and, in some cases, payment for them by students, are likely to proliferate;

● the need to demonstrate maximum value for money to a wider range of stakeholders, as part of the new compact, will demand better ways of analyzing costs and the way institutional resources are used;

● maximising the use of space by developing fully computerized central timetabling."

2.3 The Future of Higher Education: The Dearing Report

In this section, we will examine some of the suggestions made in the report of the National Committee of Inquiry into Higher Education (NCIHE), chaired by Sir Ron (now Lord) Dearing. The committee delivered its wide-ranging report on 23rd July 1997. It will have a major impact on the shape of higher education into the foreseeable future and is very forward looking. It directly addresses the impact that C&IT is having on all aspects of academic life, and foresees a future in which it is a central plank in both the delivery of material and support for that delivery in universities. In this section, we will summarize the major points of the report as they relate to C&IT, the material being drawn particularly from Chapter 13 which is the relevant part of the report.

2.4.1 Teaching

The Dearing report has a considerable amount to say about the future for teaching:

13.3   "We believe that, for the majority of students, over the next ten years the delivery of some course materials and much of the organization and communication of course arrangements will be conducted by computer. Just as most people will come to expect to be connected to, and to make use of, world communications networks in their daily lives, all students will expect continuous access to the network of the institution(s) at which they are studying, as a crucial link into the learning environment."

13.7   "Over the next decade, higher educational services will become an internationally tradable commodity within an increasingly competitive global market. For some programmes, United Kingdom (UK) institutions will rely heavily on C&IT to teach across continents. Within the UK, by the end of the first decade of the next century, a "knowledge economy" will have developed in which institutions collaborate in the production and transmission of educational programmes and learning materials on a "make or buy" basis. We must expect and encourage the development and delivery of core programmes and components of programmes, and sharing and exchange of specialist provision, to become commonplace."

13.8   "The development of a world market in learning materials, based on C&IT, will provide scope to higher education institutions to become major participants in this arena. This in turn might lead to the formation of trading partnerships between institutions for the provision of infrastructure, services and content. Such partnerships could include major companies in the communications, media and publishing industries."

From this, it is clear that there is a view at a high level that teaching is likely to become internationalized, partly as a result of, and partly as a driver for, the use of our increasingly comprehensive high bandwidth networked infrastructure and the adoption of both synchronous and asynchronous collaborative techniques. Without the innovation and effective use of appropriate collaborative techniques and the agreement of common standards, such collaborative activities will happen in a piecemeal and disjoint fashion. This will inevitably lead to unnecessary replication of work and, indeed, in extra work in translating between the different custom systems in use.

Given that the computerization of UK education is seen as a priority, Dearing has suggested concrete methods for achieving it, in terms of the necessary hardware. By 2005-6, it will be considered compulsory for students to purchase some form of notebook computer. Referred to by Dearing as the Student Portable Computer (SPC), this will be capable of connecting to networks, but is not seen as a replacement for the so-called Networked Desktop Computer (NDC). Indeed, the penetration of NDCs is expected to increase from its current ratio of 15 students to one machine to a ratio of 5:1 or better. Both of these machines are envisaged as forming part of the standard mechanism for the delivery of teaching:

13.43   "Over the next ten years, all higher education institutions will, and should, progressively move significant aspects of administration and learning and teaching to the computer medium. They should be planning for this now. The development of powerful paperback-sized 'notebook' computers, capable of sending and receiving email and accessing the Internet, is envisaged within the next few years. We expect that this technology will be harnessed by students and institutions for learning and teaching and administration through the development of a Student Portable Computer (SPC)."

13.44   "The SPC will store basic course information and enable the student to undertake a significant amount of work off-line (for example drafting of assignments). It will also allow the student, via a network connection, to access electronic information (such as timetables, course materials and library catalogues), to submit assignments, and to communicate with tutors and other students. It is possible that the SPC might be a fully mobile device accessing the network through wireless technology. We found, on our visit to the USA in January 1997, that an SPC (usually an industry-standard laptop computer) is already a requirement for courses at a number of institutions. The same requirement applies to some UK programmes."

13.45   "To use their SPCs effectively in this way, to communicate and send and receive information, students will require daily access to the network. There will, therefore, need to be adequate provision of network connection ports in institutions into which students can plug their SPCs and there should be provision of dialup connectivity for off-campus students at each institution."

13.50   "Networked Desktop Computers (NDCs) need to be of a sufficiently high technical specification to make full use of the network and networked services, and permit the use of the latest interactive multimedia learning and teaching materials and other applications (whether accessed via the network or CD-ROM). They must, therefore, incorporate up-to-date sound, video and graphics technology."

13.51   "Existing evidence suggests that, at present, the ratio of students to desktop computers in higher education institutions is only slightly better than 15:1 across the UK. In the short term, student access to NDCs needs to be improved across the sector as a whole. The required ratio will vary from institution to institution, depending on such factors as subjects taught, types of student and learning and teaching methods. A ratio of 10:1 would be a good standard at present but this needs to improve to 8:1, particularly where an institution makes extensive use of online learning materials and electronic information services. We expect that, as such methods become widespread, a ratio of 5:1, or better, will be necessary for multi-faculty institutions. Students will need information about the adequacy of an institution's provision of equipment for their use and must know in advance of study what expectations there are of students providing their own access."

"Recommendation 46

We recommend that by 2000/01 higher education institutions should ensure that all students have open access to a Networked Desktop Computer, and expect that by 2005/06 all students will be required to have access to their own portable computer."

While Dearing has little to say explicitly about software, it is clear that the aims stated in the above paragraphs cannot be achieved without a significant amount of development that will allow noncomputer-expert academics to capture their knowledge and interact with their students in a relatively straightforward way.

Although tools such as Microsoft FrontPage allow simple web site construction using concepts that are reasonably familiar to a large proportion of the academic community, producing good, pedagogically sound, sites that do more than act as a distribution point for lecture notes is hard. It is not for nothing that the salaries paid by industry to consultants who specialize in developing either web sites or commercial groupware applications are nontrivial.

It is imperative that on a very short timescale the best pedagogic methodology is aggressively explored, including both the technical issues and those of social interaction between parties using the computer to teach and learn. This is happening (*e.g.,* TLTP [5]), but in a somewhat piecemeal manner, and the move from experimental setup to widely deployed system has barely begun.

2.4.2 Administration

The problems and costs of administration are well known in both the academic and commercial sectors. Increasingly, the commercial sector has been turning to asynchronous collaborative techniques because it has been persuaded of the cost benefits to be had through using them. According to Dearing:

13.09   "As in other industries and businesses, C&IT is affecting the management and administration of higher education institutions, and is assisting institutions to manage increasingly complex activities and services such as finance, personnel, admissions, time-tabling, data collection, estates management, catering and conferencing. Progress in the successful use of C&IT for these purposes has been mixed but higher education institutions should aim to improve their economy and efficiency by making more effective and extensive use of C&IT (see Chapter 15)."

13.50   "While the effective adoption of C&IT in higher education requires appropriate technology, adequate resources and staff development, success depends on the effective management of change. The development and implementation of an integrated C&IT strategy will be one of the main challenges facing managers of higher education institutions."

It is clear from the industrial experience, from our own personal experience, and from the recommendations of the Dearing report that, to achieve the successful deployment of asynchronous collaboration systems, there must be an appropriate infrastructure, a clearly defined C&IT policy, and high-level will, effort, and understanding to make it happen. At present, there is technology available, even if it needs further development to be ideal for the needs of academia, but it is still not the case that many institutions could claim to be driving a coherent C&IT policy from the top down, with the aim of achieving the objectives Dearing has set.

2.4.3 The Changing Face of Higher Education

Increasing student numbers

"Recommendation 1

We recommend to the Government that it should have a long term strategic aim of responding to increased demand for higher education, much of which we expect to be at subdegree level; and that to this end, the cap on full-time undergraduate places should be lifted over the next two to three years and the cap on full-time subdegree places should be lifted immediately."

It is apparent from this recommendation that the numbers in higher education, which increased significantly under the last government but which were then capped, will again rise. Historically, a rise in the number of students has not been accompanied with a commensurate rise in the numbers of lecturing or administrative staff. There is some saving to be had in, for example, lectures that take little extra effort to give to greater numbers. However, it has always proved to be the case that the increase in load through extra administration, project supervision, tutorial groups, *etc.* has more than outweighed this, and members of academic staff and those that support them have had to work harder. There is little slack in the system now, particularly as many undergraduate courses are changing from three to four years (MSci, MEng type qualifications) without greatly increased resources. This simply means that staff must work more efficiently and, as argued above, groupware has a significant role to play in this.

Widening participation

"Recommendation 2

We recommend to the Government and the Funding Bodies that, when allocating funds for the expansion of higher education, they give priority to those institutions which can demonstrate a commitment to widening participation, and have in place a

participation strategy, a mechanism for monitoring progress, and provision for review by the governing body of achievement."

"Recommendation 6

We recommend:

● to the Funding Bodies that they provide funding for institutions to provide learning support for students with disabilities;

● to the Institute for Learning and Teaching in Higher Education (see Recommendation 14) that it includes the learning needs of students with disabilities in its research, programme accreditation and advisory activities;

● to the Government that it extends the scope of the Disabled Students Allowance so that it is available without a parental means test and to part-time students, postgraduate students and those who have become disabled who wish to obtain a second higher education qualification."

In these recommendations we see a commitment to widening access to disabled and otherwise disadvantaged groups; this being backed up with funds. Dearing has something to say about the way this will be achieved though, perhaps, this is something of a statement of hope rather than of certainty:

13.4   "C&IT will overcome barriers to higher education, providing improved access and increased effectiveness, particularly in terms of lifelong learning. Physical and temporal obstacles to access for students will be overcome with the help of technology. Those from remote areas, or with work or family commitments need not be disadvantaged. Technology will also allow the particular requirements of students with disabilities to be more effectively met by institutions."

It is widely believed that all forms of C&IT have, at least potentially, something to offer to everyone. However, the "disadvantaged" are not a homogeneous group and it is far from clear that we know exactly what the needs of individual subgroups actually are, let alone the extent to which these specific needs can actually be addressed by application of C&IT.

Record keeping

"Recommendation 7

We recommend that further work is done over the medium term, by the further and higher education Funding Bodies, the Higher Education Statistics Agency, and relevant government departments to address the creation of a framework for data about lifelong learning, using a unique student record number."

"Recommendation 20

We recommend that institutions of higher education, over the medium term, develop a Progress File. The File should consist of two elements:

● a transcript recording student achievement which should follow a common format devised by institutions collectively through their representative bodies;

● a means by which students can monitor, build and reflect upon their personal development."

Here we see a commitment to creating and holding records over the long term. To be effective, this will require the interfacing of existing departmental and university-wide systems to wherever the relevant central information is held. Clearly, this provides an opportunity for standardization in both the information interchange format and in the mechanisms used for keeping such information.

Staff development

"Recommendation 9

We recommend that all institutions should, over the medium term, review the changing role of staff as a result of Communications and Information Technology, and ensure that staff and students receive appropriate training and support to enable them to realize its full potential."

This is a direct realization of the fact that universities are changing and must change in terms of the ways in which they carry out their primary tasks and that all staff need to be appropriately trained in the sorts of techniques we discuss in this book.

Strategies

"Recommendation 41

We recommend that all higher education institutions in the UK should have in place overarching communications and information strategies by 1999/2000."

"Recommendation 42

We recommend that all higher education institutions should develop managers who combine a deep understanding of Communications and Information Technology with senior management experience."

Those implementing these recommendations will need to assess the current state-of-the-art in, and potential for, computer-based collaborative techniques in academia. Without specific technical input from those who know about these systems, and those who have thought about their uses in relation to more than just administration, the benefits to be had will be severely curtailed. If, in fact, the wrong choices are made and implemented, simply in order to be seen to have some sort of policy, then the consequences could be very costly.

2.4.4 Comment

The move towards greater heterogeneity in the student body, and increasing diversity in methods of study and expectations are not UK-specific. There is a growing trend in developed countries to push high-bandwidth networking technologies into every corner of everyday life; this is coupled with an increasing pressure on students to obtain formal tertiary qualifications in order to be considered for jobs. Consequently, the recommendations of the Dearing committee, which foresaw the proximity of both the need for more flexible, remote, forms of learning and the technology to provide it, represent an important roadmap that is applicable across the developed world.

However, the fact that something is increasingly possible and increasingly necessary does not, unfortunately, mean that it is increasingly a part of mainstream educational reality. The Dearing report, while outlining one vision of an ideal towards which many institutions are working, could be viewed as somewhat *naïve* when practicalities are considered.

There is undoubtedly an increase in the use of ICT within universities, some of it driven by the Dearing vision but much of it simply part of the continuous process of renewal that is a natural part of university education. Despite Dearing, developments in the UK are certainly not significantly advanced relative to other developed countries and could even be argued to lag behind them. Furthermore, much of the development that has happened is not the result of central orchestration but continues to happen either at departmental level or at the level of interested individuals.

There are many reasons for this, amongst them:

1. *Resourcing.* As with many previous ICT developments within colleges and universities, there has been a considerable underestimate of the amount of effort required to make effective use of the new technologies. A healthy cynicism amongst overworked staff means that new technologies will not be adopted until the cost-benefit analyzis has been more clearly shown to be favourable. In other words, resistance is likely to persist until it is clear that expending the time to adopt systems that are of *potential* benefit to students or the organization outweighs the *actual* (and upfront) costs to the individual member of staff. At present this case has not been made strongly, if indeed it is capable of being made at all.

    Without better products, a clearer and more convincing exposition of the benefits, a reduction in the costs, a commitment to quality central training, and extensive ongoing support, general adoption of new technologies is likely be basic at best. Naturally, institutions will parade this as evidence that they are conforming with the Dearing road map. However, greater sophistication is likely to continue to be reliant on the interest and commitment of individuals.

2. *Resourcing.* Support is a key component of the above point. However, low university salaries for support staff at the same time as a rise in unfilled vacancies for trained ICT professionals has seen the salary gap between university and industry widen substantially. This means that it is increasingly difficult to recruit and retain the highly trained ICT support staff that are necessary enablers for the deployment of new technologies in universities.

There are technical issues that cut right across all of the areas of ICT provision. So, for example, a problem as significant as computer security cannot be addressed piecemeal, or half-heartedly, or with untrained staff, or without adequate funding, and yet this is precisely what is happening.

3. *Management of change.* ICT provision in universities has tended to grow somewhat organically. There are many different machine types, operating system types, versions of programming languages and libraries, *etc.* To take a simple case in point, at UCL we know of several email systems in use in departments throughout the college.

To introduce a coherent set of different asynchronous teaching, administrative and support systems into such a heterogeneous environment, and then to maintain them, is a monumental practical challenge.

As a consequence, thought has been given as to how best to centralize service provision. This undoubtedly does help to reduce the problems described above. However, to construct such a system is a significant feat of engineering which, even if achievable, can lead to systems that are inflexible, unreliable and which need significant resources for ongoing support and upgrade. Incompatible upgrades are unbelievably painful for systems of any size.

Management information systems are perhaps the best known examples in this context, or at least those with the longest history. In many such cases, the end products have often been less capable than desired and inflexible in the face of changing requirements. A case in point is the UK Management and Administrative Computing (MAC) Initiative which, although somewhat dated, still has valuable lessons to teach concerning the overarching need for business process reengineering as opposed to a simplistic faith in the efficacy of technical solutions alone. Further, the need for appropriate (rather than forced) collaboration in large-scale ICT system deployment is another lesson learnt [6].

In spite of the difficulties, as implied by Lefrere [7], change in this context will come to higher education, perhaps because the type of investigations we see in this book will rebalance the cost-benefit analyzis or perhaps because those institutions that adopt distance learning techniques and who do go through the painful process of investing in administrative reengineering will have a competitive advantage.

However, the UK university system is not a free market and is not free of external (and in particular governmental) interference. In particular, it is difficult to believe that the scale of investment needed will be forthcoming in an era of deficit and cuts. It is therefore difficult to predict the actual rate of change.

Although there are many interesting activities taking place in the UK (*e.g.*, those forming the JTAP programme [8]) and quite passionate debate has been entered into about aspects of the Dearing report ([*e.g.*, [9, 10]), effective leadership in practical deployment within this field probably lies in the US or East Asia.

Regardless, this book is a testament to the fact that progress is being made.

2.5   Conclusion

Considerable effort has been put into support for real-time collaboration based on video conferencing but, in the academic world, less attention has been focused on the requirements of asynchronous collaboration. While academics have continued to rely largely on email and the Web, there are also numerous groupware products now available and in use in many commercial environments. In both the commercial and academic environments, more emphasis is and has been placed on having good tools for asynchronous collaboration than for synchronous collaboration. The reason can be attributed to the fact that asynchronous tools simplify business processes, remove paper from the environment, and operate on the same items that the business itself uses. The material that once was printed on paper and posted can now be delivered via email and the Web [4]. This electronic approach increases the distribution efficiency, but it does not exploit the full potential of the technology as an enabler of reengineering of the educational process itself [2].

Synchronous collaboration is important, and likely to become increasingly so as more people move away from traditional office or campus environments in such a way that they can only be virtually present at meetings and so forth. In all of these cases, however, multimedia conferencing cannot capture the nuances present in face-to-face meetings and so is less than the ideal in this respect, though it enables those who cannot simultaneously be collocated to communicate in a cost-effective way.

New tools may alleviate some of the problems of synchronous collaboration like information overload in a virtual classroom [11]; however, it is likely that universities will remain structured much as they are today until forced by external circumstances to change. Synchronous collaboration will help distance learners, but asynchronous collaboration will help both distance learners and those that are present on campus, and will also aid in the whole process of organizing teaching and research, allowing those delivering the services to act more efficiently.

In this chapter we examined teaching, research, support and administration as four main tasks of an academic environment and discussed the relevant recommendations of the Dearing report regarding these tasks. Finally, we outlined some of the practical difficulties in implementing Dearing's vision.

References

1.   http://www.leeds.ac.uk/educol/ncihe

2.   Hamalainen, M., Whinston, A. and Vishik, S. (1997) Electronic markets for learning: Education brokerage on the Internet. *Communications of the ACM*, 39, 6, 51-58.

3.   Murray W. Goldberg and Salari, S. (1997) An update on WebCT (World-Wide-Web Course Tools) - A tool for the creation of sophisticated web-based learning environments. *Proceedings of NAUWeb '97 - Current Practices in Web-Based Course Development*, Flagstaff, Arizona, June 12-15.

4.   Chellappa, R., Barua, A. and Whinston, A.B. (1997) An electronic infrastructure for a virtual university, *Communications of the ACM*, 40, 9, 56-58.

5.   http://www.ncteam.ac.uk/tltp.html

6.   Universities and College Information Systems Association (UCISA) (1999) HEFCE Consultation Paper 99/28. Fund for the Development of Good Management Practice. Available at http://www.ucisa.ac.uk/docs/reports/hefce2.htm.

7.   Lefrere, P. (2001) Virtual university? Real options for virtual universities in *Educational Environments of the Future*, edited by van der Molen H. J., Portland Press. Available at http://vu.portlandpress.com/vu_ch2.htm.

8.   http://www.jisc.ac.uk/jtap/

9.   Association of University Teachers (2001) Accreditation Proposals, LA/7012a. Available at http://www.aut.org/members/circularshtml/ls7012.html

10. Institute for Learning and Teaching in Higher Education (2001) The AUT's Accreditation Proposals: A Response.

     Available at http://www.ilt.ac.uk/news/n20010404a.htm

11. Hiltz, S.R. and Wellman, B. (1997) Asynchronous learning networks as a virtual classroom, *Communications of the ACM*, 40, 9, 44-49.

Chapter 3

Managing Distance Learning: New Challenges for Faculty

Lisa Kimball

Although the technology of distance learning receives most of the attention, it is really teaching strategies and style that have the most impact on the quality of learning in distance programs. Facilitating learning communities at a distance requires a new approach to the practice of managing the teaching and learning process. Effective faculty start with a completely new mindset about where technology fits into the equation. Rather than struggling to make up for qualities distance programs are perceived to lack when compared to traditional classrooms, faculty members who are most successful with distance technologies see them as actually providing some qualitative advantages. In addition to managing the delivery of the content to their courses, faculty teaching at a distance must learn to manage a new set of variables, which determine the extent to which their courses are effective, including: metaphor, meaning, culture, roles, time, awareness, and collaboration. Learning and practicing the skills to manage these dimensions is the key challenge for faculty development.

3.1 Introduction

What does the concept of "wait time" mean for faculty teaching students at a distance? How does one pull virtual chairs into a circle for creative dialogue?

Many institutions introducing distance learning spend a large amount of their resources (both time and money) on training faculty to manage the new technical and administrative aspects of distance courses. Instead, faculty need to learn to manage critical dimensions of the new environment in which their courses are taking place, dimensions like metaphor, meaning, culture, roles, time, awareness, and collaboration.

Distance learning can involve many different technologies used alone or in combination. Although many of the decisions to be made are about which of the many possible technologies and media will work best for specific purposes, the focus of this chapter is on the role of the facilitator as distinct from the delivery system.

The issues raised for instructors about designing and managing learning programs at a distance are really the issues that need to be raised about all learning experience including; How do you achieve the right balance between presentation and experiential activity? Between individual and collaborative learning? Between teacher-driven and learner-driven assignments?

New technology *requires* us to rethink these dynamics because we do not have the option of using familiar approaches. It gives us an opening to change the way we manage the teaching and learning process in general. The critical part of the question, "How can we engage learners via distance learning technology?" is really "How do we engage learners in more meaningful learning activities?" Facilitating distance learning is not about taking our old lesson plans and transposing them for delivery using new media. Rather, it is about expanding our available tools to create new learning dynamics aligned with the best thinking about adult learning.

3.2   A New Management MindSet

There are some critical aspects of a learning manager's mindset which must shift in order to take full advantage of new opportunities created by distance learning technology [8].

Table 3.1. Shift in mindset.

From	To
Face-to-face is the best environment for learning and anything else is a compromise.	Different kinds of environments can support high quality learning. What matters is how you use them.
Learning is what happens when teachers interact with students at a fixed time and space.	Learning happens in an ongoing, boundaryless way and includes what learners do independently of teachers.
Being people-oriented is incompatible with using technology.	Using distance learning technology in a people-oriented way is possible and desirable.
When the learning process breaks down, blame the technology.	When the learning process breaks down, evaluate our teaching strategies, not just the technical tool.
Learning to manage distance learning is about learning how to use the technology.	Learning to manage distance learning is about understanding more about the learning process.

3.3   A New Style of Management

"The European navigator begins with a plan - a course - which he has charted according to certain universal principles, and he carries out his voyage by relating his every move to that plan. His effort throughout his voyage is directed to remaining "on course". If unexpected events occur, he must first alter the plan, then respond accordingly. The Trukese navigator begins with an objective and responds to conditions as they arise in an *ad hoc* fashion. He utilizes information provided by the wind, the waves, the tide and the current, the fauna, the stars, the clouds, the sound of the water on the side of the boat, and steers accordingly. His effort is directed to doing whatever is necessary to reach the objective." [3]

The distinction between a linear and dynamic approach to navigation could also describe a major shift from the old view to a new view of managing education. The first challenge for a distance educator is to figure out how to harness the power of new media to take advantage of its capacity to support flexibility, parallel processing, and just-in-time design - not just use the new media to deliver the same old stuff.

In the old model, learning design proceeded in a linear fashion from defining objectives to lesson planning to course delivery. Educators first engaged in a comprehensive learning needs analyzis process, often based on assessments done by others about competencies and learning objectives. Comprehensive course syllabi were developed. Finally, the course was delivered as planned.

Associated with this linear approach was a set of teaching strategies that matched its linear qualities. These strategies were characterized by being predominantly one-way, centralized, and broadcast-oriented. When students appeared bored and unengaged in this type of program, the solution was to find ways to use new media to make the one-way broadcast more entertaining. Much early distance learning was nothing more than a way to generate a broadcast of an expert and his multi-media slides with good production values.

Distance learning was praised because of its ability to scale up to reach larger numbers of students at standardized levels of quality but an expert lecturing to a group of passive students is engaging in didactic one-way teaching whether that lecture is delivered from a stage in an auditorium or via broadcast television to students sitting in their living rooms.

A new mindset for teaching has emerged. Teaching and learning is seen as an ongoing process rather than a program with a fixed starting and ending point and the importance of widespread participation by learners in the design of their own learning has been recognized.

Distance learning technologies are particularly well suited to a more dynamic approach to managing learning. Good teachers have always been open to changing their lesson plans based on student input. New media makes it easier. For example, it is easy to provide additional reading materials based on student interest instead of having to rely on a textbook ordered weeks or months before the course began. Online environments can provide space for continuing conversation among students about what is working and what is not working in the course.

The same technology can also contribute to more participatory course design. In a masters level business course at George Mason University, the professor contacted most of the course members via email during the summer to find out about their interests, expectations, concerns, and skills so that he could take those into consideration when designing a course offered in the Fall semester. He was able to use that information to create preliminary project teams and develop initial assignments that reflected the specific needs of course participants.

3.4   Managing Metaphor

One of the first things it is important to think about is the kind of ambience you need to create in order to have the kind of learning experience you intend. In distance learning settings, language and metaphor are primary tools to use to create the ambience because you need to help participants evoke images to put them in a mind space conducive to learning even though they are doing it at different times and from different places. Many distance-learning environments borrow language from traditional school settings, such as classroom, lecture hall, and library, to provide cues to learners about what to expect. This can be a good strategy to help learners navigate through unfamiliar environments. However, there is a danger in using language that matches the distance-learning environment to the traditional environment because it may hardwire old models into the new medium. If you want to take advantage of the new media's ability to support more self-directed learning it is important to signal to participants that they are *not* entering a traditional classroom where they would expect to wait for the instructor to tell them what to do.

One way to start is to think about the kinds of interactions and experiences you need to support in terms of the feelings you want to evoke. Do you want participants to have intimate self-disclosing conversations like they might have late at night in a café? Or do you want to have teams of learners engage in lively brainstorming exchanges as might happen around a conference table? Putting the group in a virtual "classroom" does not help you evoke either of these dynamics.

The Institute for Educational Studies (TIES)[1] at Endicott College is a one-year intensive Masters degree program in transforming education. The design is based around communities of teachers from around the world forming a learning community that meets in a virtual campus using asynchronous web conferencing. In order to help participants "feel" a sense of being part of a virtual campus components include lectures, seminars, discussions, study groups, and guest faculty. Course participants come together in a variety of virtual lecture halls, seminar rooms, and discussions but the most important aspect of the program is to create a peer-to-peer learning community where participants share their deepest thoughts and feelings about their own personal growth and its relationship to their role as educators.

---

[1] http://ties-edu.org/

In order to support this core part of the program within the distance-learning framework, TIES made use of a metaphor from the participants' experience at a face-to-face meeting that was held to kick off the program. The meeting took place in the Vermont countryside at a house that had a big front porch. Participants spent a lot of time between sessions and in the evenings sitting on the porch sharing stories about themselves. TIES created a space online called "The Porch" where that same quality of conversation could continue throughout the year. Although the online environment was new and strange for most participants, they had no trouble understanding what to do in The Porch and immediately began sharing stories and reflections there.

At Digital Equipment Corporation, a large high-tech company, there was a thing called a "woods meeting" which at first actually did take place at the company founder's cabin in the woods of New England. Everyone knew that when you went to a woods meeting it meant that you would be brainstorming about the future of the company rather than doing day-to-day stuff. So, people started having "woods meetings" in conference rooms on site at the company - just naming it put people in a different mind-frame about what would happen. So a "woods meeting" title for an online conference could convey something similar about what needs to happen there.

In groups that do not come with a common experience to draw from you can achieve a similar shared repertoire of metaphors by taking time to elicit ideas from the participants. Have participants tell stories about previous learning experiences and engage them in dialogue about different learning dynamics and the environments where they took place. Get the group to create metaphors and names for different components of your program and use the stories yourself to provide cues, "This part of our environment is where we will have the kind of peer coaching Ted described in his story about the marketing team's white-water rafting retreat. Let us call this chat space The Raft."

Engage participants in choosing metaphors whenever possible. Have a dialogue early in the course to talk explicitly about ambience like, "What kind of interactions do we want to have in here?" Even within the larger framework of the course environment, you can use metaphors to define spaces for different kinds of interactions. For example, many groups benefit from having at least one place in the environment that uses metaphors like water cooler or *break time* to serve the same social lubrication purpose as a coffee break serves in a traditional course.

Remember, there is a big difference between facsimile and metaphor. Facsimiles can trap participants into default ways of behaving. Metaphor can be evocative and help participants create a richer mental construct about what they are doing.

3.5   Managing Meaning

Distance learners can have a harder time than those in a traditional course integrating all the different course components into a focused whole. Course managers can help by providing regular summaries of where we are and where we are going next. Weaving the multiple threads of conversation together gives all members a chance to start afresh or take off in a new direction. It can help keep the group from spinning its wheels. Sometimes, you can give people a better sense of what the virtual group is all about by simply copying the topic index or a list of all the conference messages and posting it. This may remind participants of items they want to go back to or it may reveal a gap in the conversation that can be filled by starting a new item.

It is also important to integrate the study of communication and media itself into the curriculum. Developing the learner's ability to question the process of learning will make them a more effective learner.

One of the things many distance learning programs perceive as a significant problem is the tension between delivering content resources which are essentially one-way communications (articles, books, videos, expert lectures) and providing the two-way interaction around that material which makes it meaningful to learners. It is often true that the same media environment is not optimal for both needs. An environment that does a great job of storing and organizing materials of various kinds is not necessarily a good place to hold the discussion stimulated by that material. It is very hard to conduct a role-playing exercise in a file cabinet. There is more to developing a relationship among a collaborative learning group than sharing access to a file folder.

PBS Mathline[2] is a professional development program delivered at a distance to classroom teachers. The content of the program consists of videos showing teachers in classrooms using the new ideas about teaching maths with the lesson plans and associated materials being used by the teachers in the videos. Some participating teachers tape the videos that are broadcast on private channels by local educational television, but for most it is more convenient to receive copies of the videos on cassettes. There are also other resource materials provided in print and online such as copies of articles written about the theory and practice.

However, all that material is not "the program". The heart of the program is in the learning communities of 25-30 teachers grouped by age level (elementary, middle school, and high school) and with a peer facilitator, who log into private online conferences to talk about the ideas and their experiences using and thinking about the materials. In geographic locations where it is possible, these learning communities get together during the year for face-to-face interaction. The key is that different parts of the program are delivered using different media. The online discussion provides a common room for the long term, peer-to-peer facilitated interaction which makes the program meaningful for participants.

---

[2] Public Broadcasting System Mathline: http://www.pbs.org/teachersource/math.htm

3.6 Managing Culture

Heavy-handed guidelines and rules about behavior make for a boring experience, but it never hurts to state explicitly the kind of atmosphere you hope to create. Do you hope your virtual group will be supportive, deep, amusing, fast-moving, reflective, cutting-edge, information-intensive, risky, silly, focused, unfocused? What styles and behaviors would help or hinder the atmosphere you want?

Are the participants peer learners? Team members? Neighbors in a learning community? Is the moderator expected to provide expert knowledge? Support and encouragement? A guide to other resources? If you are not sure about these roles ahead of time, the group should discuss them. Different images of roles and relationships will provide cues to different ways of participating.

A community of distance learners is like any community in that its culture is a product of shared stories, shared rituals, and shared experiences. Designing opportunities for these aspects of a program is just as important as figuring out the order of topics to be covered.

The manager of a government agency training program for high potential managers from around the country wanted to establish a collaborative culture which she hoped would help the group form a community of practice. She established a joining ritual for the program where each entering participant created a special web page with personal as well as career-related information and photographs of the participants in non-work settings. During the first week of the course, she paired up participants and replicated a familiar ice-breaking exercise of having them interview each other via email and then introduce their partner to the rest of the group by writing up a response for their online bulletin board. Participants reported that they felt that this process really made a difference in how quickly they felt like members of the community, a very different feeling from simply being among those accessing a common body of information.

3.7 Managing Roles

There are many names for the facilitator role; teacher, instructor, manager, leader, facilitator, moderator. Learners are called student, participant, member. Obviously, the choice of term can connote a lot about roles and expectations and it is an important choice to make as part of your learning design.

In the old paradigm classroom, the roles were simple. The teacher taught and the students followed directions. In the new classroom, teacher facilitators need to help all the members of the learning community (including students and other adults who may be involved) identify roles. Virtual learning communities need to define some additional roles related to their communication strategy. They may need technical support, knowledge archivists, and specialists in using different media. For all roles, virtual learning communities need to spend more time being explicit about mutual expectations (for example, how quickly they can expect responses to their online postings) because the patterns of behavior and dynamics of interaction are unfamiliar and it is easy to fall into misunderstandings and become frustrated with each other.

Distance learning provides some new ways to use people in the role of "expert" resources. Participants in the advanced management program at George Mason University invited a well-known author to join them online to discuss and answer questions about his forthcoming book. He did not want to travel in order to appear in a three-hour class so he suggested that they meet online. They were able to interact with him over time rather than for a single-shot guest lecture and so could explore his ideas in greater depth. One of the "unintended" benefits of this was that students for whom English was not their first language felt better able to think and write, in contrast to face-to-face when the conversation goes too fast.

Other members of the community can also serve in the role of teachers in a distance-learning program. Bank Street College of Education created a program focused on supporting girls so that they would continue studying science in high school. Research had shown that girls did just as well as boys in science classes in the early high school grades, but they tended to drop out before the advanced courses. This was a big problem because these courses are often prerequisites for certain college majors and are factored into college admissions. Bank Street College created a distance-learning program to link students with women mentors who had successfully entered careers in science and technology.

The program created small online groups made up of the student, her teacher, her parents, and a mentor. The student was also able to communicate one-to-one with her mentor. Students reported that they really appreciated the support of being able to ask their mentors questions about how to handle situations. For example, one student complained that the boys in her lab group made put-down type remarks to her which made her feel like quitting the course. Her mentor shared how she had had similar experiences but encouraged the student to continue with the course anyway. By expanding the notion of who could play a teaching role, the college was able to bring new resources into the program.

Distance learning also supports peer-to-peer learning by providing ways for learners to become facilitators for other learners. Creative Writers on the Net[3] is an advanced placement English program for high school students in Kalamazoo, Michigan. The essence of the course is to learn how to give and receive constructive feedback about all different kinds of writing. One of the advantages of the distance-learning model is the ease with which it is possible to post and interact with multiple drafts of writing. Although there is a team of teachers with responsibility for the course, much of the learning happens as a result of students' interaction with each other. Posting writing online makes it easy to read each others' work.

Union Institute is an accredited degree-granting program that is designed to support individual learning plans. Learners design programs with advisors that

---

[3] Creative Writers on the Net: http://www.tmn.com/efa

include combinations of traditional coursework, courses delivered at a distance, and individual study. One of the key components of this program is the requirement of Peer Days. Learners find a small group of fellow learners who share a need to explore a particular subject and pull together some kind of learning event (a guest speaker, group reading and discussion of a book, a workshop) collaboratively. Many of these Peer Days are held at a distance using online technologies that make it possible for geographically isolated learners to engage with each other. The students themselves thus take responsibility for managing a significant part of their own learning program.

3.8   Managing Time

In face-to-face and synchronous environments the challenge for the facilitator is to manage the respective airtime for different class members so the extroverts do not dominate. The same issue arises in asynchronous learning where very active participants can create information overload for others. In an asynchronous environment, some group members will check in four times a day and others will check in once a week. If you have several members who sign on very frequently, they can make it difficult for the rest to engage with the virtual group because it feels to them like the conversation has run away from them. The *rolling present* refers to differences in participants' perception of what is current. People experience everything that has been entered since the last time they checked in as current. You need to manage the pace of the group and create norms for how much time will be included in the rolling present of the community as a whole.

The fact that participants can access distance learning *any time* can be a great advantage. However, the lack of familiar time-frames, such as a class which meets on a certain day every week can make it hard for participants to manage the experience. One way facilitators can help participants is to create opportunities for explicit conversation about strategies for managing their time. For example, one moderator of an asynchronous course suggested to participants that they schedule a specific time to access the course and put it in their calendar just like any other meeting rather than leaving it to chance (in which case it often got squeezed out by other priorities).

Facilitators can also help by providing time-based guideposts to help give a learning group the feeling of making progress and moving forward. For example, in a distance course at Virginia Polytechnic University, students are given a course calendar that includes ways to check-in organized by time, topic, and medium. The course includes materials that were provided via the Web, which participants access via their corporate intranet, synchronous chat and telephone conferencing and asynchronous web conferencing led by the course facilitator. Although the participants can engage in course activities at any time, the facilitator provides the group with a pulse created by weekly "Journal" reflections where participants share their experience applying each course module to their daily experience. Participants know on which day the new conference item will be posted online, indicating time to shift the focus from one module to the next. In this way, even though learners are participating at their own time and pace, the group as a whole shares a sense of progressing through the course together.

3.9   Managing Awareness

Both facilitators and learners need to be aware of how they are performing. Distance learning students need different kinds of feedback to help them calibrate their participation with expectations. Teacher facilitators need to provide a lot more "work in progress" feedback than feedback on a final product because so much of this new type of project is process-oriented. Since using technology as a primary means to communicate will be new to most participants, they need to spend more time than usual talking about the quality of their communication. The teacher can provide some feedback but it is even better if the teacher can help participants develop a norm of providing feedback to each other about communication style, quantity, frequency, clarity, *etc*. Teachers can help team participants access more of their own feelings and reactions to messages in different media. This kind of savvy about new media is an important new skill.

In a face-to-face class, teachers watch body language and facial expression and many other signals to develop a sense of what is going on. Participants in a virtual learning community convey this same information in different ways and, much of what students will be doing will be done on their own out of sight of the teacher. Some teachers are experimenting with using the Internet as a place to store electronic portfolios of student work so that they can be accessed at any time.

Facilitation is paying attention to what is happening in your group as distinct from what you wanted or expected would happen. It is not unlike facilitating any group; if participants are not participating as much as you had hoped, do not admonish them. Instead, notice what kinds of issues they are engaged in and find ways to weave those issues into your group activity. You must detect where members are now and work with that energy to move in the direction you need to go.

3.10 Managing Collaboration

While most people agree that collaborative learning is desirable and important, it has been difficult logistically in the past. Unless students are in a residential setting, it is unrealistic to expect them to be able to find the time and space to work together full time. Distance learning provides an opportunity to support collaborative learning in ways we have not been able to do before. However, just putting participants together in some kind of common electronic space will not turn them into a collaborative group automatically. The key is to design a framework for group-work that requires the team to grapple with roles, protocols for working interdependently and mutual accountability.

For example, in the George Mason University Program on Social and Organizational Learning (PSOL)[4], participants in a graduate level course on The Virtual Organization used a wide variety of media, including asynchronous web conferences, telephone conferences, shared white board, and email to support collaborative learning. The class was divided into teams tasked with mastering sets of specific learning objectives and finding ways to transfer that learning to the class as a whole.

The distance learning cohorts within the California Institute of Integral Studies are required to present a Group Demonstration of Mastery to faculty and peers as a significant part of their doctoral program. This requires the cohort to select and commit to a common theme for learning over the course of a year or more and to integrate their distributed efforts into a shared whole.

It can be very difficult and time-consuming to self-organize into teams or small groups in an asynchronous environment. In face-to-face situations, people can quickly form small groups by making eye contact and moving physically near each other. Therefore, it is usually more effective to use synchronous media for initial group formation or for the instructor/facilitator to create teams to get a group started. You can achieve the goal of self-selection of topics by letting groups define their mission or by letting people switch groups after a while.

3.11 Managing Faculty Development

How can we help faculty make the shifts in thinking required to be effective in distance learning courses? What is the best way to learn to manage these new aspects of the learning process? The most effective strategy is to provide access to experienced faculty who can serve as coaches. Team teaching with a more experienced teacher is also a good approach.

The PBS Mathline program required more than 100 new facilitators to manage the virtual learning communities. It was not possible to bring all those people in for face-to-face training. Since audiotapes are cheap and easy to distribute, tapes were made of a panel of experienced facilitators and sent to the new group. Four to five experienced practitioners called in on a call-me audio call that was taped. In order to make the conversation feel spontaneous it was not scripted. However, it was planned and moderated. Three to four key theme questions were chosen ahead of time along with who would be first to respond to each question. After that it was a free-flowing discussion. All the facilitators on the tape were also online so the new group of facilitators were able to ask them questions after listening to the taped discussion.

---

[4] George Mason University Program on Social and Organizational Learning: http://mason.gmu.edu/~jforeman/Vorg/virtualorg.html

3.12 New Centers of Learning

"The organizations that will truly excel in the future will be the organizations that discover how to tap people's commitment and capacity to learn at all levels in an organization." [20]

Increasingly, learning managers will be found outside traditional educational institutions. The theory of organizational learning has captured the imagination of many organizations. Most have found it challenging to figure out how to connect the theory with day-to-day practice. Distance learning approaches can play a significant role in turning organizational learning from theory to reality but in a lot of companies, the first uses of distance learning technologies have been limited to creating packaged multimedia training courses either to individuals or to groups gathered to receive some kind of predominantly one-way broadcast of information. This does not do much to support organizational learning.

To harvest the knowledge and experience of people and make them available to the organization as a whole, distance learning technologies need to be managed differently to support dialogue rather than just databases.

In the information age, education and training in organizations consisted of large amounts of explicit knowledge made available to them through huge archival databases. Quantifiable facts, formulas, and procedures were, and still are, available to anyone in these organizations. In contrast, today's knowledge or learning organizations create environments where experiential knowledge is learned through dialogue and interaction day-to-day. Communication technologies are needed which support this interaction. Previously tacit knowledge based on extremely valuable experience now supplements the quantifiable data.

The environment should stimulate and nurture the complex network of interpersonal relationships and interactions that are part of an effective management communications and decision-making process. People must be allowed to make choices about with whom they need to communicate and learn without regard to traditional organizational boundaries, distance and time. In other words, they need to manage their own learning, to form new groups and teams as requirements develop and change.

The new framework for managing distance learning should be about managing the learning process rather than managing courses. The kinds of questions we need to be asking ourselves are not about how to plug one kind of technology into another or how faculty can be more effective on video. The more important questions are about how to use technology to leverage resources and group dynamics in new ways to make fundamental changes in every part of the learning process.

References

1.   Bates, A.W. Tony (1995) Technology, Open Learning and Distance Education. Routledge.

2. Beer, V. (2000) The Web Learning Fieldbook: Using the World Wide Web to Build Workplace Learning Environments, Jossey-Bass.

3. Bentley, T. (1994) Facilitation: Providing Opportunities for Learning. McGraw-Hill.

4. Berreman, I. (1997) An improvisational model for groupware technologies. *Sloan Management Review,* Orlikowski, W. and Hofman, D., Winter, 1997.

5. Collison, G., Elbaum, B. Haavind, S, and Tinker, R. (2000) Facilitating Online Learning: Effective Strategies for Moderators, Atwood Publishing.

6. Digenti, Dori (1999). Collaborative learning: A core capability for organizations in the new economy, *Reflections (Society for Organizational Learning) Journal.* Winter 1999.

7. Eunice, A. and Kimball, L. (1997) Zen and the art of facilitating virtual teams. *Conference Proceedings, Organization Development Network Annual Conference,* Organization Development Network, 76 South Orange Avenue, Suite 101, South Orange, NJ 07079-1923.

8. Eunice, A., Kimball, L., Silber, T. and Weinstein, N. (1998) Boundaryless Facilitation, in *Pushing the Boundaries: Learning Organization Lessons from the Field*, Pamela Dodd (Ed), Kennedy Press.

9. Farry, S. B. (1994) From Managing to Empowering: An Action Guide to Developing Winning Facilitation Skills. Quality Resources.

10. Hanna, D., Glowacki-Dudka, M. and Conceicao-Runlee, S. (2000) 147 Practical Tips for Teaching Online Groups: Essentials of Web-based education, Atwood Publishing.

11. Kimball, L. (1997*) Intranet Decisions: Creating Your Organization's Internal Network*, Miles River Press.

12. Kimball, L. (1995) Ten ways to make online learning groups work. *Educational Leadership*. Association for Supervision and Curriculum Development, Alexandria, VA, October.

13. Martinez, M., and Bunderson, C. (2000), Foundations for personalized web learning environments. *ALN Magazine*, 4.2, December 2000.

14. Oravec, Jo Ann (1996) Virtual individuals, virtual groups: Human dimensions of groupware and computer networking. Cambridge University Press.

15. Passmore, D.,(2000) Impediments to adoption of web-based course delivery among university faculty. *ALN Magazine*, 4.2, December 2000.

16. Porter, Lynnette R. (1997) Virtual classroom: Distance learning with the Internet. John Wiley.

17. Salmon, G. (2000) E-Moderating: The key to teaching and leaning online, Stylus Publishing.

18. Schrage, Michael. (1996) No more teams!: Mastering the dynamics of creative sCollaboration. Doubleday.

19. Schwartz, Roger M. (1994) The skilled facilitator: Practical wisdom for developing effective group, Jossey-Bass.

20.   Senge, P.M. (1990) The fifth discipline: The art and practice of the learning organization, Currency/Doubleday.

Chapter 4

Collaborative Interactions in Support of Learning: Models, Metaphors and Management

Kent Norman

New electronic educational environments invite almost unlimited possibilities for interactive learning and collaboration in the digital university. However, to support quality education, learning activities need to be guided by principled models of interaction, guidelines for the design of user interfaces, and policies for the management of interaction and collaboration. In this chapter, a model of interaction among instructors, students, and educational material will be introduced to help define the types of collaborative interactions among instructors, among students, between instructors and students, and with materials. To further define learning activities, the structure of the human/computer interface will be discussed in terms of interface metaphors and a prototype system that provides tools for accessing materials, submitting assignments, asking questions and providing feedback, engaging in dialogue, and working on team projects. These metaphors and resulting systems add necessary structure, meaning, and limits to learning activities. Finally, both instructors and students need to manage the interaction by scheduling, organizing, and focusing activities. Policies may be implemented in the system to provide scheduled roll-out of materials and assignments, automatic filing and storage of materials, and deadlines and constraints on submissions. Illustrations and applications will be drawn from ten years of experience in the Teaching Theaters at the University of Maryland and other collaborative projects.

4.1   Introduction

New electronic educational environments, however construed on networks and computers, offer a full range of computer and communication facilities. In principle, everything that we might want to do in education can be done in the emerging electronic educational environments. These environments, supported by local area networks and the Internet, provide new channels for collaborative models of learning, training, teaching, and ultimately the authoring of science and knowledge. Multimedia browsing and authoring, desktop video conferencing, and specialized animations, simulations, and games provide new media for learning.

As the infrastructure for this environment unfolds, the question is how to use it in new and effective ways to support not only current models of education but new methods of student-student, student-educator, and educator-educator collaboration in the educational process. New levels of interactivity, communication, and collaboration are now possible. However, the unlimited range of possibilities poses a design problem. The design and implementation of the interface to host these new activities is critical to its success. The creation of this environment and the tools to support it involve at least three disciplines: (a) human/computer interaction for the design and evaluation of the interface; (b) cognitive psychology for theories of learning, knowledge comprehension, and collaborative thinking and problem solving; and (c) education for the models of pedagogy, curriculum development, and evaluation of learning effectiveness.

In this chapter, a model for the interaction among students, instructors, and educational materials will be presented. A new model for spatially directed/ spatially privileged collaboration will be used in conjunction with new techniques for visualizing and constructing shared collaborative spaces. Research and teaching experience collected over the last ten years in the Teaching Theaters at the University of Maryland as well as other projects will be used to formulate new directions for software development for collaboration.

4.2   A Model of the Interaction Space

Collaboration requires media, methods, and members. Substantial bodies of literature already exist pertaining to computer supported collaborative work (CSCW) [2] and computer based instruction (CBI) [3]. On the other hand, research is only beginning within the overlap of learning technology and collaborative tools. In this section, a foundation for collaborative learning technology will be laid by discussing: (a) the infrastructure of electronic classrooms; (b) the development of software methods of allowing collaboration to happen electronically; and (c) collaborative efforts across disciplines and distance.

4.2.1 Teaching Theaters become Stages for Collaboration

In 1991, the AT&T Teaching Theater opened at the University of Maryland. The room was equipped with 20 workstations for the students (for up to two students per workstation) and two for the instructor as shown in Figure 1.

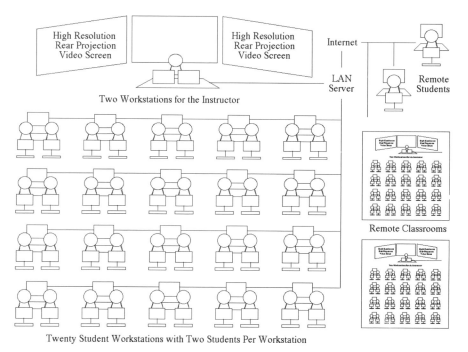

Figure 4.1. The electronic classroom.

The computers were networked to allow for communication and collaboration among the students and the faculty. Two large 4x6 foot (1.2 x 1.8m) displays were used for group viewing of material and a video switcher employed for exchanging screens. Three additional classrooms have been completed since then: the IBM-TQM Teaching Theater in 1994, the OITS Teaching Theater in 1997, and the Plant Sciences Teaching Theater in 2000. These classrooms have been the result of efforts on the part of a Steering Committee composed of faculty and administrators and the Teaching Technology staff in the Computer Science Center (see http://www.inform.umd.edu/TeachTech/).

Much has been learned about: (a) what technology works and what doesn't work in the classrooms; (b) how to configure and manage the servers and networks; and (c) how to support and maintain the system reliably. However, more importantly, much has been learned about how the technology can be used for collaborative learning. Over the years, a number of faculty at the university have taught a wide variety of courses to a large number of students. The trend has been for lectures to evolve from presentations to explorations, from passive learning to active engagement, and from the "sage on the stage" to the "guide on the side". Shneiderman *et al.* [14] note, "We originally called our electronic classrooms Teaching Theaters, but as faculty experimented with new teaching styles the Steering Committee shifted to the term Learning Theaters to convey an increased emphasis on student-centered learning styles."

During these years of operation a large number of collaborative learning exercises and approaches have been tried. Collaborative activities have ranged in size from small group projects to whole class and even groups of classes, and in scope from short in-class sessions (*e.g.*, brain storming and idea formation) to whole semester projects (*e.g.*, create a web site for a community organization or write a computer program). Many of these have been summarized in journal articles and technical reports [1, 11, 14]. Additional background and theory on the electronic classroom can be found in Chapters 4 and 5 of *The Switched On Classroom* (http://www.lap.umd.edu/ SOC/) [9] and a chapter on desktop distance education in [10]

4.2.2 Collaborative Spaces

Collaboration in education, however, is broader than the stereotypical illustrations generally cited as examples. Collaboration is an inherent part of education, from teachers co-laboring with students in one-to-one tutoring to learning communities such as the one-room schoolhouse, and from teachers collaborating in the preparation of materials to students collaborating in studying and even in attempts to cheat.

To help comprehend the range of collaboration in learning activities a model of interaction will be used. In 1990, Norman proposed a model of interactions to help define the interaction spaces [5]. At its most trivial level, education can be viewed as the flow of information from one generation, however construed, to the next. Although education is a much richer event embodying not only the hopes and purposes of humanity but our very destiny as well, the technological schematic need only consider the flow of information from one point to another. Figure 4.2 gives a schematic diagram of some of these spaces and some of the interactions that may occur in them.

To this schematic we add the content of the information and the interaction of human agents about this information. The collaborative classroom and the underlying educational environment supporting it is a multi-faceted electronic space involving complex interactions among two sets of agents (instructors and students) and two sets of objects (course materials and course products). The interactions among these sets form a complex network of relationships. On the left side of the figure, the double arrows indicate that instructors interact among themselves. In the hard copy classroom, this is by way of formal printed media such as books and journals and by way of informal methods such as conversation and the exchange of notes and ideas. On the right side of the figure, the double arrows indicate that students also interact among themselves. In the traditional classroom, student interaction is generally limited to informal methods of communication such as in-class discussion and out-of-class study groups.

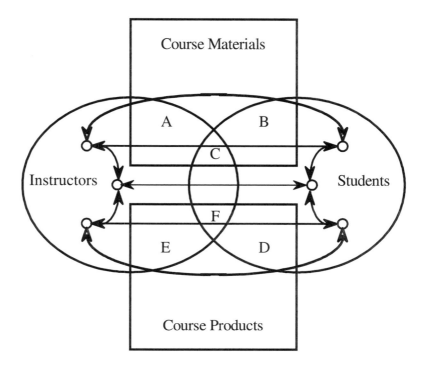

Figure 4.2. A schematic of the interaction spaces and the sets of agents and objects in the instructional process.

The instructional process basically involves interaction across sets of agents. Instructors convey information to the students and students convey information back often in the form of questions, answers, and reports. In general, however, interactions are conveyed by means of the two sets of objects, the course materials and the course products. Course materials consist of previously existing texts, lesson plans, and compendia of materials such as references, collections, and databases. Course products are the result of educational activities and include such things as test results, class dialogue, original works produced by the students, and evaluative feedback. In general, the originating source of the information is the set of course materials; it is conveyed by means of the instructor to the students or by students directly interacting with the information and finally, results in the observable products of education which, hopefully, are diagnostic of lasting changes in the students themselves.

Switching to the digital media, the course materials and course products are contained in hypermedia databases and interaction with these databases is by way of the human/computer interface. The interface is represented in Figure 4.2 as the intersection of areas covered by the domains. There are six intersecting areas. The Instructor-Material Area A pertains to the instructor's access to course material outside of their direct interaction with students. Course preparation would be a major activity in this area. Similarly, the Student-Material Area B pertains to student access to course material outside of direct interaction with the instructors. This would include the activities of independent reading and studying. The Instructor-Material-Student Area C is a three-way interface of the instructors and the students together interacting with the course material. This area basically represents the activities of delivering lectures and classroom interaction with course material. The Student-Product Area D pertains to student authoring of papers, completion of assignments, and taking of exams. Since students may also be grouped, this area may also contain collaborative work. The Instructor-Product Area E pertains to instructor access to course products for evaluation and grading. Finally, and central to collaboration and mentoring, the Instructor-Products-Students Area F is a three-way interface of instructors and students with the products. Instructors and students may work together on collaborative class projects.

With this as a schematic, one may then translate each space to a file server or device storing the course materials and course products. Each interaction among agents can be translated to some tool for transmitting information such as email, Listservs, file transfer protocol (FTP), multi-party chat channels, or "browsers" on the world wide Web. The question then is how to design the educational space so that it is integrated, understandable, and usable by students, instructors, and administrators. The abstract information space must be instantiated, given substance, and made meaningful.

To further conceptualize the collaborative aspects of this interaction a spatially directed/spatially privileged model of collaboration is proposed in Figure 4.3 as a frame for organizing past efforts and for identifying new innovations and requirements for collaborative tools. Collaboration is spatially directed in the sense that it can be lateral (with peers at the same level, *e.g.*, students), hierarchical (between members of different levels of the same hierarchy, *e.g.*, student, teaching assistant, and instructor), diagonal (between members of different levels of different hierarchies, *e.g.*, a student in one class with an instructor teaching a different class), nested (with members in the same class or discipline), or crossed (with members of different classes or disciplines).

Collaboration is spatially privileged when team members have different privileges to read and write to shared areas. Each student has his or her own personal space in addition to a space to which they can write and from which others can read. In Figure 4.3 for example, Student B can read part of Student A's space but cannot write to it. Outside of their personal spaces is a shared area from which all students on that team can read and to which they can write. Part of that area is a common space between teams and in that space part of Team 1's area can be read by Team 2, part of Team 2's area can be read by Team 1, and part can be both read and written to by both teams. This structure of privileges allows members within teams to work individually, to share products for review, and to combine group-work for the final report. It also allows groups to share work and ideas and to collaborate at higher levels.

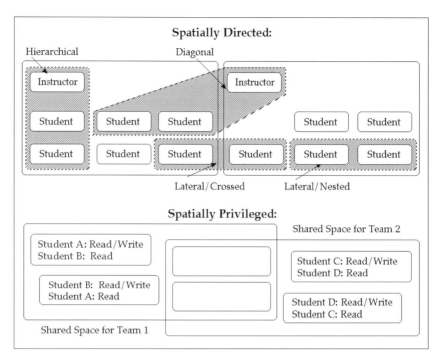

Figure 4.3. A spatially directed/spatially privileged model of collaboration.

4.3 Metaphors and the HyperCourseware Prototype

How we use things depends on how we think they work. In the case of new technologies, we often use metaphors and graphics to make them look like things with which we are already familiar. A multiple choice exam on computer uses the same structure of a stem and foils and can appear on the screen to look just as it might on paper. Only minor modifications are necessary so that a mouse click replaces a pencil check mark to indicate the selected alternative. Changing one's answer does not require an eraser but merely another click invoking the graphic metaphor of a radio button. Similarly, a listing of dates, lecture topics, readings, and homework assignments may look like a typical course syllabus, but a click on the topic jumps to the lecture notes, a click on the reading displays the text, and a click on the homework assignment opens a form for submitting the work.

In the new electronic educational environment, the interactions in Figure 4.2 and the relational structures in Figure 4.3 are channeled through software tools. Many tools have been developed specifically for this purpose and other generic tools have been used in creative ways to provide for interaction and collaboration through email, listservs, and internet relay chat as well as complete courseware shells on the world wide Web. In this section, one prototype called HyperCourseware will be used to illustrate the use of metaphors and the need for an integrated electronic environment in education.

One of the greatest needs in collaborative learning in electronic environments has been an integrated software package that seamlessly ties all of the aspects of the learning, teaching, and collaborative processes together. The problem in education has not been the existence of software but the fact that most programs have been either: (a) small-scale, one-off, subject-specific, platform-dependent programs written by educators; or (b) general-purpose programs for business applications retro-adapted for educational use. To bridge the gap, Norman [5] proposed an electronic educational environment that has now become known as "HyperCourseware". It is based on the idea of collaborative hypermedia, a system that allows multiple users to explore the same materials and to communicate with each other while making use of dynamic metaphors in education.

4.3.1 HyperCourseware Prototype

The conceptual interactions and spaces shown in Figures 4.2 and 4.3 have been instantiated in an easy-to-use interface in HyperCourseware. The objective embraced by HyperCourseware has been quite broad: to provide an integrated and seamless hypermedia infrastructure to support the full range of classroom activities [7, 11]. Over its years of development, HyperCourseware has become quite extensive. Samples of screens of an early version written in stackware can be viewed at the HyperCourseware web site at http://www.lap.umd.edu/hcw, and its current web-based version can be seen at http://cognitron.umd.edu. To illustrate a part of the interface, Figure 4.4 shows the Home Screen and a number of the current modules available around its perimeter.

At the global level, HyperCourseware is organized around educational tools, materials, and objectives rather than around semantic or domain specific knowledge. It is only at the local or content level in the materials that knowledge structure becomes important and is incorporated into the materials by the instructor or instructional designer. Consequently, HyperCourseware was written to host any subject and to support many different learning activities common across many different types of courses. These activities range from record keeping and online testing to hypermedia presentations, and from individual exploration to group collaboration and team projects [12].

HyperCourseware uses the conventional objects of classroom instruction and implements them in digital form in the electronic classroom. Objects such as the course syllabus, the lesson plan, the lecture notes, the class roll, *etc.* are instantiated in graphic form in a hypermedia database. Furthermore, in HyperCourseware the database is used to provide the same sort of natural links between objects as one would expect in the educational materials themselves. For example, the syllabus is a natural navigational mechanism to jump to lectures, readings, and assignments;

the class roll is a natural navigational jump to information about students and grades; and the grade list is a natural navigational jump to exams and assignments.

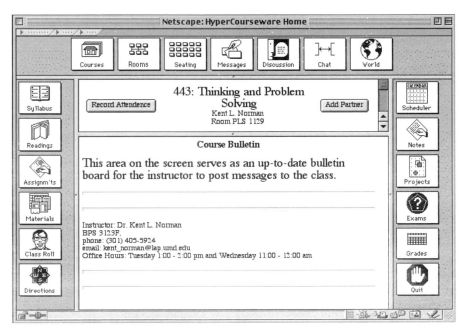

Figure 4.4. The "Home" screen of HyperCourseware which displays a number of linked modules making up the current educational environment.

In addition to the multimedia course materials, the real advantage of the electronic environment supported by HyperCourseware has been the wide range of collaborative tools. Each tool can be used in different ways depending on project goals and course objectives.

Dialogue as collaboration

A number of collaborative exercises in the electronic classroom have used different forms of multi-party chat sessions. These have been used for brainstorming, focused discussion, and group planning. Tools for organizing, monitoring, and analyzing chat sessions have been partially developed. At present these tools are used to count student entries and cluster them by topic and by contributor. Additional tools that allow for visualization of threads, clustering of ideas, and better integration with other tasks are needed.

Collection and dissemination of ideas

Initial collaboration begins with the generation and polling of ideas, materials, or parts of a project. Several tools have been used for facilitating discussion by having the students start with an initial contribution. These contributions are aggregated and then disseminated to the group for inspection. Once the group has seen everyone's contribution, it can go to the next level of discussion. Other applications have involved collecting parts of a larger project from either individuals or from subgroups. For example, subgroups might contribute parts (*e.g.*, subroutines for a program, sections of an article, or designs of rooms in a building). The parts are collected, aggregated, and disseminated. The group evaluates whether the aggregation works and/or what needs to be changed.

Project spaces

Structured project spaces have been used for team collaboration. A structured project space is a template that allows different members of the team to contribute to their prescribed parts while also allowing all members to view and comment on any part of the project. Parts of the project space are write protected so that only certain members may change the information. This approach helps to manage and track the contribution of individual members of the team and hold members accountable for their individual work rather than only being able to assess the overall project for assigning grades.

Ordered file exchange

Collaboration is often serial. One person creates the first part, the next member adds the second part, and so on. Routing handlers are used to direct materials from one student to another. In one application, the first student wrote an article which was then passed on to four other students who read the article and critiqued it. The critiques were then passed back to the first student. Similar procedures can be programmed for other routing of materials in learning environments.

4.3.2 Interface Design for Collaboration

The challenge to the software engineer and the instructional designer is to develop interfaces for these tools that are easy to use and that assist both the students and the instructors in using the collaborative tools in a productive and efficient manner. A number of books and articles deal with the problem of interface design [4, 6, 8, 13]. These outline the methods of interaction, the principles of screen layout, the importance of consistency, the need for clear directions, and the need for the interface to match user expectation.

In the area of interfaces for collaboration there are some additional concerns that need to be mentioned. First, navigation is a pervasive problem in all software; however, in collaborative tools it is often critical. Clear navigational tools are needed to find where to go for a particular collaborative session. There are many times when all of the students need to be at the same point in the system to perform an exercise. A homing function that jumps all of the students to an instructor defined location is one solution for group navigation.

Second, clear displays are needed to inform the student of important parameters of the interaction and controls to set those parameters. For example, student identity or anonymity in collaboration is an important factor. The screen should clearly indicate whether the contribution is to be anonymous or whether identification is to be associated with the transmission. Figure 4.5 shows such controls on a chat tool in HyperCourseware.

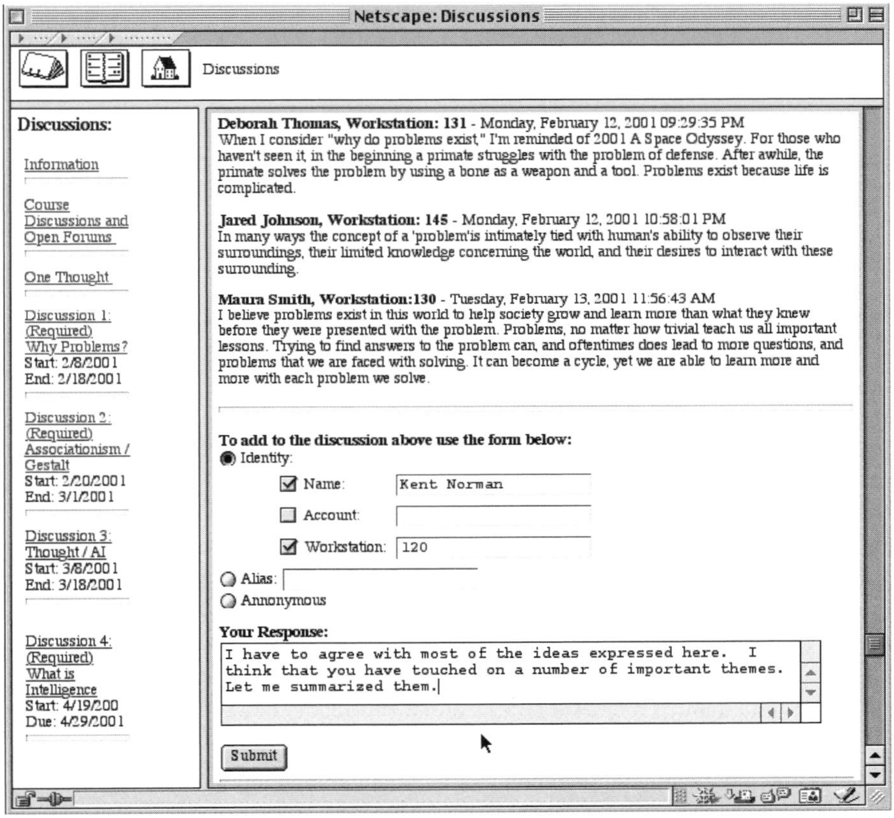

Figure 4.5. A chat channel screen in HyperCourseware.

Finally, the interface needs to provide information and feedback on how collaborative information is shared among the students, who can see and modify information, and how group consensus is achieved for the final product.

4.4   Policies for Managing Learning Activities

The tools for collaborative learning activities are only effective if they are put to good use. Just setting up a Listserv for a class does not ensure that it will have any educational use or redeeming value. It must be put to the right use and monitored to ensure that it is properly used. In this section we will look at some of these uses and ways of monitoring and managing the collaboration to ensure that learning objectives are being met.

As indicated in Figure 4.1, there are many areas for collaboration in education in addition to the stereotypical "group project". A sampling of collaboration is listed below.

Collective Note Taking. Students vary in their ability and readiness to take notes in class or to write notes on readings. Collective note taking distributes the responsibility for digesting the information across a group and provides a collective set of perspectives that can be discussed and edited to provide a set of study notes that will be more complete and balanced than individual notes. Collaborative word processing tools can be used to collect individual notes, sort by time and topic, and allow for editing by the students and the instructor.

Study Groups. Students study together discussing topics, explaining concepts to one another, working problems together, and quizzing one another. Dialogue tools can be used for discussion and explanation. Shared workspaces can be used for problems and illustrations. Quizzing can be done using chat tools. However, for each of these activities, the current generic tools need to be refined and linked to facilitate the specific activities.

Collective Information Search. The skills of information search and retrieval are becoming more and more important in education. Collaborative information search on the part of the students helps them to share ideas, techniques, and resources. Students may search individually at first or they may divide the task among themselves and then combine the results at the end. They may share needs so that if one hits upon a source of interest to another that student can be informed of the lead. Again, generic search tools and communication tools need to be designed to make these tasks easy and efficient.

Group Projects. The intent of the group project is to allow students to work together on a project that involves more work than any one individual could perform during the course of the semester. It involves the collective skills of dividing the project into subtasks, assigning subtasks to group members, overseeing the progress of the work, and finally bringing the parts together for completion. Rarely, however, are students given instruction on project management let alone tools for scheduling and monitoring the overall project. They are left to struggle with failure, missed deadlines, and inequities. It is here that easy-to-use tools for group project management are desperately needed in education. In a number of instances instructors are beginning to use tests to assess the abilities and skills of team members, to pre-assign them to roles on the team, and to use project planning and tracking software. A successful approach is to assign students to the following roles:

- *Collectors* who go out and gather interesting and relevant information from multimedia.

- *Commentators* who write commentaries and discuss the collections.

- *Constructors* who are involved in the construction of the virtual space housing the collection. (This involves technical and programming skills.)

- *Curators* who serve as managers of the collection, guide the progress, and oversee its progress.

Collaborative Exams. In many courses, after we expound on the virtues collaboration and cooperative learning activities, we then give a traditional competitive final exam. However, tools exist and can be further developed to create exams that assess the collaborative abilities of individuals while testing the collective knowledge of the group. These exams monitor contributions to group answers to essay questions and the division of labor in answering objective questions.

The many interactive collaborative activities of the students require new levels of monitoring and control. Listservs and chat sessions can go off onto extreme tangents, useless volumes of banter and filler, and sometimes destructive directions and flaming. Group projects can become resentful one-person efforts or total stalemates. In general, it is a good idea to specify as many initial rules as possible and to employ continuous monitoring and control to alleviate problems. Such rules and methods are listed below.

Setting Rules of Interaction. Unrestrained discussion can quickly go awry. In general, it is best to avoid anonymity and aliases in online discussion. Furthermore, it is useful to set rules for entries and to assign grades based on compliance with those rules. For example, in a focused discussion on the pros and cons of some issue, one might require each student to make three reasoned entries, the first being an opening position, the second being a criticism of the opposition, and the third being a defense of the original opinion or a repositioning of opinion.

Roll Out Subtasks Over Time. Another method of controlling collaborative activities is to reveal and assign parts of a larger task over time. For example, the first step might be to assign a brainstorming task to the group, then an evaluation of possible alternatives, then a decision of the preferred alternative, and so on until the final report is turned in. Scheduling helps to structure the task, reduce procrastination, keep milestones on a timely basis, and even out distribution of work. The down side is that this entails additional work on the part of the instructor. However, much of this may be handled automatically with assignment tools, as in HyperCourseware, that distribute materials at predetermined times.

Rotating Exposure to Information. Collaboration can also be controlled by rotating the exposure of materials among the members of a group in a set order. In a three-person group, for example, initial input from Student A could be handed to

Student B, B's initial input to C, and C's to A. After each has reviewed the initial input and modified it, it would be handed to the third student. A round robin approach ensures that all students are active in the collaborative process and routing tools help to structure and subdivide the process.

Continuous Monitoring of Group Interactions. It is assumed in the new electronic educational environment that many, if not all, collaborative interactions leave records in a database. Thus, over the course of a project, one can look at the number of transactions and contributions by each member of a group. At the end of the semester the instructor can assign grades not only on the final product but also on the level and type of interactions by the students. Furthermore, during the semester, the instructor can monitor the progress of the groups and spot problem groups and problem members and plan interventions to correct the problems. Needless to say, tools are needed so that the instructor can see at a glance the progress of each group and the patterns of collaboration. Figure 4.6 shows a mock-up of one possible system in which the instructor can select teams, members, and tasks for observation. Graphs at the bottom show effort over time as vertical bars, and effort by members as horizontal bars. Graphs among the members show the structure of the group as hierarchical, egalitarian or independent.

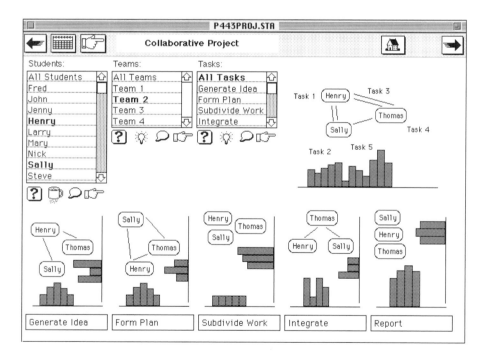

Figure 4.6. A visualization of collaborative activities.

4.5 Conclusion

A key to effective learning has always been collaboration in one form or another between the instructor, the students, and the material. However, the question through the ages has been whether or not the key has been turned to unlock the power of collaboration to engage the interest of students, allowing them to relate meaningfully to the information and to learn to work together. In the past, it has been the exceptional teacher who has drawn the students into engaging dialogue and constructive projects or the adventurous student who has explored and interacted with others. Today, the new media of instructional technology in an electronic educational environment presents new tools to suggest, enhance, and facilitate collaboration that has not been possible in the past. While many possibilities exist, this chapter emphasizes the importance of interface design and new tools for managing collaborative activities so that educational objectives will be met in the process.

References

1. Alavi, M. (1994). Computer mediated collaborative learning: An empirical evaluation. *MIS Quarterly*, 18, 159-173.

2. Baecker, R. (1993). Readings in groupware and computer-supported cooperative work: Assisting human-human collaboration, San Francisco, CA: Morgan Kaufmann.

3. Chambers, J. A., & Sprecher, J. W. (1983). Computer assisted instruction: Its use in the classroom. Englewood Cliffs, NJ: Prentice-Hall.

4. Neilson, J. (1999). Designing web usability: The practice of simplicity. Indianapolis: New Riders Publishing.

5. Norman, K. L. (1990). The electronic teaching theater: Interactive hypermedia and mental models of the classroom in *Current Psychology Research and Reviews* (Special Issue: Hypermedia and artificial intelligence) 9, 141-161.

6. Norman, K. L. (1991). The psychology of menu selection: Designing cognitive control at the human/computer interface. Norwood, NJ: Ablex Publishing Corporation.

7. Norman, K. L. (1994). HyperCourseware for assisting teachers in the interactive electronic classroom in *Proceedings of STATE 94: Fifth Annual Conference of the Society for Technology and Teacher Education*, Washington, DC, 473-477.

8. Norman, K. L. (1994). Navigating the educational space with HyperCourseware in *Hypermedia*, 6, 35-60.

9. Norman, K. L. (1997). Teaching in the switched-on classroom: An introduction to electronic education and HyperCourseware. (http://www.lap.umd.edu/SOC/).

10. Norman, K. L. (2000). Desktop distance education: Personal hosting of Web courses in A. Aggarwal (Ed.), *Web based learning and teaching technologies: Opportunities and challenges*, Ideal Press.

11. Norman, K. L., & Carter, L. (1994). An evaluation of the electronic classroom: The AT&T Teaching Theater at the University of Maryland in *Interpersonal Computing and Technology: An Electronic Journal of the 21st Century, 2,* 22-39. (Gopher: guvm.ccf.georgetown.edu; Listserv: listserv@guvm.georgetown.edu.

12. Sebrechts, M. M., Silverman, B. G., Boehm-Davis, D. A., & Norman, K. L. (1995). Establishing an electronic collaborative learning environment in a university consortium: The CIRCLE project in *Computers in Educatio, 25,* 215-225.

13. Shneiderman, B. (1997). Designing the user interface: Strategies for effective human-computer interaction (3rd ed), New York: Addison-Wesley.

14. Shneiderman, B., Alavi, M., Norman, K., & Borkowski, E. (1995). Windows of opportunities in electronic classrooms in *Communications of the ACM*, 38, 19-24.

Chapter 5

Managing Tertiary Education in a Global Virtual Environment: Networked Educational Management

Philip Uys

Many conventional tertiary educational institutions have been incorporating internet-based (networked) education. Entirely virtual universities are emerging. Networked education naturally leads to participation in the global educational arena. What are the implications for academic, administrative and student management when embracing networked education? Some argue that networked education is essentially an alternative delivery mode and its management is thus no different than that of other modes. Others posit that networked education is a new educational paradigm and a response to the educational needs of the emerging information society, in the same way as the traditional class was a response to the educational needs of the industrial society. Management of networked education is therefore fundamentally different from conventional educational management particularly in a global environment. This view correlates with new forms of private enterprise management including management of the learning organization, the information-based organization and the networked organization. The writer proposes a new form of tertiary educational management for the operations of networked education in a global environment: *networked educational management*. The following dimensions of networked educational management are discussed: networking, student focus, globalization, its flexibility, its boundary orientation and its being information based.

5.1 Introduction

"… as soon as a company takes the first tentative steps from data to information, its decision processes, management structure, and even the way it gets its work done begin to be transformed." [1, p. 100].

The widespread implementation of internet and intranet-based education (networked education) in tertiary education globally necessitates a careful consideration of appropriate corresponding academic, administrative and student management approaches. Networked education is being implemented on an exponential scale due to: its flexibility; its links to the emerging culture of post-modernism [2]; its potential to increase the cost-effectiveness of delivery [3] and quality of learning; its pertinence as an appropriate educational response to globalization; and its ability to help address the global increase in demand for tertiary education [4]. Tiffin [5] believes that the "…concept of the virtual class is the kernel of a new educational paradigm that matches the needs of an information society" (p. 1). Tiffin further states that "… networked education is an information technology system for education and training which could become to an information society what the conventional classroom is to an industrial society, the core communication system for preparing people for the society they live in" ([6], p. 2).

A fundamental difference between networked education and conventional face-to-face or distance education is that it relies on a telecommunication infrastructure rather than a transport infrastructure to bring together the essential elements of education [5] and provide a new level of connectivity within the educational process. Networked education therefore deals primarily with the movement of bits of information rather than with the movement of atoms [7].

The term "*management*" is used in a broad sense to describe planning, organizing, leading and control [8, 9] on all levels of a tertiary educational institute. There has been a clear and consistent call from prominent writers on management and organizational design like Drucker [10, 11, 12], Senge [13], Peters [14], Marquard [15], Tapscott [16], Limerick and Cunnington [17] that these functions of management are to be practiced in an entirely new way in the context of the emerging global information or knowledge society.

Tapscott [16] states, "It is fairly widely accepted that the developed world is changing from an industrial economy based on steel, automobiles, and roads to a new economy built on silicon, computers and networks. Many people talk of a shift in economic relationships that's as significant as the previous displacement of the agricultural age by the industrial age" (p. 43). Peters [18] contends, "the definite shifts described indicate that the organization of the learning process in the post-industrial society might become entirely different in many ways" (p. 53).

Rayport and Sviokla [19] argue that every organization (including educational organizations) "…today competes in two worlds: a physical world of resources that managers can see and touch [the "place"] and a virtual world made of information [the "space"]" (p. 75). They illustrate and argue that these "…two value adding processes are fundamentally different" and that "...a company's executives must embrace an updated set of guiding principles because in the marketspace many of the business axioms that have guided managers no longer apply" (p.83).

Paul [20] posits that an institution that is dedicated to the values and practice of open learning needs to have an "open management style" (p. 72). Thomas, Carswell, Price and Petre [21] argue for the "...transformation of practices (both teaching and administrative) to take advantage of technology in order to provide needed functions, rather than superficial translation of existing practices". Bates [22] contends that the introduction of networked education "...will mean a thorough re-examination of the core practices of the organization, from advertising to registration to design and delivery of materials to student support to assessment of students, in order to analyze the most effective way of providing these services in a networked, multimedia environment."

Drucker [11] constructs an analogy between the introduction of computers in education and that of the book, and argues that a revolution in education based on the underlying technologies is occurring: "The printed book, fiercely resisted by the schoolmasters of the fifteenth and sixteenth centuries, did not triumph until the Jesuits and Comenius created schools based on it in the late seventeenth century. From the beginning the printed book forced the schools however to change drastically how they were teaching.... We are in the early stages of a similar technological revolution, and perhaps an even bigger one" (p. 243).

This research argues that the management of networked education is fundamentally different from conventional educational management, particularly in a global environment. A new kind of educational management is required in tertiary education for managing the operations of networked education on the strategic (long term), tactical (resource allocation) and operational (day to day) levels of management.

This chapter is based on the action research findings of the Hydi Educational New Media Center [23, 24] in implementing networked education since September 1995 at Massey University, and on case studies in other countries. This chapter presents some aspects of the writer's doctorate research of the last four years [25].

5.2 Conventional Educational Management

"The historic continuity of the institution is unbroken, and many of the medieval university's unique features remain characteristic of today's universities: features, for example, such as...structures of governance, such as the division of major branches of learning into faculties, and the hierarchical positions such as deans, chancellor and rector" ([26], p. 7)

Garrison [27] points to higher education when contending that as "...formal education grew in size and complexity, bureaucracies became the controlling mechanism" (p. 38). In contrast to the institutional management structures, the teaching and research functions of academic staff as professionals are typically more client oriented, less formal and less concerned with hierarchy [20]. While institutional conventional educational management operates on a largely bureaucratic model, academic staff operates on a "collegial model" ([20], p. 32). The anarchic model [28] depicts the modern university as an organized anarchy that, according to Paul [20], illustrates such ambiguities and uncertainties that it renders the traditional forms of management meaningless or inept (p. 37). It seems, however, that the bureaucratic elements of conventional tertiary education are pre-eminent and also in constant conflict to the self-management ideals and processes of academic staff.

This description of management in conventional tertiary education aligns itself clearly to what Burns and Stalker [29] call a *mechanistic* control process in contrast to an *organic* control process. The mechanistic management structure links with a stable external environment. According to Daft ([30], p.61) in this structure tasks are broken down in specialized, separate parts; tasks are rigidly defined; there is a strict hierarchy of authority and control, and there are many rules; knowledge and control of tasks are centralized at the top of the organization and communication is vertical.

The management model on an organizational level in conventional tertiary education is one of tension between a centralized administrative approach and a decentralized academic approach in which the centralized, bureaucratic and hierarchical dimensions seem to be pre-eminent.

The generic conventional management paradigm in tertiary education can be described as being: largely mechanistic, formal, centralized, focussing predominantly on the local environment, insular, inflexible, rigid, bureaucratized with strong institutional control, segmented, with a high degree of division of labour, variable participation; and often politicized.

5.3   New Forms of Educational Management

In view of the new technologies and the emergence of the information age, education

"…is experiencing a shift from formal, centralized, and segmented operations to increasingly complex, decentralized, and integrated levels of organization" ([27], p. 38).

Rumble [31] refers to the operations of distance education as a "highly distributed system" that "looks very different to the residential or non-residential campus-based university" (p. 95). Garrison [27] points to the potential of computer-based distance education to transcend the barrier to "…both decentralize education and individualise or personalise it at the same time" (p. 88). Peters [18] contends that in the post-industrial society there will be in distance teaching institutions a "departure from a highly centralized organization of the teaching-learning process and a move to small decentralized units which can be made transparent by the means of new technology" (p. 53). Forsythe [32] contends ".... the use of such communication systems is seen as part of a large learning system that may well be a network of institutions" (p. 60).

Paul [20] suggests that a value-driven leadership approach can address the different models of educational management and that, in this approach, leadership is committed to ensure that people find meaning in life through their work by creating things of value (p. 68). Paul argues that an institution that is dedicated to the values and practice of open learning needs to have an "open management style" (p. 72) and that "those responsible for the leadership and management of these institutions must emulate the principles they espouse in the performance of their day-to-day activities" (p.22).

5.4   New Forms of Private Enterprise Management

"Networks of networks along the Internet model are beginning to break down walls among companies – suppliers, customers, affinity groups, and competitors. We will see the rise of internetworked business, internetworked government, internetworked learning, and internetworked health care…" ([16], p. 55).

Aspects like the globalization of education, the role of private enterprise in tertiary education and pressures on the funding base impel tertiary institutes increasingly to operate in ways that closely resemble private enterprise. At the same time, private enterprise is concerned with, and heavily involved in, education ([11], p. 243; [27], p. 38). Drucker [1] asserts that the "…need to organize for change also requires a high degree of decentralization" in the structure of the "new society of organizations" (p. 117). Beare and Slaughter [33] contend, "…a business which operates on bureaucratic lines cannot compete in a post-industrial economy…" (p. 35). Peters [34] highlights the importance of boundary management in the organization of the future in which the boundaries are described as wavy, thin and transparent. Marquardt [15] describes the learning organization as being "boundaryless" (p. 83).

Burns and Stalker [29] indicate that an *organic* control process, in contrast to a *mechanistic* control process, is coupled with an unstable external environment. According to Daft ([30], p.61), in this structure, which is appropriate for the modern organization operating in a turbulent environment, employees contribute to the common tasks of the department; tasks are adjusted and redefined through employee interactions; there is less hierarchy of authority and control, and there are few rules; knowledge and control of tasks are located anywhere in the organization; and communication is horizontal. Two major transformations (or megatrends) in society are a transformation from centralization to decentralization (in effect distribution) and from hierarchies to networking ([35], p. 1).

Marquardt [15] contends that in this "…faster, information-thick atmosphere of the new millennium… 'old' companies [cannot] compete with more agile and creative learning organizations" (p. xv). A learning organization has a streamlined, flat hierarchy and is seamless and boundaryless (p. 83). It is further built on networking and "…realizes the need to collaborate, share, and synergise with resources both inside and outside the company… they provide a company with a form and style that is fluid, flexible, and adaptable" (p. 84).

The characteristics of the management required in tertiary education to match the educational needs of the information or knowledge society include being complex, decentralized or distributed, networking of peers, personalized delivery, dealing with networking and collaboration internally and with other institutes, increased boundary management, an integration of on- and off-campus learning and being highly adaptive and flexible in a volatile external environment.

Conventional management of tertiary education struggles with the desperate need to reform its management because of the external and internal environment but is often ineffective at doing this because of its current management approaches. It seems from the above that the inefficiency of the current models of managing conventional tertiary education calls for a meta-model or a new management paradigm to transcend the discrepancies between these management models.

5.5   Networked Educational Management

The writer proposes a new educational management paradigm for managing the operations of networked education: *networked educational management.* Networked educational management incorporates the key elements of the new forms of private enterprise and educational management. This term is chosen since a central aspect of networked education and the management thereof seems to be the *connectivity* or *networking* that it facilitates often across the boundaries of space and time. This term correlates with "network management" [17] and terms that writers like Tapscott [16] ("internetworked organization"), Beare and Slaughter [33] ("network organization"), Limerick and Cunnington [17], ("network organization"), and Tapscott and Caston [36] ("open networked organization") use when describing the organizational model for the emerging information age. Drucker [12] calls the society in which tertiary education currently operates the "networked society" (p.65) because of the centrality of networking with other organizations through alliances, partnerships and outsourcing.

Networked educational management has twelve dimensions: networking, student focussed, globalization, transitory, adaptability, transcending time, market orientation, computer mediation, collaboration, convergence, boundary orientation and information based. The dimensions of networking, globalization, flexibility and boundary orientation are discussed in this chapter.

5.5.1 Networking

Networked educational management postulates that a distributed model of management is appropriate for networked education on both learning and institutional levels. Networking is therefore the central premise of networked educational management. The distributed nature of networked educational management is based on the new connectivity within networked education, the distribution of learning and control, the distributed nature of the Internet and intranets, and the globalization of education.

Networked educational management has its control, power and resources distributed throughout the organization. It links to an *organic* control process [29] in contrast to a *mechanistic* control process, in which "knowledge and control of tasks are located anywhere in the organization" ([30], p. 61).

Managing the connectivity that networked education facilitates is a key difference between managing the conventional class and managing the operations of networked education. It connects or networks student and student, teacher and student, student and resource, teacher and resource, past and present independent of geographical or time differences. The learning control as well as online learning and teaching materials are distributed to both local and distance students using the same interface (*i.e.,* a web browser) because of the convergence of learning modes which traditionally have been called "distance education" and "on-campus education" through networked education. This implies that the management of learning is no longer linked to physical locality (on-campus/off-campus) but distributed to study networks comprising local, distance, national and international students, that operate as virtual teams.

Bates [37] acknowledges the challenge to create a congruity between centralized and decentralized management aspirations in tertiary education: "When it comes to organizational structures, the challenge is to develop a system that encourages teaching units to be innovative and able to respond quickly to changes in subject matter, student needs, and technology. At the same time, redundancy and conflicting standards and policies across the institution must be avoided" (p. 181). A similar tension within the organization of information systems activities and communications has been transcended in computer and communication systems using distributed approaches. Networked educational management will ensure conformity to central principles and values and simultaneously encourage diversity. Active progression towards networked education opens an institute to the impact of the distributed nature of the new educational technologies (specifically the Internet and intranets).

The globalization of education may furthermore necessitate collaboration and partnerships. These partnerships can exist to ensure the local support of distance students in networked education, to address accreditation and certification issues or for more effective participation in networked education. Institutes might therefore find themselves physically or logically distributed through partnerships and collaborations with other national and international institutes. This calls for a distributed management system in education that also addresses "…the need to interact on learning highways across borders…. all nations, in future, will have to design their educational systems in such a way that they not only have internal coherence but also have an open architecture - that they can network with other educational and learning systems" ([38], p. 199).

5.5.2 Globalization

"…if the virtual class was going to be distance independent then like the information society it was going to be global rather than national" [6]

The global nature of networked education is possible because the new educational technologies facilitate and lead naturally to the globalization of education since the central technology in networked education is the Internet. Networked education is accessible from anywhere in the world where access to the Internet is possible [23] and is further information-based ([11], p. 258). The global nature of networked education means that institutes in tertiary education can project themselves into a global educational market of providers and students, which places new demands on management.

Networked educational management through its global nature also includes the management of relationships with collaboration and consortium partners and needs to address cultural differences in an international educational arena.

5.5.3 Flexibility

"The emerging consensus is that successful Universities of the next millennium will be those that embrace continuous change as an education paradigm. Such Universities will be able both to adapt to changes in the social market for their students and to lead this market in directions optimal to the society's goals by continually adapting their education plans, methods and strategies of teaching, and educational infrastructures to changes in the environment" ([39], p. 1607).

Control is an integral part of management [8] that is hugely impacted by the transitory nature of the operations of networked education. Tapscott ([16], p. xv) holds that "Far more than the old western frontier, the digital frontier is a place of recklessness, confusion, uncertainty, calamity and danger." The controlling position of the student in networked education and the changing nature of the student body contribute to an uncontrollability of huge proportions, which challenges the essence of conventional educational management. In this paradigmatic shift, the focus and control transfer to the student who can select from various international offerings, access web sites and people across cultural, national and philosophical boundaries, while constructing their own learning and meaning through a constructivist educational approach ([40], p. 157). Networked education is further unbound in space and time and provides students with enormous flexibility.

The environment in which networked education in tertiary education occurs at the beginning of the millennium is exceptionally dynamic and volatile. This can be attributed largely to the emergence of a global information or knowledge society that many view to be "… as significant as the previous displacement of the agricultural age by the industrial age" ([16], p. 43). Drucker [11] draws an analogy between the introduction of computers in education and that of the book, and contends that a revolution of similar or even greater proportions in education is occurring. Even the nature of the change process from conventional to networked education itself is not stable; Morrison [38] describes the "process of evolution in terms of dislocations, dilemmas and uncertainties rather than projections from "what is" to "what is needed"." The global dimension of networked educational management furthermore increases the boundaries of the institutes using networked education and exposes them to further factors and influences from a turbulent international environment.

In the emerging information or knowledge society, education has to contend with exponential growth in the amount of information available for use by organizations, governments, businesses and people. There are estimates that "today information is doubling every eighteen months and that by the year 2012 it will be doubling every day" ([41], p. 264).

Managing the dynamic nature of online material requires tight change control and quality assurance systems (NOT documentation systems!) while at the same time addressing the flexibility of online materials that can be changed continuously and immediately. This is clearly different from using other publishing mediums like paper or CD-ROMs.

JIT teaching, that is teaching that can change rapidly and immediately based on the needs of students and is available when students need it ([42], p. 154; [15], p. 177; [40], p. 158), calls for the management of teaching to be particularly adaptive.

The factors above point to the need for a high level of adaptability in the administrative, academic and technological management of networked education.

5.5.4 Boundary Orientation

"Competitive industries are clustered … are linked as customers and suppliers, through people, research institutions, university programmes and related diversification. This is typical. It is how a competitive industry is created and sustained" ([43], p. 53)

Boundary management within the university environment has become more relevant as "… the external environment has impinged more directly on university operations..." ([44], p. 56). An emphasis on boundary management correlates with the organization of the future proposed by Peters [34], Tapscott [16] and Daft [30]. It also correlates with an "essential element of effective network management" which is to "develop your boundary roles" ([17], p. 89).

The extensive use of the Internet in networked education further leads to an extension of the boundaries of an organization's academic and administrative systems. Networking now often transcends national boundaries so that the Global Alliance for Transnational Education [45] describes the current educational environment as the "...new borderless educational arena". This correlates to one of Fullan's [46] six themes of educational change namely "From going it alone to alliances".

A major boundary management issue in networked education is to provide adequate access to courses. There are initiatives to address this like cyber cafés, internet access in public spaces like libraries, arranging adequate on-campus computer access, collaboration with other educational institutes to provide access to remote students, as well as telecentres, which are widely used in Australia and Europe and growing in Africa ([47], p. 90). "Drop-in" computer labs can be provided for on-campus students participating in networked education via the Intranet and computers can be placed in public access areas like the library.

With increased access and extended boundaries comes an increase in the possibility of abuse, which highlights another boundary management issue that is ensuring security of the ICT systems in networked education. Addressing accreditation and certification across national and academic status barriers is a further prominent issue in boundary management of networked education.

5.6   Conclusion

"...the medium of print, so long our almost exclusive means for preserving knowledge, has yielded significant ground to the remarkable storage and retrieval capacities of the computer; and that, further, this loosening of the keystone of the modern educational past allows us to glimpse, and demands that we define, a new educational future no longer constrained and shaped by the exigencies of print/textbook-based education" [48]

"...the widespread use of new technologies in an organization does constitute a major cultural change. Furthermore, for such change to be successful, leadership of the highest quality is required" ([37], p. 42)

"... a successful innovation aims at leadership... if it does not aim at leadership from the beginning, it is unlikely to be innovative enough, and therefore unlikely to be capable of establishing itself" [10]

Conventional tertiary educational management has struggled with a dichotomy, which led to some describing it as organized anarchy. The administration is often characterized by bureaucratic, hierarchical management approaches with a preference for centralization. In contrast, the teaching and research functions of academic staff as professionals are typically more client oriented, less formal and less concerned with hierarchy with a preference for decentralization. Networked educational management can ensure conformity to central principles and standards while it simultaneously encourages diversity and may contribute to transcending this tension and facilitating harmony in the management of tertiary education.

Lack of funding is often touted as a key stumbling block in the implementation of networked education in conventional tertiary education. More important though, from a management perspective, is to create an enduring vision and a strategic implementation framework for the effective implementation of technological innovations like networked education. Berge and Schrum [49] contend that "The most important function of institutional leadership may be to create a shared vision that includes widespread input and support from the faculty and administration, articulates a clear educational purpose, has validity for stakeholders, and reflects the broader mission of the institution" (p. 35). "Passive stewardship as a concept of management…is no longer a useful option when the continued viability of the institution over which stewardship is being executed is threatened.[it] demands enlightened, innovative, and aggressive leadership" ([50], p. 246).

The extensive management and wider implications for a conventional tertiary educational institute when implementing networked education might further be pointing to the emergence of a new kind of educational institute. Networked educational management needs to occur at all levels of an institute that seriously engages in networked education. It follows that the kind of institute that fully adopts networked education will display fundamentally different characteristics than that of a conventional tertiary educational institute. In terms of an overall organizational structure it seems possible therefore that *networked educational institutes* might emerge that will actualize networked education and use networked educational management to its fullest extent.

"There is no alternative but to face the inevitability of a profound impact of new technology on teaching and learning and to work to establish a rich educational environment within that framework…" ([51], p. 120)

"In a time of drastic change it is the learners who survive; the 'learned' find themselves fully equipped to live in a world that no longer exists" Eric Hoffer.

References

1.   Drucker, P.F. (1998) Peter Drucker on the profession of management. Boston, MA, Harvard Business School Publishing.

2.   Hartley, D. (1995) The 'McDonaldization' of higher education: Food for thought. *Oxford Review of Education*, vol. 21, 409-23.

3.   Romiszowski, A (1993, June) Telecommunications and Distance Education. ERIC Digest, June 1993. [Online]. Available at:
gopher://ericir.syr.edu:70/00/Clearinghouses/16houses/CIT/IT_Digests/Telecom. [1997, July 11]

4.   Daniel, J. S. (1998) Mega-universities and knowledge media: Technology strategies for higher education. London, Kogan Page.

5.   Tiffin, J. (1996b, November) In search of the virtual class. Paper presented at the Virtual University Symposium, Melbourne, Australia.

6.   Tiffin, J. (1996, February) The Virtual Class is coming in *Education and Information Technologies*, 1 (2).

7.   Negroponte, N. (1995) Being digital. New York, Knopf.

8.   Newman, W. H., Warren E. K., McGill A. R. (1987) The process of management. Strategy, action, results. Englewood Cliffs, NJ, Prentice-Hall.

9.   Schultheis, R. & Sumner, M. (1989) Management information systems: The manager's view. Boston, MA, Irwin.

10. Drucker, P.F. (1985) Innovation and entrepreneurship. London, Heinemann.

11. Drucker, P.F. (1989) The new realities – in government and politics, in economics and business, in society and world view. New York, Harper & Row.

12. Drucker, P.F. (1995) Managing in a time of great change. New York, Truman Talley/Dutton.

13. Senge, P. M. (1990) The fifth discipline: The art and practice of the learning organization. London, Century Business.

14. Peters, T. (1988) Thriving on chaos: handbook for a management revolution. New York, Knopf.

15. Marquard, M. J. (1996) Building the learning organization – a systems approach to quantum improvement and global success. New York, McGraw-Hill.

16. Tapscott, D. (1996) The digital economy: promise and peril in the age of networked intelligence. New York, McGraw-Hill.

17. Limerick, D. C. & Cunnington, B. (1993) Managing the new organisation - A blueprint for networks and strategic alliances. Chatswood, Australia, Business & Professional Publishing.

18. Peters, O. (1993) Distance in a postindustrial society. In Desmond Keegan (Ed.), *Theoretical Principles of Distance Education* (pp. 39-58). London, Routledge.

19. Rayport, J. F., & Sviokla, J. J. (1995) Exploiting the virtual value chain in *Harvard Business Review*, November - December 1995, 75-85.

20. Paul, R. H. (1990) Open learning and open management: leadership and integrity in distance education. London, Kogan Page

21. Thomas, O., Carswell, L., Price, B., Petre, M. (1998) A holistic approach to supporting distance learning using the Internet: transformation, not translation in *British Journal of Educational Technology*, Vol 29, No 2, 149-161.

22. Bates, A. W. (1999) Strategies for the Future. [Online]. Available at: http://bates.cstudies.ubc.ca/strategies.html [1999, July 10]

23. Uys, P. M. (1998, April) New educational technology and the global village: key management issues in higher education in *Proceedings of Towards the Global*

University: Strategies for the Third Millennium Conference. Tours, University of Central Lancashire.

24. Uys, P. M. (1999, July) Towards the Virtual Class: Technology Issues from a Fractal Management Perspective in *Proceedings of the ED-MEDIA 99 - World Conference on Educational Multimedia, Hypermedia & Telecommunications.* Seattle, AACE

25. Uys, P.M (2000) Towards the virtual class: key management issues in tertiary education. PhD thesis, Victoria University of Wellington.

26. Patterson, G. (1997) The university from ancient Greece to the 20th century. Palmerston North, NZ , Dunmore Press

27. Garrison, D. R. (1989) Understanding distance education: A framework for the future. London, New York, Routledge.

28. Cohen, M.D. & March, J. G. (1974) Leadership and ambiguity. New York, McGraw-Hill.

29. Burns, T. & Stalker, G. M. (1961) The management of innovation. London, Tavistock.

30. Daft, R. L. (1989) Organization theory and design. (3rd ed). St. Paul, MN, West Publishing Company.

31. Rumble, G. (1992) The competitive vulnerability of distance teaching universities. In Tait, A. (Ed.), *Key issues in open learning* (pp. 94 -118). Harlow, Longman.

32. Forsythe, K. (1984) Satellite and cable. In Bates, A.W. (Ed.), *The role of technology in distance education* (pp. 57 - 65). London, Croom Helm.

33. Beare, H. & Slaughter, R. (1993) Education for the twenty-first century. London, Routledge.

34. Peters, T. (1988a) Restoring American competitiveness: Looking for new models of organizations. Academy of Management Executive 2, 103-109. In Daft, R. L. (1989). *Organization Theory and Design.* (3rd ed). St. Paul, MN, West Publishing Company.

35. Naisbitt, J. (1982) Megatrends: Ten new directions for transforming our lives. New York, Warner Books.

36. Tapscott. D. & Caston. A. (1993) Paradigm Shift: The new promise of information technology. McGraw-Hill.

37. Bates, A.W. (2000) Managing technology change: Strategies for college and university leaders. San Francisco, Jossey-Bass.

38. Morrison, T.R. (1995) Global transformation and the search for a new educational design. in *International Journal of Lifelong Education*, vol. 14, (3), 188-213.

39. Esquer, G. N. & Sheremetov, L. (1999, July) Process engineering model and tools for a collaborative learning environment. In *Proceedings of the ED-MEDIA 99 - World Conference on Educational Multimedia, Hypermedia & Telecommunications.* Seattle, AACE.

40. Mason, R. (1998) Globalising education: Trends and applications. London & New York, Routledge.

41.   Nugent, D. (1996) Teaching and learning for a changing world. In Zepke, N., Nugent, D. & Roberts, C. (Eds.), *The new self help book for teachers* (pp. 247-263). Wellington, WP Press.

42.   Tiffin, J. & Rajasingham, L. (1995) In Search of the Virtual Class: Education in an Information Society. London, Routledge.

43.   Caulkin, S. (Ed.). (1990) Drucker, Ohmae, Porter & Peters. Management briefings. (Management Guides. Special report No.1202). London, The Economist.

44.   Middlehurst, R. (1993) Leading academics. Buckingham, Open University Press.

45.   GATE (1999) The global alliance for transnational education. [On-line]. Available at: http://www.edugate.org/ [2000, January 17].

46.   Fullan, M. G. (1991) The new meaning of educational change. 2nd edition. London, Cassel Education Ltd.

47.   Naidoo, V. & Schutte, C. (1999) Virtual institutions on the African continent. In Farrell, G. M (Ed.), *The development of virtual education: a global perspective.* (pp. 89 - 124). Vancouver, The Commonwealth of Learning. [Online]. Available at: http://www.col.org/virtualed/index.htm [2000, January 8]

48.   Chou, L., McClintock, R. , Moretti, F. , Nix, D. H. (1993) Technology and Education: New Wine in New Bottles. Choosing Pasts and Imagining Educational Futures. New York, New Lab for Teaching and Learning.

49.   Berge, Z. L. & Schrum, L. (1998) Strategic planning linked with program implementation for distance education. In CAUSE/EFFECT, 21(3), 31-38.

50.   Karol, N. H. & Ginsburg, S.G (1980) Managing the higher education enterprise. New York, John Wiley & Sons.

51.   Johnston, R. & Challis, K. (1994) The learning relationship: A study of staff development and satisfaction in relation to distance learning teaching. *In International Journal of University Adult Education*, vol. 33, no. 1, 62-76.

Chapter 6

eClass

Jason A. Brotherton and Gregory D. Abowd

The eClass project and its predecessor, Classroom 2000, is an attempt to show how automated capture of live lectures for later access by students and teachers can impact the teaching and learning experience. In this chapter, we present the major motivations for the development of the eClass prototype software system. We also describe in some detail how the software system was structured to facilitate the development of a living laboratory for experimentation over the past six years. We end with a brief discussion of the major evaluation lessons learned and advice for continuing this valuable service in the educational domain.

6.1 Introduction

Much of the technology and research on the classroom is geared toward providing instructors with the ability to present more information during a lecture, with the goal of providing a deeper learning experience. However, we feel that students, still left with pen and paper, are drowning in information because the tools they have cannot adequately capture the richness of a modern classroom lecture. As a result, many students wind up practicing a "heads down" approach to learning - they are too busy writing down everything presented in the classroom instead of actually paying attention to the lecture material.

eClass (formerly Classroom 2000) is a project started by researchers in the Future Computing Environments Group at the College of Computing, Georgia Institute of Technology, to help alleviate some of the students' burden. In simplest terms, eClass is a suite of programs enabling a classroom to "take notes" of live lectures on behalf of its occupants. Through the automation of the capture of live courses and then making them available on the Web, we hope to empower students to pay attention in class, free from the obligation of copying everything down. We also hope to create a new approach to multimedia authoring - live teaching as courseware production.

As the project grew, we focused more on supporting the capture and access of live experiences and less on the goal of automatically creating online courses. As a result, we feel that the notes for a lecture created by eClass are best suited for those students who were actually in the lecture, though we have seen other effective uses as well. Therefore, we describe our work here as an enhancement for traditional lectures, not as a replacement for them.

In the remainder of this chapter, we describe our motivation and the underlying roles and activities that we assumed in building eClass. We then take a closer examination of the tools and services of eClass and how the suite of clients and servers work together. We will discuss some of our evaluation results and finish with a constructive view of what can be done to improve eClass, and the directions in which we think further research could explore.

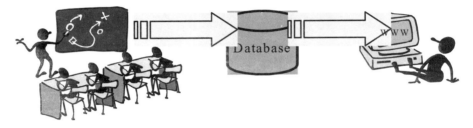

Figure 6.1. A simplified view of eClass. eClass takes everything that is written on the electronic whiteboard, said in class, and shown on the Web, and places it in an online database where the materials can be later accessed via a web browser.

6.1.1 An Overview of eClass

eClass began with the goal of producing a classroom environment in which electronic notes taken by students and teachers could be preserved and accessed later, augmented by audio and video recordings. The initial idea was to produce media-enhanced records of a traditional lecture. eClass has since evolved into a collection of capture-enabled programs that attempt to preserve as much as possible of the lecture experience, with little or no human intervention.

To the students enrolled in a course taught using eClass, the in-class experience is not all that different from a typical classroom. A professor lectures from prepared slides or web pages or writes on a blank whiteboard. Then, shortly after class is over, the students can access the lecture via the Web, choosing to replay the entire lecture, print out any slides that were created, search for related materials, or just go over a topic that was not well understood.

From the professor's viewpoint, using eClass is not much different from any room equipped with modern presentation equipment. Before class, materials to be shown (if any) are prepared in PowerPoint®. Upon entering the classroom (Figure 6.2), the instructor starts some client software from our system and proceeds with the lecture, showing prepared slides on the electronic whiteboard, and writing on it. As the lecture progresses, a partial history of it can be seen on separate displays at the front of the room. After class, the instructor closes our program and a series of web pages are automatically created, integrating the video, visited web pages, and slides. This is normally completed before the instructor leaves the room.

Figure 6.2. eClass in use. On the right, the instructor annotates PowerPoint® slides or writes on a blank whiteboard. Previous slides (or overviews of more than one slide) are shown on the middle and left screens. The screens can also be used to display web pages.

Figure 6.3 shows an example of the captured notes. In the upper left panel, students see a timeline of the class, from start to finish, decorated with significant events that happened in the class such as the instructor visiting a new slide or a web page. Clicking on the black timeline plays back the audio and video of the class at that point in the timeline while clicking on the blue slide links takes the student to that slide, and clicking on the red web links takes the student to that web page (shown here in a new window). Below the timeline is an embedded video player. The student has the option of using an external or embedded player.

The right side of the interface is where all of the slides and their annotations are shown in a single scrollable frame. This allows for scanning a lecture to find a topic quickly. For slower network connections, only one slide at a time is loaded into the frame. Clicking on any handwritten annotations will launch the video of the lecture at the time the annotations were written.

Other features of the notes that are not shown include generating a printable version, searching for keywords in the lecture, and editing a collaborative web page for the course.

6.1.2 Motivation

Figure 6.3. An example of the notes taken by our classroom. On the left a timeline is decorated to indicate significant changes of focus, from whiteboard slides to web pages. The frame beside the timeline contains a scrollable list of whiteboard slides to facilitate browsing. Web pages are brought up in a separate browser window, as shown. Directly above the timeline is a link that allows students to bring up help on using the system.

Our general research goals are centered on the idea that the automated capture of everyday experiences for later playback or searching is a valuable service for people. Automated support can help computers do what they do best - record an event - in order to free humans to do what they do best: attend to, synthesize, and understand what is happening around them, with full confidence that specific details will be available for later perusal.

One reason why we chose the college classroom for our first attempt at building an automated capture and access support system is because of the obvious need for students to record what goes on in it while at the same time paying attention to the lecturer. Additionally, the items to be recorded in the classroom (what the instructor says and writes) are easy to specify and not too difficult to capture. Cameras and microphones can record what the instructor says, and electronic whiteboards can be built to capture what is presented and written.

It was not enough, however, to show that we could build a capture and access system for the classroom; we also wanted to show that such a system, once incorporated into the everyday educational experience, would provide a valuable service for the population of students and instructors. We initially had a hunch that note taking with pen and paper could interfere with the act of paying attention and that students in classrooms might be paying more attention to copying down information presented in class than to the information itself. After our first prototype and a few interviews with students, we found that this hunch turned out to be correct.

When asked, "Briefly describe your note-taking practices in traditional classrooms utilizing a traditional whiteboard and overhead projector," students answered (emphasis ours):

- "I **copy all the notes** written on the board."
- "Many times I lose what the professor is saying because **I'm too busy writing notes** on what she said previously."
- "I'm usually more busy trying to write/decipher what the instructor is writing on the board, and **don't really have the time to understand** the concept."
- "**I spend all my time scribbling frantically** without listening to what the professor is saying."

These responses are from undergraduate and graduate students enrolled in classes using eClass at the Georgia Institute of Technology. Automated capture can help relieve the students of the burden of copying down everything that goes on in the class, thereby enabling them to concentrate better on the lecture or take fewer, more personalized notes. The whole point of capture, however, is in the access to the materials. Integrating the audio and video of the class with the instructor's handwriting should increase the value of the handwriting by providing more context of what was going on at the time of writing. Access to captured materials should aid students in studying for exams or whenever in the future that information is again needed. Again, investigating access in the classroom domain was a good match for our research because the access of classroom materials can initially just be a replay of what was presented during the lecture.

Although we knew that automated capture would have applications in distance learning and general business meetings, we explicitly focused on the standard university lecture, with access made available to those who had attended the lecture in the first place. There are some who would argue the effectiveness of this age-old didactic form, but the fact remains that a vast majority of education occurs this way. Producing a system specifically tuned to the traditional lecturing style would allow us to experiment with a large number of users and also put us in a position to observe how automated capture affects the form of the traditional lecture.

6.2   Definition of Terms, Roles, and Activities

Because many different images and preconceptions come to mind when one envisions a classroom, this section makes explicit our definitions and descriptions of a typical classroom environment. While much of this may seem obvious, we feel that before we describe the tools and services eClass provides, we need to define precisely the underlying classroom model and the assumptions that eClass was built upon.

6.2.1 Roles

We have defined three roles in our classroom environment: instructor, student, and outsider. The tools and services of eClass support each role to some degree. A student is any person who wants or is required to learn or study a topic of information and is paying an institution or instructor to teach them about the topic. An instructor is the person who is charged with the task of sharing or giving information about the topic. An outsider is any person who has an interest in what is being taught, but is not paying for the information or would not otherwise be considered a student at the time the information was taught.

6.2.2 Situation

A topic is defined as a collection of knowledge about a particular subject. Topics can be broken down into smaller segments where each segment is discussed in a lecture. A single lecture may cover many segments, or one segment may span many lectures. A lecture is a meeting where at least one instructor and two or more students come together in a scheduled location at regular intervals for dissemination of knowledge from the instructor(s) to the students or, in some cases, from students to students. A course is thus a collection of these lectures over a period of time and the classroom is simply the location where lectures are taught.

6.2.3 Tools

Both the instructor and students use tools in the classroom to help them with their roles. Two of the most familiar items in the classroom are chalk/markers and the chalkboard/whiteboard. It is hard to imagine a classroom where the instructor does not have some large markable surface to display information. Slowly, these surfaces are becoming electronic, but whatever the technology used, each classroom typically has a large surface where the instructor can write information for the students.

Oftentimes, an instructor has too much information to write during class, or needs to display intricate drawings or photos where physically drawing the information is impossible. In this case, acetate slides and an overhead projector are commonly used. Here, the instructor can write on the projected slides to further explain key points. In some modern classrooms, overhead cameras and television sets are used to achieve the same purpose. Recently, instructors have started using presentation software (such as Microsoft PowerPoint®) to prepare their lectures. During class, a computer with a projected display is used to give the lecture. In all cases, the instructor is using some tool to prepare materials in advance for use in class in order to save time during the lecture.

In classrooms equipped with networked computers and projected displays, some instructors have taken to using the Web as an instructional tool. Essentially this is the same as an overhead projector, but with no marking capabilities. Instructors can use the Web to show either prepared presentations or information created by other people, or in some cases, other students.

The students have traditionally had access to only a few tools to help them learn the material presented in a lecture. Some instructors prepare handouts of their prepared material either before or after the lecture. Paper and pen are the icons of any student and a strong note-taking ability is often the mark of a successful student. Audio recordings are sometimes permitted, but using the audio to study from is often hard enough that it is not worth the effort.

6.2.4 Tasks and Activities

After identifying the tools of the classroom, we are now ready to identify the activities that make use of them. The instructor has one main objective - to disseminate knowledge among the students and assess if they have learned it. The instructor has many common activities for doing this: lecturing, meeting with students outside of class time, and assessing performance on assignments (such as projects and homework) and tests.

Homework assigned during a lecture typically consists of work done outside of class designed to reinforce the topic taught in lecture. Projects are typically more lengthy assignments, usually done in teams, and extending for the duration of several lectures. Projects are designed to show competency in several lecture topics, the ability to work as a team, and the ability to integrate knowledge from different subjects.

Tests are the familiar assessment method bemoaned by many students. They are designed to show a comprehensive knowledge over an entire course's worth of material. Tests are the most common method of determining grades, and passing tests is usually a student's main motivation for the class.

Students are also charged with other tasks in the classroom. The most obvious ones are attending the class, taking notes during the class, and studying after the class. Many instructors also insist on discussion from the students and, via assignments, that they review their notes outside of class.

6.2.5 What eClass Supports, and the Assumptions eClass Makes

eClass assumes, not unreasonably, that a course and all of its lectures take place in only one classroom throughout the semester. With a little manual effort, our software supports courses that consist of two or more classrooms. eClass can also support a lecture (but not very well) given in two different locations if it is given in two parts. We attempted to use eClass with lectures that take place in more than two locations at the same time and were met with mixed success. eClass was not designed to support distributed lectures and the amount of manual effort required to "force" the system to fit this model made it clear that eClass was not a good solution for distributed classes.

We do not assume that the students or instructor of a course are the only people who will access the online notes. We have discovered that access to captured materials can also aid other instructors teaching a course that was previously taught by a different instructor. eClass helps instructors prepare for a new lecture on a topic already discussed by allowing them to see the materials used in class and how they were presented. Students of other courses and outsiders often look at the online notes for a captured class in which they were not enrolled. The system supports in some way access from instructors and non-students, but our intent was to provide an access service for the actual students of the course.

We do not mean to imply that eClass directly supports all of the roles, tools, and tasks specified above. Recall that the main goal of eClass was to build a classroom that could take quality notes for the students enrolled in a course. In trying to meet this goal, we have noticed our system being used in ways we did not predict. For example, professors have had open-note tests using eClass and have created class projects that require the use of eClass to build publicly critiqued artefacts. In most of these cases, we then refined our system to facilitate and encourage this unexpected behavior. This has resulted (for better or worse) in eClass being used to some extent to support the people and activities described above.

6.3   eClass in Detail

In order to instrument any environment for automated multimedia content generation we need to provide computational services in that environment that are effectively pervasive without being overly intrusive. This is a goal in common with much of the work over the past decade in the area of ubiquitous computing, yet one that is essential for a classroom environment where instructors are not going to want to deviate from their normal teaching styles.

Rather than build new tools for instructors to use, we chose to augment existing classroom tools with capture capabilities. In this way, we hope to have a win-win situation; instructors do not need to change their teaching style or do any extra work, and the students get the benefit of automated capture.

6.3.1 The eClass Model of the Classroom

Our initial work focused on treating a classroom lecture as an example of multimedia authoring. Taking parallels from movie production, we identified four separate phases of the execution of a capture and access system and built or bought tools to support those phases. These phases, pre-production, live recording/capture, post-production/integration, and access, are described below. Later, we will discuss the tools used to support each phase.

Initially, the effort involved to support a single class was so great that we were only able to experiment with one class per term. The chief advantage of adopting this four-phase model of the classroom is that we constructed each phase of the system to be independent and, because of this, over time, we were able to streamline all features of the system to support many enhancements at a time.

Pre-production

Before a lecture begins, some lecturers may prepare a presentation as a series of slides or web pages. In the pre-production phase, we are concerned with providing a simple way to reuse existing classroom material. Since most preparation tools that instructors use allow for the exportation of GIF or JPEG images, we built our system to support the annotation of a series of images. In the degenerate case, the instructor annotates a set of blank images, and this is equivalent to writing on a blank whiteboard.

There is no work required of the students during the pre-production phase. If the instructor's lecture style consists of writing on a blank whiteboard, then there is also no work required of him. If the instructor wishes to lecture from prepared slides, then he must transfer his materials into eClass.

The classroom can be a hostile environment and although there is not much demand on the students and instructor in this phase, there is a small amount of maintenance that needs to be done before each class. Users sometimes turn off machines, or terminate our software, which should be always running on general-purpose computers in the classroom, and these need to be restarted. Users sometimes use the projectors to display other electronic materials and forget to return the projector to a computer that other users expect always to have its display projected. Users sometimes turn down volume settings on recording equipment or move cameras. In an ideal setting, once eClass is running, things just work, but in a dynamic classroom environment where wires are pulled and equipment can by used by anyone, some effort must be spent in returning the room to its "default" settings. It is this "small" amount of work that surprisingly accounts for nearly all of the researcher's time in running eClass. It is interesting to note that some "expert" users have taken it upon themselves to learn how to set up the classroom. Although the room only takes a minute to configure, we feel it is still too complicated to expect instructors to do this.

Live recording / capture

The capture phase begins when the instructor is ready to give her presentation. Once a lecture starts, we want to record as much information as possible. There are two distinct methods for solving the capture problem. The first is to have the room provide all the computational needs and the second is to have the user carry with them all of the required computational needs. The former leads to "smart" rooms that record activity in them, and the latter leads to personal electronic notebooks. Our research has experimented with both approaches, but in eClass we augmented the room with the technology, as this seemed the least intrusive method for instructors and students. Indeed, we tried to make eClass "walk up and use" as much as possible for the instructors and students.

During the capture phase, we focused on recording what was presented (slides, web pages), written, and spoken. We also recorded a wide angle, low quality video of the instructor focused on the front of the room. Student questions were also recorded, but they were generally out of the camera's field of vision.

In this phase, the work of the instructor should be exactly what she would be doing anyway - teaching a class. The work of the students however is greatly reduced. They can now focus less on capturing everything and more on paying attention to the lecture.

Post-production / integration

Once class is complete, there is some effort necessary to provide for the integration between the captured electronic whiteboard activity and the audio/video stream of the class. There is also some post-production work necessary to produce a web-based interface that makes it easy for the students to access the augmented notes from a class home page.

The instructor or students do not need to be concerned with this phase. All work happens invisibly and automatically at the end of a class. Occasionally, system errors occur resulting in a lecture not being properly processed and a student, not finding the lecture, will email our help team. These errors are generally trivial and we can fix them as soon as they are reported (if they are not automatically reported by our software).

Access

In the access phase, students and teachers are provided with a web interface to browse past lectures. Access is the most critical step of any capture application. If the captured material is not available whenever the user needs or wants it, the system will not be used. Furthermore, since capture applications often deal with personal notes and annotations, each user will want (and expect to be able) to modify the presentation of their materials. We had to compromise in this, as eClass did not initially support personal note taking or modification of captured lectures. We have extended portions of the system to enable these features, but have not used them on a reliable basis.

In this phase then, instructors no effort is required of instructors, while students hopefully will be more productive in their study time as a result of the captured notes.

6.3.2 The Tools of eClass

We have built or bought many tools to help automate the four phases of the capture and access of a classroom lecture. In this section, we will describe the tools and in the following section, explain how they work together to capture and make available access of classroom activity.

Transfermation

We originally provided for the ability for instructors to create slide images manually and import them into our system. The tool was crude and required instructors to know how to use an FTP-like browser, but enabled instructors to import content into eClass without our intervention.

The process of converting presentations and then importing them to eClass was time-consuming and tedious. It was also too complicated for new users who were not familiar with file transfer protocols, presentation packages or computers in general. Over time, we found that nearly all instructors were using Microsoft PowerPoint™ to prepare lecture presentations. Because of this, we were able to help automate this process by creating a tool called Transfermation, which takes an existing PowerPoint™ presentation file and automatically extracts slide images and uploads them into eClass.

Transfermation was written as a wizard interface using Visual Basic. This was necessary in order to use the PowerPoint® libraries needed to create images from slides. As a result, Transfermation only runs on PCs running Microsoft Windows 98. This turned out not to be a great limitation in our work because most of the machines used to create the presentations could be used to run Transfermation. It was also possible to run Transfermation on the electronic whiteboards we used in all of our classrooms at The Georgia Institute of Technology.

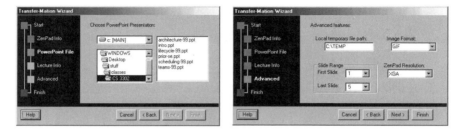

Figure 6.4. Transfermation is a wizard that allows for easy importing of PowerPoint® presentations into eClass.

Electronic whiteboards and ZenPad

eClass requires the use of an electronic whiteboard to capture the instructor's handwriting and, optionally, to display prepared materials. Electronic whiteboards come in many shapes and sizes. They can be illuminated screens with ink-less markers, or modified whiteboards that use real ink markers, or even traditional whiteboards with augmented sensing technology such as cameras and radio-transmitting pens.

Illuminated screens can be front-projected or rear-projected and have the advantage of being able to display, capture, and control dynamic computer screens. Advantages of rear-projected boards (LiveBoard [5], SoftBoard [12], SmartBoard [11], TeamBoard [14], Ibid [8], PanaBoard [7]) are that they are self-contained and have no occlusion from the instructor standing in front of the projector. Front-projected whiteboards are generally cheaper and take up less space since the projector is usually ceiling mounted. Modified whiteboards (some versions of the SmartBoard, and others) have no computer display and only show the ink physically written on them. Electronic whiteboards built from traditional whiteboards (BrightBoard [13], ZombieBoard [3], eBeam [4], Mimio [16]) are typically the least expensive since all they require is the sensing technology to detect and capture handwriting. While both modified and traditional whiteboards can have prepared materials projected on them with an overhead projector, the projected information cannot easily be captured.

For our classrooms, we chose a rear-projected electronic whiteboard made by Xerox Liveworks, called the LiveBoard. A LiveBoard is a pen-based computer running Windows® with a large, 62" interactive display (Figure 6.2 shows a

Liveboard in use during a class). For other eClass installations, the choice of which electronic whiteboard to use was mostly a matter of price and whether the instructors would be presenting prepared presentations or simply writing on a blank whiteboard.

The main capture tool for eClass is ZenPad (Figure 6.5), a program that runs on an electronic whiteboard and allows us to capture what is presented and written. ZenPad is one part of a client-server Java system, and the main component of what we call Zen*, the collection of generic capture tools that comprise eClass. The eClass servers (described later) coordinate classroom sessions and store and process all of the captured data.

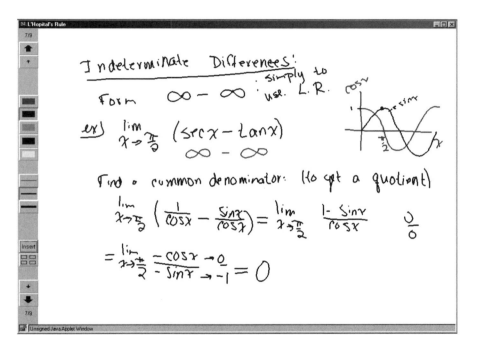

Figure 6.5. Screen shot of ZenPad running on an electronic whiteboard. Navigation and ink marker buttons are on the left panel while the rest of the interface is a blank writing surface.

ZenPad provides a very minimal interface that maximizes the actual screen surface for writing. Earlier prototypes provided more functionality to the end user, but those features were not used very much and subtracted from the all-important screen real estate teachers wanted for a writing surface.

ZenPad keeps information about when various activities occur. For example, we know when a lecture began, when slides were displayed, when every single pen stroke was created, and when the lecture ended. This information is required for the integration of the teacher's lecture material with the audio or other streams of information, such as audio, video, and web pages that are recorded during class.

Recall that the teachers we supported had differing lecturing styles, resulting in the need to support different presentation styles. Teachers with prepared slides wanted to have ZenPad move slide by slide through the lecture with the ability to display a slide and annotate on top of the slide. Other teachers simply wanted ZenPad to provide a continuous scrollable blank writing surface upon which the entire lecture could be handwritten, similar to an overhead projector with a scrollable film.

Beyond fulfilling that simple requirement, ZenPad provides a minimal interface, attempting to conserve screen space. Instructors can change pen thickness, pen colors (depending on the electronic whiteboard, this feature is either automatic, by picking up a colored pen, or manual, by clicking on the software button), and can insert slides if needed. Some users have complained that ZenPad does not provide more support for structured drawing but, in general, we have found that this simple interface has been the best one.

Extended whiteboards and ZenViewer
The LiveBoard is a large display, but it is about one-quarter the width of a traditional classroom whiteboard. Initial use suggested that whereas a LiveBoard is great for small meeting presentations, it was just too small for a classroom. We extended the size of our electronic whiteboard by using two additional computers with their displays projected next to the LiveBoard. When used with ZenPad, this gives the illusion that the electronic whiteboard is really the size of three LiveBoards instead of just one. The extended displays can also be used to display web pages.

These extended display machines run a Java Applet called ZenViewer that allows viewing of the current or previous slides written on a whiteboard running ZenPad. The applet displays the slides and the ink written on them in real time. ZenViewer can be run from anywhere on the Internet and has the ability to display just the current or previous slide, or an overview of many previous slides.

Capturing visited web pages
Since it is difficult to take traditional notes when viewing web pages, we capture the URLs visited and integrate them with the slides written so that students can revisit them again after class. Originally, we tried to modify existing web browsers in a Macintosh environment to save their access histories. Now, we can use any commercial browser on any operating system to do this by having the web browser go though a proxy server (discussed later) which then relays the URLs back to our eClass database where it is integrated with the presented slides and ink.

Audio / video recording and ZenStarter
Our main classroom employs one video camera, used to capture a low quality video of the instructor and all of the projected displays. We used six individually adjustable ceiling-mounted mini microphones used to record the audio of the

instructor and the students. Our second classroom does not record video, but records audio through the use of two microphones mounted in the front and rear of the classroom. These microphones do a fair job of recording the instructor and students, but we occasionally need higher quality recordings of the professors to generate voice transcripts, used for later searching. For this reason, the instructor has the option of wearing a wireless lapel microphone. Some instructors prefer to use the wireless microphone just for the increased audio quality alone.

All of these audio and video signals are sent to a computer that encodes the video and audio using RealVideo® and RealAudio®. Our audio/video medium choice allows us to provide audio and video to students over slower modem connections.

Although using the commercial RealEncoder® allows us to generate streamable content easily, the instructor still needs to start and stop this program. To alleviate this problem, we wrote ZenStarter, a general-purpose program that can start and stop other programs (with optional parameters) based on a ZenPad session. When the instructor starts a class by running ZenPad, all relevant ZenStarters will start any programs that need to run. We have also used ZenStarter to start and stop ZenViewers automatically and to turn on the projector for the computer display, but we have not implemented this for everyday use.

Ending a lecture - StreamWeaver
After class, the instructor exits ZenPad and leaves the room. All of the captured data is sent to a central server where it is processed and woven together, using a Java program we have written called StreamWeaver to merge together time-stamped streams of information into classroom notes in the form of HTML documents. These notes (see Figure 6.3) consist of each slide that was written in class along with a timeline that shows the order in which slides and web pages were visited. By clicking on a stroke, a RealPlayer® is spawned which plays the audio at the time of writing. Clicking on the timeline also indexes into the audio at the appropriate point. Within one minute after class, a syllabus of all the lectures for that class is automatically updated, and the captured notes are automatically made available.

Access – From StreamWeaver to PHP
In the beginning, ZenPad provided a browse-only mode that students could access to replay lectures. We had to abandon this dynamic interface in favor of static, more constrained HTML documents because at the time, most browsers were not capable of running Java programs robustly. StreamWeaver was written to generate enhanced HTML documents of the integrated classroom activities.

Although StreamWeaver made our online notes accessible to virtually everyone, it blurred the line between the integration and access phases making enhancements to the program difficult. For example, if StreamWeaver was enhanced to create a better HTML interface, it would have to be run again on all previous lectures to generate the new HTML code. As the project matured, we modified StreamWeaver to populate a MySQL database and then used PHP scripts (a web-based scripting language) to create dynamically the access interfaces for the students.

Having all of the captured materials stored in a database with a dynamically generated interface allowed us to make many enhancements to the online notes. Instructors were now able to add comments to their lectures after the fact, perhaps clarifying a complicated topic. We were able to custom configure browsing interfaces tailored to the student's request, and we were able to generate searchable notes for the first time.

Students were able to search the online notes by specifying a keyword to find. The data that could be searched depended on the course, but we were able to support the searching of a keyword over what a slide contained, what was written, what was spoken, web pages, instructor notes, and collaborative web pages for a course. We were able to generate the searchable content automatically, except for handwriting and speech transcriptions.

Searching over handwriting required that the instructor manually transcribed her writing. In practice, this only took a few minutes per lecture, but only a few instructors bothered to do it. We experimented with automated handwriting recognizers, but they were unable to produce any usable output.

Voice transcription was done using a commercial recognizer trained to one of two instructors. We were able to achieve around 80% word accuracy, which turned out to be sufficient for searching over the audio. The recognizers required that the instructor wear a wireless microphone and much manual effort, so we eventually stopped supporting this feature.

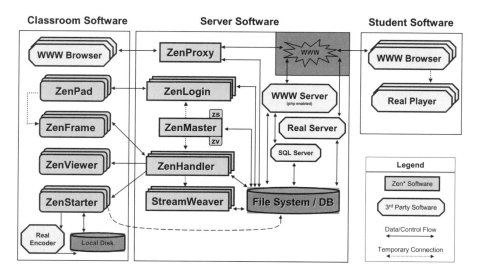

Figure 6.6. The complete Zen* system that comprises eClass.

Behind the scenes – the servers

All of the programs described above only tell half of the story. Behind the scenes, we have several servers running to enable all the eClass components to work together. The servers, together with the client software, comprise the Zen* system diagram shown in Figure 6.6.

eClass relies on the use of several third party servers to help store and retrieve information. We use an Apache Server (Apache Software Foundation [2]) as our web server, a Real Server (Real Networks [10]) to stream video and audio, and a MySQL Server (Open Source [9]) as our database server. Once these three commercial servers are running, we then run our two servers, ZenMaster and ZenProxy.

The heart of our system is the ZenMaster server, a multi-threaded Java program that runs on the system server machine. Classroom sessions are initiated through ZenPad, invoked either as a stand-alone program or through a web browser in the classroom. Multiple classrooms can run ZenPad clients simultaneously.

Each ZenPad client goes through the ZenMaster server and establishes a connection with a ZenLogin server module. This module handles all of the pre-production tasks such as user authentication, lecture creation, and slide imports.

Recall that the classroom uses ZenViewers to display previous slides and ZenStarters to record audio and video automatically. These programs connect to ZenMaster and essentially announce their presence by specifying the IP address of any ZenPad machines they want to monitor. ZenMaster stores these requests in a global address space.

Once a lecture is ready to begin, ZenPad launches ZenFrame (shown in Figure 6.5) that again connects to the ZenMaster server and then instantiates a connection to a ZenHandler server module. ZenFrame sends to this module all of the ink and slide navigation events from the instructor. Meanwhile ZenHandler also establishes connections to any ZenViewers and ZenStarters that have been started for the room in which ZenFrame is running. ZenViewers receive all of the ink and navigation events of ZenFrame through ZenHandler and therefore act as an extended display showing the current ZenFrame screen, the previous screen, or an overview of screens, updated in real time. ZenHandler tells ZenStarter that a class has started and ZenStarter runs the RealEncoder program that begins encoding audio and video for the class. As the class is proceeding, ZenHandler is saving all of the captured lecture material to the server disk.

The other server, ZenProxy, is a simple web proxy that records all web pages visited by browsers configured to go through the proxy. When the class is over, ZenStarter sends the encoded audio and video files to the server disk while ZenProxy sends all of the URLs visited to the server disk. ZenHandler then invokes StreamWeaver, which takes the time-stamped streams of information and creates web-accessible artifacts by generating GIF and JPEG images of the slides with ink transposed on them and placing all of the data into the system database.

The entire post-production process takes about one minute to complete. After the class, students can access the captured lecture materials by using their Web browsers with streaming audio capabilities to access PHP scripts that in turn query the database for classroom information and data.

Summary

All in all, there is nothing remarkable about the tools that eClass uses, but the way that we integrate them enables us to build a complex note-taking system. Table 6.1 highlights all of the eClass components and the phases in which they are used.

From a hardware point of view, there is no "standard" eClass setup. We have had several installations at The Georgia Institute of Technology, Georgia State, Kennesaw State University, McGill University, and Brown University, and no two installations utilize the same equipment. We view a typical installation instead as the minimal services that the room can provide and the hardware needed to provide them. How this is actually accomplished may be through several different hardware configurations using different products and infrastructures. For example, one computer could control all the services for an entire classroom, or there could be multiple computers for each service. The important thing is that the captured notes are independent of the physical equipment used in the classroom.

Table 6.1. A summary of eClass components and the phases they support. Software we created is listed in a bold font and third party software is listed in italics.

	Pre-Production	Live Capture	Integration	Access
Client	**Transfermation**	**ZenPad** **ZenViewer** **ZenStarter** *WWW Browser* *RealEncoder*		*WWW Browser*
Server	**ZenMaster**	**ZenMaster** **ZenProxy**	**StreamWeaver** *MySQL Server*	**PHP Scripts** *WWW Server* *Real Server* *MySQL Server*

6.4   Evaluation Results

Over the four-year lifetime of the project, we have gained extensive experience in the use of eClass. We have captured parts or all of 98 courses at The Georgia Institute of Technology. Courses have ranged from graduate to undergraduate and have been in areas of computer science, electrical engineering, and mathematics. Installations at Kennesaw State University, McGill University, and Brown University have experienced less use, capturing only 12 courses combined. At The Georgia Institute of Technology, we have captured over 2,300 lectures by 27 instructors and have received over 100,000 online note accesses. During this time we have collected over 1,000 student questionnaires and studied over 2,200 online note access sessions. In this section, we will briefly discuss some of our evaluation results based on the observational data collected.

6.4.1 Students Find eClass Worthwhile

Overall, students found eClass to be an effective enhancement to the classroom. They reported that eClass helped them pay more attention during class (59% agree, 27% neutral, 14% disagree) and helped to make the classroom more engaging (67% agree, 23% neutral, 10% disagree). Students overwhelmingly would prefer to take a class taught with eClass than a traditional course (81% agree, 14% neutral, 5% disagree) and felt that eClass helped them learn the material presented in the course (63% agree, 25% neutral, 12% disagree).

Despite the design of eClass to support presentation-style lectures, other instructors who employed more discussion-style lectures used it as well. Surprisingly, students thought that eClass was well suited for the courses they took regardless of the teaching style (81% agree, 14% disagree, 5% disagree).

Again, by focusing on building a system that supported current teaching styles and lectures, we found that we did the right thing. 50% of students thought that the lecture was the most important component of the course and 25% thought that it was second most important. As a result, nearly 100% of all students have accessed the online notes, most of them (40%) to view a lecture that was previously attended. Other top reasons given for accessing the notes were to review a missed lecture (16%), to study for an exam (17%), to get help with a homework assignment (12%), and to follow up an interesting point in class (17%).

6.4.2 Students Take Less Notes

We have found, not surprisingly, that eClass results in students taking fewer notes. We believe that eClass encourages students to take more summary-style notes, and we are currently looking into ways of testing this hypothesis.

While eClass notes are useful, they are not a substitute for taking notes. If students were forced to choose between only having their own notes and only having eClass notes, they would rather have their own notes (54% agree, 23% neutral, 23% disagree). Not surprising then is that they feel eClass notes would increase in value if they were able to make personal annotations on them (59% agree, 29% neutral, 12% disagree).

6.4.3 eClass Does Not Encourage Skipping

Many people ask us if eClass might encourage students to "skip a lecture and catch the highlights at home". As we have said before, we designed eClass as a supplement to attending a lecture rather than a replacement for it. Because eClass lacks so many features found in distance education systems, we did not think that students would prefer to watch what eClass captures to attending the class.

Two attendance experiments have supported our hunch. In the first experiment, attendance records of two sections of the same course were compared. In one section, the instructor used eClass; in the other, she did not. We found that there was no negative impact of eClass on attendance and, in fact, attendance was better and more consistent in the section taught using eClass. A second experiment counted the attendance of several courses at The Georgia Institute of Technology, some using eClass, some not, over a one-month period. We again found that the use of eClass did not result in lower attendance.

Student surveys also support the claim that eClass online lectures are not a substitute for being in the live lecture. Student reactions to whether eClass encourages skipping are mixed (29% agree, 36% neutral, 35% disagree), but they do feel that eClass relieves them of the worry of missing a class on those few times when it cannot be helped (51% agree, 20% neutral, 29% disagree).

6.4.4 Augmentation of Pen and Paper Notes is Worth the Effort

eClass is not just about creating automated notes, it is about creating a new type of notes. By having online notes, we can integrate pen and paper notes with audio, video, and other artefacts found in the classroom. Overall, students found the audio augmentation of the notes valuable (55% agree, 33% neutral, 13% disagree). Video augmentation was less useful (39% agree, 38% neutral, 23% disagree), probably because of the poor video quality. Linking web pages with the online notes was viewed as a valuable service as well (57% agree, 36% neutral, 7% disagree).

Of course, one of the drawbacks to online notes is that they can only be viewed from a computer and not, say, on the bus ride home or in bed (not yet anyway!). We provided a printing function for students and they found it to be useful (56% agree, 25% neutral, 19% disagree), showing that the enhanced online notes were also valuable in the unaugmented but printed form.

6.5   What Can Be Improved

There is no doubt that eClass has been a tremendous success for our research group. It has been accepted and demanded by instructors and students and several other researchers have used it. eClass, however, is far from perfect. There is much about eClass that is now either inefficient or obsolete.

One major problem with eClass is that it was written in Java while the language was still in early development. As a result, we custom built (sometimes not very well) many libraries that are now a standard part of the system. Examples of these routines include our own object serialization, FTP functions, custom GUI components, and network functions. These routines are now easily replaced with the latest version of Java and Swing, Object Serialization, and Remote Method Invocation. As a result, many parts of our system are quite antiquated and inefficient and, ultimately, error prone.

Reliability has always been a concern. Our software is reliable enough when used properly, but often fails in the face of unplanned events, like network outages. Moreover, the general reliability of eClass is affected when the physical equipment in the room is disturbed, such as audio cables being disconnected, or video cameras being turned off. We could easily improve reliability by fixing our code but, since our recording equipment is located in the classroom, we cannot avoid these types of failures. Therefore, one easy way to improve our system is to have all equipment located outside the classroom where it is not as easily disturbed.

eClass has a few design flaws, with the major one being our networking model. The result is that eClass can only support one-way interactions between ZenPad and ZenViewer, and there can only be one writing surface (ZenPad) per classroom. Instructors would greatly benefit from the ability to annotate slides shown or to be able to control the presentation from a ZenViewer. Students would greatly benefit from the ability to take their own notes on top of the instructor's notes in real time. While we were able to introduce student note-taking devices (StuPad, discussed below), we had to cobble our system so much that we decided that it would be better just to rebuild the system.

The video quality eClass provides is very low. This was done because it was believed that video would provide more information than audio and therefore be more useful. In order to be able to still provide online note access to dialup modem users, we had to encode the video at such a poor rate as to make it barely usable. Also, the instructor could not easily control the video cameras. It would have been nice to have camera control from within ZenPad so that the instructor could change camera angles, zoom in when needed, or even turn it off.

Although eClass can use PowerPoint® presentations, it does so by creating static images of the presentation. This is fine for most users, but a few instructors have complained about the loss of any custom animations as a result of the conversion. Rather than build a whiteboard that can accept an impoverished version of PowerPoint® slides, we should instead have augmented PowerPoint® with ZenPad features. At the beginning of the project, however, we did not anticipate the widespread use of PowerPoint® and, even if we had, we would not have been able to eClass quickly build or evaluate its use if we had chosen that route.

Collaborative web sites (CoWebs) are quickly becoming commonplace for courses here at The Georgia Institute of Technology. CoWebs [6] are a collection of web pages that anyone can edit using just their browser and without being familiar with HTML. We tried to integrate CoWeb technology into eClass with some success. Students and instructors were able to create content and have it linked from the eClass notes, but it required knowledge of HTML and was not very easy to do. We feel that the ability for students to post comments and content publicly was a great asset to eClass and something the students wanted, even if we did not do a good job of integrating the two technologies.

Keyword searching was not heavily used in our system, despite the fact that we think it was easy to use. One reason for the lack of use might be attributable to the ease with which topics could be scanned. For a course, each lecture usually has a germane title and, while viewing a lecture, it is very easy to scan all of the slides quickly. It might be that searching is not needed for students enrolled in a course, but is more useful to other viewers of the notes. One obvious way to improve our searching is to create a topic search rather than a keyword search, but we have not explored that option.

In the beginning of eClass, we wanted to give students electronic note-taking devices. After a few prototypes, we realized that the big win came from supporting the capture of the public information in the lecture first. Once we succeeded in building eClass and having it used regularly, we again turned to incorporating student annotations. This resulted in StuPad, a note-taking device for students that had the ability to act like a ZenViewer, but with more navigational freedom [15]. A StuPad server interfaced with eClass masquerading as a ZenViewer, and then interacted with all StuPad clients. In this way, a StuPad client could receive all the information of a ZenViewer without being tied to the architectural design of eClass.

The only problem with StuPad was in the expensive pen tablet computers that it required. We have since looked at less expensive (and less powerful) note-taking devices and are currently working on a new design of eClass based on a capture/access toolkit we are building. The new design will incorporate all of the improvements discussed above as well as enable future developments that we have not yet specified.

6.6   Conclusion

We have introduced four phases to any capture/access application: pre-production, live capture, integration, and access. We have shown how this separation of concerns allows for easy, fail-fast designs and an increased longevity of the system. eClass has been a successful research project for us and a useful system for instructors and students. We were lucky in that we chose the right domain to explore capture and access. The lessons learned have since allowed us to generalize our capture and access work into other domains, most recently into the home environment. For more information about the history or evaluation of eClass, please see our previous work [1] or visit: http://www.cc.gatech.edu/fce/eclass.

References

1. Abowd, G. D. (1999) *Classroom 2000*: An experiment with the instrumentation of a living educational environment, in *IBM Systems Journal*, Special issue on Pervasive Computing, Volume 38, Number 4, pp. 508-530.

2. Apache (2000) Apache software foundation. http://www.apache.org.

3. Black, M., Bérard, F., Jepson, A., Newman, W., Saund, E., Socher, G. and M. Taylor (1998) The digital office: Overview, in *AAAI Spring Symposium on Intelligent Environments*, Palo Alto.

4. Electronics_for_Imaging, *eBeam* (2000) http://www.ebeam.com.

5. Elrod. S.E.A. (1992) *Liveboard:* A large interactive display supporting group meetings, presentations and remote collaboration, in *CHI '92*. 1992. Monterey, CA.

6. Guzdial, M., Rick, J., Kehoe, C. (2001) Beyond adoption to invention: Teacher-created collaborative activities in higher education, in *Journal of the Learning Sciences*.

7. Kintronics (2000) *Panaboard*. http://www.kintronics.com/panaboard.html

8. MicroTouch (2000) *Ibid*, Virtual ink Corporation, 56 Roland Street, Suite 306, Boston, MA 02129. http://www.microtouch.com/ibid

9. MySQL (2000) *Open Source*. http://www.mysql.com.

10. Real Server (2000) *Real Networks*. http://www.real.com.

11. SMART Technologies (2000) *SMARTBoard*, SMART Technologies, Inc, #600, 1177 - 11th Avenue SW, Calgary, AB, Canada, T2R 1K9.

12. SoftBoard (2000) *SoftBoard*. SoftBoard, 7216 SW Durhan Road, Portland, OR 97224.

13. Stafford-Fraser, Q., and Robinson P. (1996) BrightBoard: A video-augmented environment, in *CHI '96*. Vancouver, Canada.

14. TeamBoard (2000) *TeamBoard*. http://www.teamboard.com.

15. Truong, K.N., Abowd, G. D., and Brotherton J. A.. (1999) Personalizing the capture of public experiences, in *User Interface Software and Technology*. Asheville, NC.

16. Virutual_ink (2000) *Mimio*, Virtual ink Corporation, 56 Roland Stree, Suite 306, Boston, MA 02129. http://www.mimio.com

Chapter 7

Learning Gains in a Multi-user Discussion System used with Social Science Students – The coMentor Experience

Graham R. Gibbs

MUDs (Multi-User Domains) are multi-user programs that were amongst the first to be used to support student collaborative learning on the Internet. Their operation in a variety of contexts has shown the potential for educational gains through the use of virtual learning environments (VLEs). The coMentor system was developed to support learning amongst social science students by adapting the discursive and collaborative elements of MUDs to operate within a web interface. Evaluation of the software with a group of students studying philosophy on sociology and psychology 106 courses suggests that learners can develop both deep and strategic learning styles in such environments and that they can learn from seeing the work of their peers. coMentor retains the spatial metaphor central to MUDs and there is still much to be gained from such metaphorical usage in VLEs. coMentor is also being used to test the use of IMS to exchange information between different VLEs and other university systems. Early results suggest there are gains to be made from such inter-operation.

7.1 Introduction

There is a good deal of research about collaboration in learning in traditional settings that has demonstrated its utility. Some show that the benefits arise from the motivation and encouragement that collaboration can create. For instance, Madden and Slavin [1] and Slavin [2] suggested that students in collaborating classes felt that their peers wanted them to learn. However, more centrally, there is evidence of improved learning through collaboration. Dansereau [3] had students cooperate by taking turns as recaller and listener. They read a section of text, and then the recaller summarized the information while the listener corrected any errors, filled in any omitted material, and thought of ways both students could remember the main ideas. Learners working together on structured cooperative tasks learned technical material or procedures far better than those working alone. The utility of elaborating explanations to peers was confirmed by Webb [4] who showed that students who gained the most from collaborative learning were those who provided elaborated explanations to others. There is some evidence that peer learners have to take appropriate roles, for instance the one with more to say taking the role of task-doer while others might become observers, monitoring the situation [5]. This does not necessarily mean that only the more active collaborators will gain; even the observers may learn from the exchanges. As McEndree *et al.* argue, students can learn much from observing the dialogues of other learners. This they refer to as "vicarious learning" and it often consists of learning from the (observed) mistakes in the dialogues and discussions of others [6].

The development of a range of computer-based communications technologies has provided new opportunities for designing systems to support collaborative learning.

7.2   MUDs and MOOs

7.2.1 Definition

The MUD or MOO (MUD, Object Oriented) derives from the interactive, role-playing, multi-user dungeon games:

"MUDs...are programs that accept network connections from multiple simultaneous users and provide access to a shared database of "rooms", "exits", and other objects. Users browse and manipulate the database from 'inside' the rooms, seeing only those objects that are in the same room and moving between rooms mostly via the exits that connect them. MUDs are thus a kind of virtual reality, an electronically-represented "place" that users can visit." [7]

The creation, through a text-based interface, of an imaginative world is fundamental to many MUDs. Users often refer to the distinction between life in the MUD and life outside the MUD, referred to as RL – real life. Text descriptions of rooms, places, people and objects are used to give a sense of place and reality along with a general atmosphere to MUDs and MOOs. For example, Figure 7.1 shows the introductory "page" to the VUW (the Virtual campus at the University of Waterloo) MOO at the University of Waterloo, Canada, which sets the tone for an academic campus.

One of the most commented-on aspects of MUDs and MOOs is that users can adopt different characters or personas from those they have in real life. A new user can create a description of themselves along with a gender (which may be male, female or neutral) and their identity may even be plural (as in a flock of seagulls) [8, 9]. This description guides their own behavior and especially how others behave towards them, since initially the description is the only information other users have about the player.

```
<*>The University Of Waterloo - Virtual Campus Information Kiosk<*>

~~~~~~~~~~~~~~~~~~~~~~~~~~~~~~~~~~~~~~~~~~~~~~~~~~~~~~~~~~~~~~~~~~~~~~

You are standing on the outskirts of campus. A welcoming white booth
rests on a low grass hill. Below it, there's a comfortable red plank
bench. You can find out lots of things about the Virtual Campus
here. Just type `enter' to go into the Information Kiosk. North
leads you onto campus, south leads to Off-Campus and student
housing.

It's quite chilly. The setting sun is obscured by low-hanging
clouds. There is a light breeze wafting in.

---Contents: Objects and People---
You see VUW INFORMATION KIOSK here.

---Available Exits---
<north> to Ring Road -- Southern Intersection
<south> to University Ave -- South of Kiosk
<west> to A grassy hill
<enter> to Inside VUW Information Kiosk
```

Figure 7.1. Introduction "Page" for VUW MOO

7.2.2 Educational MUDs and MOOs

The potential of MUDs in education has been recognized in a variety of ways [10]. Not surprisingly, one use is to support creative writing, building upon the creative and imaginative dimensions of MUDs. However, in general, it has been the support for rooms and chat that has most attracted educationalists. The technology offers new opportunities for conducting classes and seminars. Long distance learning is one obvious example, but, with the hypertextual qualities of text-based virtual realities, opportunities abound for unusual student projects that engage imaginative and structured thinking in written texts. In higher education, the uses of MUDs and MOOs have divided into four main areas: writing, language learning, general campus and research community support.

A typical example of using MUDs to teach writing is the "Composition in Cyberspace" course that attempted to achieve a kind of engaged writing [11]. It involved pairing composition classes at two US universities, and used both an asynchronous email journal and synchronous class meetings on Diversity University MOO to connect the classes and to create a public forum for the students' writing. Students submitted examples of their writing and others were able to read them, comment on them and learn from them. As Harris notes:

"students wrote much more carefully... They learned to express their ideas clearly and convincingly – and they wanted to do so, because they knew how easy it would be for others to challenge unsupported claims. They were thus more effective, engaged writers, not only in the "informal" or "fun" settings of MOOs and email lists, but also in the work they submitted to their instructor" [11].

There are quite a number of language MUDs and MOOs. A typical example is MundoHispano, a Spanish language MOO [12]. It creates a community of native speakers of Spanish from around the world along with teachers and learners of Spanish, and computer programmers. A key advantage that organizers and users of language MUDs and MOOs claim is that students get the chance to "chat" (albeit in writing) with native language users. Although the language experience may be far from the structured programme of the language class, the experience of native speakers' conversation constitutes a kind of ultimate authenticity in the electronic exchanges.

One of the largest and best known general campus MOOs is Diversity University [13]. Designed as a virtual campus the program provides facilities for large numbers of students, teachers, and administrators worldwide to use its classes, literature, and consulting services. Other examples include the Virtual Online University at the University of Athena, USA, which has submitted a formal application for accreditation as a university, and VUW (the Virtual campus at the University of Waterloo). VUW was developed in 1995 for use with an entirely online Technical Writing undergraduate course.

The fourth common use for MUDs and MOOs is to support research communities. They are used to support academic research activities rather in the way that conventional conferences and workshops do. Examples include BioMOO [14] and MediaMOO [15]. At MediaMOO media researchers from around the world discuss current projects, teachers meet weekly to discuss ways of using computers to teach writing and there is a large group of rhetoric and composition subscribers who meet weekly in the (virtual) Netoric Cafe to discuss a wide range of issues, particularly integrating technology and writing. Two important points about MUDs and MOOs are illustrated by these activities. First, MediaMOO is acting as support for the same kind of informal meetings, discussions, and chats that are often some of the most stimulating parts of traditional face-to-face academic conferences and workshops and through this it fosters a sense of belonging to a community. Second, although it is possible to "drop in" at any time, most users and operators of MUDs and MOOs find it necessary to schedule online meetings and events, just as in "RL".

7.2.3 Pedagogy in MUDs and MOOs

Several advantages for the use of MUDs and MOOs in education are claimed. Most can be linked to the kind of imaginative virtual reality created by users and the object and room descriptions found in MUDs. Moock suggests that the natural conversational and community features of a MOO encourage users to converse and conduct themselves in ways that are close to those of real-life meetings and conversations. In this way, remote learners, and even those from different cultures, can experience not just the language and discourse of those in the MOO but also some of the social and communal features of people meeting together [16].

Many MUDs and MOOs also seem to foster strong senses of mutual help and peer support. This has been noted by Bruckman in her account of learning to program in a MOO, where, in the absence of good manuals and offline support, the learner was helped by other participants in the MOO who gave freely of their time [17].

However, there are also some problems associated with the use of MUDs in teaching. One can arise simply from the popularity of the medium. If many people are chatting at the same time then there is a tendency for discussions to break into many threads and, as discussions overlap, the situation becomes very confusing and hard to moderate.

Another problem that comes with success is that of overload of students or teachers.

"With larger groups of students, the email journal can produce significant work for the students and for the faculty members. If a collective group of 40 students write two or three email messages a week, instructors and students end up reading 80 to 120 messages each week. Although some of us are used to that volume of mail, many students are not (and many faculty members are on a number of Internet discussion lists already), and so the journal can become tiresome if not over-burdening" [11].

However, probably the most serious problem in traditional, text-based MUDs, is the need for students to master a command-line interface using a Telnet application to undertake tasks such as moving around the environment, adding work or commenting on others' and reading documents deposited in the system.

7.3   coMentor

7.3.1 Introduction to coMentor

The coMentor project is an attempt to address the Computer Aided Learning (CAL) needs of the social sciences. The potential for CAL in the social sciences like sociology, politics and social policy is large. In 1998 there were over 9,100 academics and researchers in social science departments in higher education in the UK and over 133,000 students. However, teachers in these disciplines have been relatively slow to adopt CAL. An important reason for this is the difficulty of applying CAL to subject matter that is mainly textual, discursive or disputational; in other words to those disciplines and topic areas, such as those found in much of the social sciences, where the subject matter is predominantly theoretical or non-empirical and essentially contested. Many computer-based approaches, such as modelling and visualization are inappropriate because they generally assume an empirical subject matter and/or a universally agreed paradigm. In contrast, in disputational topics there is no real empirical content and debate is the essence. Typical examples are philosophy, methodology and social theory.

The use of MUDs or MOOs to support such teaching and learning therefore seems to hold much promise. The majority of research results about the educational use of MUDs has come from those using command-line and non-web compliant interfaces that appear to students to be isolated from web resources. Social science students are among the least enthusiastic about computers and departments commonly do not have good access to high-end equipment. The coMentor project addresses these issues by using a MOO modified to operate through standard web browsers to support teaching and learning in theoretical subjects. To this end coMentor supports the following facilities:

- graphics, icons, visual tools, identification of users;

- users may adopt persona for different philosophical positions (*e.g.*, sceptic, rationalist);

- debate – encourages chat and discussion;

- rooms – or at least virtual spaces where groups can meet in relative privacy;

- objects – including documents, notes, URLs, FAQs. They can be left by teachers, mentors or learners. Unlike most MOOs these are not programmable by users;

- both synchronous and asynchronous communications;

- annotation of texts produced by others;

- learning tools, *e.g.*, concept mapping tools.

The technical approach used by coMentor is based on the APECKS/WOOM system. This makes use of frames and forms on the web page to eliminate the need for a separate Telnet application. This system, developed by Jeni Tennison at the University of Nottingham, uses a modified MOO database to generate HTML "on the fly". In addition there are Java applets, Perl scripts and Java applications to extend the functions of the browsers and to support MOO to HTTP communications on the server. Students can use standard browsers such as Netscape Navigator and Microsoft Internet Explorer without any separate, extra software. The server runs LambdaMOO on a UNIX (or Linux) workstation. This is a MOO developed at the Xerox Palo Alto Research Centre and there are versions for PowerMac, several kinds of UNIX and WinNT. A linked HTTP server (Apache) delivers images and Java applets, to give full graphical and interactive functionality.

There are several other systems combining MOO and web in development, and it seems inevitable that the future of MUDs and MOOs will involve some kind of MOO/web combination. [18, 19, 20] There is, therefore, a degree of convergence between systems like coMentor and web-based VLEs. Nevertheless, a crucial distinction remains, reflecting the different starting points of the two approaches. This centers around the core metaphor used by each. MUDs and MOOs are based on a metaphor of place. Users construct rooms and populate them with objects that have certain behaviors. In contrast, web-based systems tend to be based around a filing system metaphor. They are constructed hierarchically as an efficient way to navigate around large numbers of different files. Users add information and files at the appropriate point in this hierarchy and in general the information has no associated behaviors.

7.3.2 coMentor Design Philosophy

Early formative evaluation using observation of current teaching sessions, group interviews and a web-based questionnaire with undergraduate and postgraduate students suggested that needs fell into four main areas:

Group and Seminar Work. Students wanted to choose who was in their group and to be in different groups for different topics while maintaining access to work done by other groups. They wanted greater linkage between the lecture topics and associated group-work or seminars. Although they wanted to be able to ask some questions anonymously, they did want rewards for contributing to group-work.

Individual Work. Again, students wanted access to each other's work and they wanted access recorded to reward good work and prevent problems of plagiarism. They also wanted input from tutors on work in progress and feedback on presentations from tutors and fellow students.

Resources. Students requested three main types of resource: course support, such as an FAQ of queries to lecturers, lecture notes and supplementary material, framework-giving summaries, and key articles; a pre-course pack, including such things as an introduction and contextualization of philosophy and its relation to other social science subjects, a guide to writing theoretical and philosophical essays, and examples of past essays and exam answers; and, lastly, outside resources, such as discussions and seminars with or between external experts, and audio-visual material such as talks, interviews, and documentaries.

Access. Some students, such as those on Masters' programmes, were part-time and only came into the university one day a week. Many said they did not use the university computer laboratory and so would be unlikely to use coMentor unless they could use it from home or work. Many Masters' students also wished for more communication with fellow students in between their seminar days.

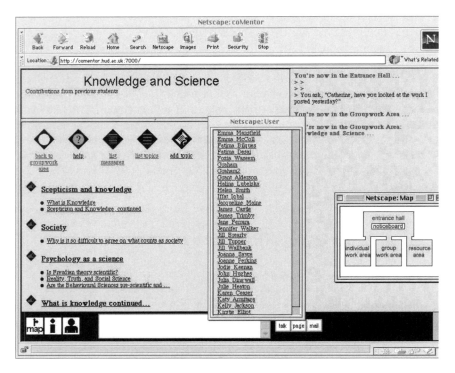

Figure 7.2. The coMentor system.

To meet these needs, the facilities in coMentor are situated within a common environment, which allows learners to chat and send messages while working together in a particular area (see Figure 7.2). These facilities include:

● Allowing many learners to connect simultaneously to a server and allowing identification of learners (both personal and ideological). In coMentor users have the option of choosing identities which have relevance to social theory or philosophy and are expected to "stay in role" while on the MOO. Thus a user could adopt the identity of a rationalist, and would be expected to take that viewpoint and defend it in debates.

● A spatial organization of contents so that learners interact in "places" or can "visit" depositories of information on previous discussions. Virtual group-work is supported by providing the facility for students and teachers to establish groups and virtual places where they can meet and discuss. Such "places" include groups for specific purposes, for instance to prepare a paper, or thematic or topic-based groups.

● A "library" of reference materials. This includes selected texts from student discussion, specially constructed FAQs and other materials (*e.g.*, good texts to read) deposited by students and teachers. This includes examples of previous year s' essays and exam questions and answers. The issues of plagiarism, consent and copyright this raises are, in part, addressed by the provision for audit trailing and user tracking.

- Synchronous and asynchronous communication tools. The former includes chatting with those in the same place (room) and paging those logged on but "elsewhere" in the system. The latter includes email (i.e., the ability to leave messages on the system), threaded discussion lists and an annotation tool. In this way students can comment on contributions made by others and annotate reference materials available in coMentor.

This design constitutes coMentor as a learning tool [21, 22]. By using the facilities of the web to provide much content, and student and teacher discussion to provide the rest, the software itself is almost free of content. coMentor can thus be seen as a CAL package which assists learning but which itself has little knowledge content. Knowledge content is added by the users and especially by the learners. The function of the learning tool is not to get students to learn by acquiring surface knowledge from manifest information in the software, but to get them to master new concepts by manipulating the program in ways made possible by the latent concepts on which its design is based. The bias away from surface learning and towards deep learning can be seen in the evaluation results discussed below.

A key advantage of the learning tool approach is that the software is not made specific to one teaching context or to one educational institution or department. Although for the purposes of development and evaluation, coMentor supported the teaching and learning of philosophy and social theory for social science students, the design of the system is such that with relative ease, and with a little knowledge of HTML, it can be adapted to support learning in other knowledge domains. The system has already been used to teach sociology, cultural studies and nursing.

7.3.3 Evaluation

The system was evaluated in 1997-8, with a group of full-time social science undergraduates taking a compulsory Methodology and Philosophy module. Several types of data were collected. All contributions posted to any of the areas were recorded. Transcripts and logs of all movements around the system and synchronous chat were kept. A questionnaire was administered after the end of the module. This contained a series of questions about students' use of the system, both fixed response and open-ended, along with the ASSIST Learning Styles Inventory [23].

As is common when introducing CAL, the use of coMentor involved several changes in the teaching and organization outside the VLE. Indeed, experience suggests that CAL works best when it is integrated into other elements of the course [24]. Changes made included some of the lecture topics and face-to-face group-work sessions. These were focused much more on student activities such as presentations and linked to work in the VLE. For instance, summaries of debates were put in the virtual resource area along with copies of OHPs from student presentations and material from teaching staff lectures. A change made to the form of assessment had major implications. Previously students were assessed by a short essay and a one hour, unseen examination. This was changed to allow students who wished to, to take an assessment on coMentor based on at least 5 short contributions made in each of 5 different weeks instead of the final examination. Students were encouraged to write their contributions in a word processing package (*e.g.*, Word), then cut and paste them into coMentor, so they had a back-up copy. To address student anxieties about the criteria that would be used to mark the online contributions they were told that they would be assessed using the same criteria as the module essay. Thus the contribution was expected to have structure and organization, and an introduction and a conclusion. It was required to focus on the question, demonstrate a good understanding of theoretical concepts, discuss relevant criticisms and identify and challenge assumptions. Students were expected to show an awareness of relevant sources and evidence in the literature and use a proper system of citation.

7.3.4 Results

106 students took the module and 54 replied to the questionnaire, a response rate of 50.9%. 56% of respondents claimed to be using the system about once a week or more. The logs of activity showed a pattern of use that gradually increased during the semester until by the last 6 weeks about 70% were using the system once a week or more often. There are two likely reasons for this. First, the assessment required postings in each of 5 separate weeks and, thus, the closer the end of the exercise became, the less time was available in which contributions could be made.

Table 7.1. Average learning style by frequency of use of coMentor.

	Frequency of use				
Learning Style	Not at all	Just a few times	About once a week	More than once a week	
Deep	73.0	70.0	79.9	80.4	
Surface	35.3	46.9	37.1	39.4	
Strategic	44.7	54.6	71.6	80.6	***

*** - significant at $p<0.001$. Scores range from 0 to 100.*

Second, informal feedback suggests that the whole environment became more attractive as there was more activity online and there was more work to see. This increased the perceived benefits to students of using the system.

Table 7.1 shows the learning styles scores derived from the ASSIST inventory. Those doing the coMentor assessment and those claiming to use the system more frequently showed significantly higher scores on deep and strategic learning and lower scores on surface learning [25]. They were also high compared with scores from other universities and other courses. The latter were more in line with scores of those not using coMentor regularly. The ASSIST inventory derives from work by Entwistle and Ramsden [26] who made a distinction between various orientations to study. They contrasted the deep approach, in which the learner is concerned to understand both the facts of the matter and the underlying principles, with the surface approach, in which the intention is only to complete the task requirements. More recently, Entwistle and colleagues developed the ASSIST Learning Styles Inventory. In this they clarified a third approach, the strategic, to reflect their finding that an identifiable group of learners adopted elements of deep or surface approaches in a judicious manner in order to get the task done efficiently. Learners taking this approach focused on organizing their work and their time and were alert to the demands of assessment in order to do well.

It is perhaps not surprising that students learning philosophy should show high deep learning scores. It suggests that they recognized that the best way to learn such a theoretical subject was to adopt a style that focussed on the conceptual and underpinning ideas. Without further research, it is difficult to say whether learning philosophy with coMentor promoted such learning styles or whether those adopting such styles found amenable support for their approach in coMentor and therefore chose to use it more.

What was unexpected in coMentor was the significantly better scores on the strategic approach to learning shown by regular users of the system. Bearing in mind that students had the freedom to choose how much to use coMentor and that many did so because they had chosen to take an online assessment, this seems to suggest that these learners were using the learning environment strategically. This required both flexibility in learning and a degree of organization. Those lacking these were left having to opt for the examination.

Although there was relatively little evidence of engagement by students in discussion (many threads contained just one message, for example) it is clear that by posting work students made available to their peers a large body of relatively accessible work and some helpful hints (readings, explanations *etc.*) that others found useful.

> "It was more "accessible" than some of the texts, *i.e.,* less jargon used".

Several students noted that the effort of having to write and post the contribution helped to clarify issues. As one said,

> "In order to place info in the work areas you had to understand it".

It is also clear that the content of the environment helped students clarify what the expectations of the module were. They shared their study problems with others, looked at the sample essays from the previous year and identified what kind and level of work was required of them.

"It helped me to understand other perspectives. Also ways in which to write a philosophy essay".

Table 7.2. Features and activities on coMentor students thought helped them learn philosophy (percentages)

Looking at the content of others' contributions	63
Looking at others' style of presentation (*e.g.*, structure, argument, referencing)	41
Getting feedback from other students	28
Contacting tutors, and teachers. Asking them questions.	28
Chatting with others online	4
Just keeping in touch with others	18
Giving help to others/replying to others	24
Information provided by others (*e.g.*, references)	41
Seeing others' mistakes	22
Having administration details online (*e.g.*, handouts, lecture details, timetable, assessment details)	72
Having general web philosophy resources available online	28

7.4   Extending the Spatial Metaphor of Rooms

As discussed above, coMentor draws on and enhances the familiar MUD spatial metaphor of rooms. However, the system avoids simply reproducing the geographic character of rooms and places associated with a real university. Many educational MUDs, especially the campus MUDs do this. For instance, schMOOze is a MOO-based system to support the teaching of English as a second language or as a foreign language (ESL/EFL). Figure 7.3 shows the text-based campus map with which users are presented.

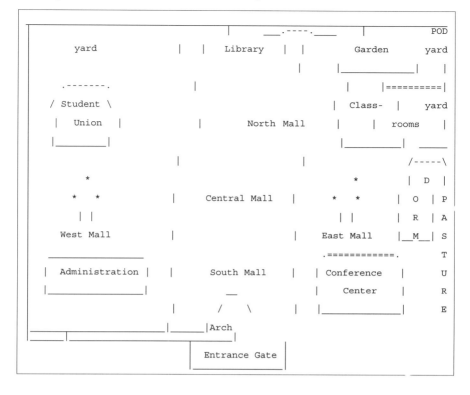

Figure 7.3. Text-based map of schMOOze.

As some have noted [27], this can easily undermine many of the advantages and opportunities for collaborative learning a MUD can offer. Of course there is much utility in the current metaphor of rooms in a teaching context. It makes implicit references to a periphery, a context, which helps create a set of expectations in the users of the system. This is what Brown *et al.* have referred to as "genre" [28]. It is possible to extend this without undermining the usefulness of the room metaphor to give users a much richer set of expectations about the nature of what will take place in a VLE. Creating virtual lecture theatres and seminar rooms may have the advantage of familiarity, but just as they are not always the best forums for promoting dialogue and discussion in real life, so in the VLE they may not be the best metaphor for promoting learning. Giving the right cues to students about what is expected in the system is important. *What* is taking place and its ground rules may be significantly influenced by *where* it is taking place. To this end the coMentor project is exploring ways of visualizing the places where debate and discussion take place in ways that give strong messages about the kind of activities and behavior expected there. The underlying motive is to help clarify to students the nature of the discussion in which they are taking part and hence promote a more active style of learning. Table 7.3 shows some of the possible metaphors for learning places and the expectations they should promote in learners. They suggest other ways of structuring debates and discussions in coMentor and suggest other objects that might be useful (*e.g.*, manifestos for philosophical positions, agony aunts for those with philosophical/theoretical problems) and other forms of ground rules for discussions and debates.

Metaphor	Related concepts, issues
Seminars	focus on "leaders", topics
Debates	taking sides, argument, evidence, propositions
Meetings	Diaries, slots, members, work, tasks, minutes
Chats	informal, my friends, unfocused
Visits	arrangements, guides, occasional
Journeys	trips, going somewhere, fellow travellers, companions, landscape
Groups	members, set (learning) tasks, group processes.
Clubs	interests, hobbies, membership, newsletters, meetings
Elections	votes, winners, soundbites, manifestos
Battle/fight	sides, weapons, winners/losers, reinforcements/support
Advice desk	Expert support, focused on my problems
Agony Aunt	Sympathetic, personalized
Play	make-believe, acting out, preparation/learning
Sport	practice, competition, skill, trainers.

Table 7.3. Alternative metaphors and users' expectations.

7.5   VLE Interoperability

There are now many virtual learning environments in use. Most are based around a web server, but others take distinctive routes to supporting student learning. It is clear that, just as MUDs have gained by being adapted to integrate with the web, in the long term, VLEs cannot operate in isolation. There are facilities and approaches that are offered in some environments but not in others and it would be useful if such functionality could be shared. Moreover, universities are finding it more and more important to be able to link these environments with the rest of their information systems. In this way they can ensure that student registration on the

VLE can be done easily and is consistent with their other registration data and they can also take assessment data from the VLE and incorporate it into their examinations database.

One development that may meet all these needs is IMS, Instructional Management System [29]. It is hoped that this will become an international standard for the exchange of a wide range of educational data. The specification not only covers educational content but also includes information about students, groups, costing, credits, ownership and so on. At the moment this is a developing standard and the UK academic community, through JISC, is a member of the international consortium working on the specification. Currently some aspects of the specification have been published, but others are still in earlier stages of development. Learning environment software and university corporate database systems will need to be adapted to export and import data in IMS format.

coMentor is now being developed, in a collaborative project, Co3, with teams from the Universities of Staffordshire (representing COSE) and Bangor (representing Colloquia) to test the application of some aspects of the IMS specification. COSE and Colloquia are also learning environments, but operate in quite different ways from coMentor. The aim is to create output in IMS format in each of the three systems and then import it into one of the others. At one level this is not difficult. IMS uses XML which is relatively simple to generate. However, there is still a good deal of leeway in interpreting what the entities referred to in the IMS specification mean in the respective VLEs. This is further complicated by the fact that the IMS specification is still subject to change.

The coMentor experience has demonstrated the educational gains that can be made from linking the creative and spatial elements of traditional MUDs with a web interface and web resources. Similar gains may also be possible from linking together VLEs with distinct pedagogic models and from linking them to university registration and examination systems. At the moment, the size and openness of the IMS specification make it unclear whether it will be able to provide the complete answer to such integration. Nevertheless, it seems that for at least a basic set of educational data and a limited set of learning functions, import and export of data in IMS format will be possible and will deliver considerable gains in effectiveness and efficiency to universities using conforming systems.

Acknowledgement

The coMentor project was supported by the JISC Technology Application Programme, Project JTAP 2/75.

The Co3 project is supported by the JISC Committee for Integrated Environments for Learners (JCIEL) programme.

References

1. Madden, N. E. and Slavin, R. E. (1993) Cooperative learning and social acceptance of mainstreamed academically handicapped students. *Journal of special education*, 1993, 17, 171-182.

2. Slavin, R. E. (1990) Cooperative Learning: Theory, Research and Practice. Prentice Hall, London.

3. Dansereau, D. F. (1988) Learning and Study Strategies: Issues in Assessment, Instruction, and Evaluation. Academic Press, New York.

4. Webb, N. (1985) Learning to cooperate, cooperating to learn. Plenum Publishing. New York.

5. Dillenbourg, P., Baker, M., Blaye, A. and O'Malley, C. (1994) The Evolution of Research on Collaborative Learning. http://tecfa.unige.ch/tecfa/research/lhm/ESF-Chap5.text

6. McKendree J., Stenning, K., Mayes, T., Lee, J. and Cox, R. (1998) Why observing a dialogue may benefit learning. *Journal of Computer Assisted Learning*, 14, 110-119.

7. Curtis, Pavel and Nichols, David A. (1996) MUDs Grow Up. Social Virtual Reality in the Real World, Xerox PARC, Palo Alto, CA.
ftp://ftp.lambda.moo.mud.org/pub/MOO/papers/MUDsGrowUp.txt

8. Bruckman, A. (1993) Gender Swapping on the Internet. *The Internet Society*, San Fransisco, CA, August 1993

ftp://ftp.media.mit.edu/pub/asb/papers/gender-swapping.txt

9. Reid, E. (1995) Virtual worlds: Culture and imagination. *CyberSociety: Computer Mediated Communication and Community*, Jones, S. G. (Ed.), Sage, London, 164-183.

10. Haynes, C. and Holmevik, J. R. (Eds.) (1997) High Wired: On the Design, Use, and Theory of Educational MOOs. The University of Michigan Press, Michigan.

11. Harris, L. (1998) Composition in Cyberspace: A Model for Collaborative Teaching and Learning. Susquehanna University, in

http://www.cyberstation.net/hf/rtic/moo/lharrisj.htm

12. http://www.umsl.edu/~moosproj/mundo.html

13. http://www.du.org

14. http://bioinformatics.weizmann.ac.il/BioMOO/

15. http://www.cc.gatech.edu/fac/Amy.Bruckman/MediaMOO/

16. Moock, C. (1996) Communication in the Virtual Classroom.
http://colinmoock.iceinc.com/nostalgia/virtual_classroom.html

17. Bruckman, A. (1994) Programming for Fun: MUDs as a Context for Collaborative Learning. *National Educational Computing Conference*. Boston, MA, June 1994.
ftp://ftp.media.mit.edu/pub/asb/papers/necc94.txt

18.   http://sensemedia.net/sprawl/

19.   http://www.cm.cf.ac.uk/htbin/AndrewW/moo_browser?look+79

20.   http://www.education.monash.edu.au/projects/moo/

21.   Gibbs, G. R and Robinson, D. (1998) CAL as learning tool: Lessons from educational theory. *Using Technology Effectively in the Social Sciences*, Henry, M. (Ed.) Taylor and Francis, London.

22.   Chute, D. L. (1995) Things I wish they had told me: Developing and using technologies for psychology. *Psychology Software News*. 6, 1, 4-9.

23.   Tait, H., Entwistle, N. and McCune, V. (1997) ASSIST: A Reconceptualisation of the Approaches to Studying Inventory. Paper to the 5th International Improving Student Learning Symposium, University of Strathclyde, September.

24.   Ravenscroft, A., Tait, K. and Hughes, I. (1998) Beyond the media: Knowledge level interaction and guided integration for CBL systems, *Computers and Education* 30(1/2), 49-56.

25.   Gibbs, G. R. (1999) Learning how to learn using a virtual learning environment for philosophy *Journal of Computer Assisted Learning*, 15(3), 221-231.

26.   Entwistle, N. J. and Ramsden, P. (1983) Understanding Student Learning. Croom Helm, London.

27.   Fanderclai, T. L. (1995) MUDs in education: New environments, new pedagogies. *Computer-Mediated Communication Magazine*, 2, 1, (January 1, 1995) page 8 http://www.december.com/cmc/mag/1995/jan/fanderclai.html.

28.   Brown, J. S. and Duguid, P. (1996) Keeping it simple. *Bringing Design to Software*, Winograd, T. (Ed.), Addison-Wesley and ACM Press, New York, 129-145.

29.   http://www.imsproject.org/

Chapter 8

The Application of Business Groupware Technologies to Support Collaborative Learning with Face-to-Face Students

Clive Holtham, Mark D'Cruz, and Ashok Tiwari

This chapter reviews the support of asynchronous teams utilizing intranet-based mini-case study publication with web-based conferencing The specific situation relates to large groups of one-year full-time MBA students. The chapter reports on this exercise from both pedagogic and groupware perspectives. Implications, and planned future developments of this approach, are reviewed.

The key pedagogic assumptions behind this exercise were based on theories of collaborative or cooperative learning, particularly peer tutoring, discussion in learning, and learning from case studies.

The exercises involved students preparing work individually, then publishing that work to a groupware or intranet database. Small groups then had to work asynchronously on group tasks, using the groupware, and drawing on their individual material. Students were assessed primarily on an individual basis.

A great deal was learnt about the academic issues arising from this type of work, as well as technical issues. Very considerable emphasis needs to be placed on clear pedagogic goals. It is also essential to have confidence both in the computer network and in the technical support facilities available.

The overall feedback from the exercise was very positive, but the clear academic benefits need to be assessed alongside the relatively greater actual and opportunity costs of running this type of intensive exercise.

8.1   Educational Context

The key pedagogic assumptions behind this exercise were based on theories of collaborative or cooperative learning, as outlined in [3] and [18]. There is a subset of this theory which focuses on peer teaching or tutoring [9]. [6] and [10] define this as "the system of instruction in which learners help each other and learn by teaching". These authors examine the specific topic of tutorless groups, which "aim to motivate students to become more involved with their own learning, so that they become more active and self-directed in their work".

There is also closely related theory to be derived from the role of discussion in learning [27] and from the use of syndicates and small groups in higher education [2]. There is, in addition, a specific concern with learning from case studies, a method that was refined at the Harvard Business School using relatively substantial, teacher-led cases [17]. Six different types of skills that can be developed through cases [6] are: analytical, application, creative, communication, social, and self-analyzis. In this exercise, the skills of particular relevance were:

Analytical: The basic research of a case; analyzis of the whole set of cases created by team members.

Application: students need to be able to apply basic information management concepts *e.g.*, the McFarlan Grid and the Balanced Business Scorecard, and latterly differing models of e-commerce.

Communication: The ability to edit and present a mini-case in an unfamiliar structured format, published to a large group electronically

Social: The development of social skills in asynchronous computer supported communications.

8.2   Computer Supported Collaborative Learning

Even though the term CSCW was not used at that time, the first generation of CSCW application and research was during the 1960's, arising from Englebart's work at Stanford [7]. The second generation began during the 1970's and was primarily based around innovations in higher education. One major center was at the University of Illinois where PLATO was developed [1]. PLATO involved both a multimedia intelligent tutoring system, as well as groupware-style conferencing and shared databases. Another major center was at the New Jersey Institute of Technology (NJIT) where the pioneers Murray Turoff and Starr Roxanne Hiltz [13] still continue to evolve what they call the Virtual Classroom [12, 26].

As networked technology has become widely available in higher education, the related concept of Computer Supported Collaborative Learning (CSCL) has been developed. It is worth noticing that much of the historic evolution of CSCL has been rooted in the needs of distance education [16]. There has been relatively less research concerning the use of CSCL with students who are otherwise wholly face-to-face. This imbalance can be expected to change, both as conventional teaching resources become more constrained, and as face-to-face institutions seek to enrich the range of learning experiences available [19].

8.3   Other Relevant MBA Experiences

Apart from the general use of case studies there have, in the last decade, been a wide variety of experiments, pilots and implementations of collaborative learning approaches within business schools and specifically MBA programmes. Many examples relate to distance education *e.g.*, Henley Management College, New York University's Virtual College and the University of Texas executive MBA programme.

The largest single initiative has been taken at the University of St. Gallen, Switzerland, where, for some time, the whole academic and administrative infrastructure has been conducted through a Lotus Notes based environment. The example with the most similar context to that of City University is probably that of the University of Ohio MBA programme [24]. Another innovative approach is that of the University of Pretoria [5].

One of the most sophisticated approaches to date developed for MBA work was the CATT (Computerized Argumentation Based Teaching Tool) prototype [10]. This was "built around the concept of asynchronous, distributed, multi-party interaction". It used a specific argumentation methodology - IBIS. Its developers argued that "the creation of a truly global classroom environment requires the development of groupware-based systems to support the case discussion method...that spans the boundaries of time and space".

8.4   Specific Context

This chapter specifically describes the utilization of groupware technologies on the City University Business School Full-Time MBA course. It specifically relates to the "Information Management Core Course", a compulsory course for over 100 students. The average age of students is 29, with almost all having good previous business experience.

Since 1989, use of the Internet on the course has been compulsory, and has evolved from email only, through telnet and FTP to gopher. As soon as the Web became available it was incorporated in the course. Hands-on skills in these technologies are provided at the beginning of term one, with the Information Management course itself provided over nine weeks in term one. All MBA students are expected to have PC facilities at home. Virtually all have modems at home. The relevant university IT facilities are based around central Unix servers, with clusters of PCs and Unix workstations linked to the core.

The Business School has been researching the use of groupware in business since the late 1980's, *e.g.*, [14]. It has also been developing network-based educational use since 1989 [20, 22]. This has particularly involved use of "virtual teams" of both MBA and undergraduate students based at business schools in France, the USA, Finland and Ireland. They are given a management case study which they need to discuss and resolve electronically via email, closed usenet groups, and customized conferencing facilities provided by the COMCONF consortium in the USA.

There has been use of Lotus Notes and a wide range of other groupware tools in researching executives' business use of groupware [15], and to support this Lotus Notes has been available since 1993 on a research LAN under OS/2. It has also been provided on the university's Unix servers for student use since 1994. As a result of other groupware research and development work, the Business School had, by the start of academic year 1995/96, also developed a web-based conferencing system. This required a Netscape client. It was later replaced by a Notes server requiring, at that time, Notes clients. A major change in 1999/00 was to move from the proprietary Notes client to a web browser as client.

8.5 Specific Pedagogic Objectives

The Information Management Core Course is concerned not with the mechanics of e-business, but rather with its strategic application. It is taken for granted that students will make practical use of IT during the course, but all hands-on technologies are taught ahead of time so the Core Course syllabus is entirely academic and business based. Three formal objectives were set for the core course exercise.

1. The software should be used to prepare MBA students for experiences they were certain to face on returning to work, and which benefited from an experiential approach. The theme chosen was "working in global virtual teams". Surprisingly few of the students had prior experience of using conferencing software for this purpose in their business careers but many have used non-work chat systems and there is an increasing number who are either technically proficient in commercial groupware, or previous power users of it.

2. It should directly familiarize students with key business issues they need to be aware of, for example the social and process dimensions of technology-supported virtual teams.

3. There was a need to apply information management and e-business theories covered in lectures and reading.

Other objectives that were set were:

4.   The exercise should involve creating particular types of pressures on students, especially those relating to timeliness and to timing.

5.   The exercise should not only be challenging, but enjoyable and even fun.

6.   It was decided early on that this exercise would comprise a major part of the coursework for the course. It now comprises the whole of the coursework. Explicit criteria for student assessment were therefore set, and published, in advance. This importance of compulsion had been learnt from earlier year's use of groupware with MBA students [21].

8.6   Design Considerations

During the period before January 1996 when the first exercise was being finalised, it was discovered that ICI had just completed an exercise using Lotus Notes to support a global virtual team of over 40 fast-track middle managers [25]. The concept that had actually been used by ICI was unexpectedly close to that already envisaged for the MBA students. This involved the participants researching, and writing up in a structured format, a mini-case study concerning the strategic use of IT in business. The ICI case studies were input and published via Lotus Notes, which then provided the platform for subsequent discussions among the virtual team.

The Business School had a difficult decision to make between using Lotus Notes or its own proprietary web conferencing software. The decision was eventually taken to use the web conferencing primarily because there was no time in the MBA schedule to run even the brief training sessions necessary for Lotus Notes. However, the intention was always to reverse-engineer the content into a Notes database both for marking and for research purposes. So the web conferencing system was customized in a format largely indistinguishable from Lotus Notes in its input forms. The database and "viewing" functionality of Notes was not, however, easy to reproduce economically, so a bulletin board type of output was used. The move to a Notes client greatly improved functionality, but limited most students to the use of university computer laboratories. This was solved by the move to a browser as client.

8.7   The Exercise

The objectives of the exercise were published in the course handbook in week one of term two, and explained at the week one lecture. The basic stages were as follows, and relevant statistics for a typical year are shown in Table 8.1:

1.   Students "bid" for the subject of the mini-case study; the bids submitted are immediately published to the respective virtual teams.

2.   Students research the case and input a mini case via online forms. There are an immense variety of topics covered both within and across specialisms (assessment is individually based).

3.   After the deadline, the mini cases are published to the four virtual teams. Teams were organized across specialisms, now ranging in size from 12 to 15 participants, but in earlier years groups of up to 45 were used.

4.   The first discussion phase in virtual teams, responding to a topic set by the virtual MD (assessment is individually based).

5.   Feedback from the MD on the first discussion.

6.   The second discussion phase in virtual teams, responding to a second topic (assessment is team based).

7.   Feedback from the MD on the second discussion.

8.   Reflection and conclusions (assessment is individually based).

9.   Assessment of students' individual performances.

Table 8.1. Statistics of the MBA discussion database.

Groups	A	B	C	D	All
Nos. Male	33	7	31	17	88
Nos. Female	12	11	10	16	49
Total Participants	45	18	41	33	137
No. of comments for discussion 1	133	84	120	249	586
No. of comments for discussion 2	148	67	86	87	388
Range of comments per participant discussion 1	1-21	2-8	1-12	0-29	1-29
Range of comments per participant discussion 2	0-10	0-9	0-5	0-11	0-11
Range of comments per participant for both discussions	2-24	4-15	1-16	4-29	1-29

8.8   Post-Exercise Phase

After the discussions were completed, it was essential to be able to assemble all the contributions into a single, easily-viewable location, to enable marking to take place readily. Once the course was finished, the student case studies were transferred to CD, so students had a personal and permanent record of the aggregate of the case studies.

8.9 Practical Problems

As with any novel approach there were both unexpected problems and unexpected benefits. Starting with the problems, there was little doubt that the tight weekly deadlines ran counter to the preferred *modus operandi* of a minority of students who tended to hand in material at or near deadlines. In this exercise, there were either advantages (as in the bidding phase) or desirabilities from participating other than at the very last moment.

Technology factors have almost always been of key significance. In the early years, many students did not have electronic access at home and many more than expected decided to print out their virtual team case studies, and also the discussion lists. This put, during certain time periods, the normally good printing facilities into very heavy overload, causing frustration to many students. As almost all students now have access to modems, the need for continuous (24 hours a day, seven days a week) reliable access to the university network has become critical. Laptop points for students are now provided in the library, but these have generated a new set of problems relating to the diverse configurations of the laptop.

8.10 Benefits

In the assessment of the exercise by students, it received very positive feedback by the great bulk of students, despite the logistical problems. The ability to use collaboration technology, becoming common in many businesses, was very positively rated. It also has to be said that there was a novelty element for face-to-face students in carrying out group interactions via this asynchronous method. For a highly-rated MBA course there is a very substantial amount of group-work, which can be both energizing and frustrating (especially in synchronizing meetings). Carrying out parts of the coursework via quite large asynchronous teams did not place the students under even further pressures to have meetings. This was generally welcomed, although a small minority of students strongly disliked the lack of face-to-face contact, even where they recognized the inevitability of use of the asynchronous approach in many businesses.

There is little doubt that from the Course Leader's point of view, asynchronous coursework offers one great benefit, namely that the contributions being assessed are all physically visible, and group-work can be marked on a wholly individual basis. There was nothing to prevent students discussing matters face-to-face but there could be no marks allocated for such discussions. Our impression was that the time pressures involved meant that there was little scope for offline discussion the nearest we could observe was where a group of students were working on individual input at the same time in the same laboratory.

As the exercise has evolved, the use of electronic media to search for and find relevant material has extended very significantly. By the time of writing, students are provided with access to two major online resources. The first is Proquest

Online, with over 1000 business journals available in full-text online. The second is Lexis-Nexis Executive, which is more newspaper orientated, and in particular includes the fulltext of both the *Financial Times* and the *Harvard Business Review*. Both are now available not only, as was initially the case, from university machines, but also via passwords from staff and student home machines. This has proved to be of very significant value for MBA students who work long hours at the university and who thus tend to do most of their research from home. By carrying out practical intensive use of these key information resources very early in their MBA year, students develop a skill of continuing value throughout the course.

Students were asked to comment on the advantages and disadvantages of collaborative technologies generally. From their answers, it was clear that overall, even in the short time available, mostly sound insights were achieved out of the student's own experiences.

8.11 Generic team skills

[2] provides a checklist for effective small group-work. In our experience these valuable guidelines developed for face to face syndicate work in higher education apply almost directly to groupware-based interactions. Most of these were followed in the MBA exercise:

1. **Exchange Information.** Make sure the students know what it is all about; teach them how people work in groups; hold a preliminary procedural meeting.

2. **Engineer Cooperation.** Insist on participation; anticipate conflict; use subgroups; encourage any moves to assume responsibility for their own learning.

3. **Playing Roles.** Certain roles must be filled if the group is to function efficiently; variations in roles of individuals fits wider educational objectives.

4. **Controlled Informality.** Make time specifically for less formal chat.

8.12 Roles of Asynchronous Participants

For the purposes of the exercise, instructions were issued to students in the name of the Managing Director of the company they were working for. The MD also reviewed the performance of teams overall at the end of each of the electronic conferences. The MD assessed teams in business language in much the same way as any senior executive would do. At the same time, the performance of teams was reviewed by the Course Leader in both process and academic terms.

The exercise was directed by the Course Leader, with input and advice from a departmental colleague with considerable experience of mail-based simulations.

Technical support was provided by a "technographer". The individual involved was already expert in web authoring, as well as being an experienced Lotus Notes developer. When using innovative technologies the importance of a highly-qualified technographer cannot be over-stated.

Initially, no explicit briefing was given to students on roles. Teams found the first week of discussion quite difficult as they had to learn by experience how to function in this unfamiliar environment. The most critical roles needed were for participants who could shape the discussions towards convergence on the questions set by the MD. Not all groups appeared to have equal shares of individuals with these skills in Week 1. Explicit reminders were given concerning the need for convergent behavior. Subsequently, the advice on roles has been increased and made more explicit, but it still does not require, for example, named roles to be performed by specific students.

8.13 Groupware Issues: Web and Notes Facilities

The Business School's groupware strategy has been based around the use of Lotus Notes for electronic publishing and discussion conferencing. Since Notes was introduced in the early 1990's, there has been growth in the business use of the Internet, plus the availability of new forms of groupware based on the intranet. The exercise as undertaken by the MBA students was effectively an intranet exercise, with the exception that external moderators were able to access the system and the servers were not physically isolated from the Internet, protection being via a secure ID and password system.

The Business School strategy has envisaged active use of the Internet as a window on the outside world, with the groupware being a parallel internal world. This strategy was revised as a result of the release of Lotus Domino. This software enables a Notes server also to be a web server. Notes databases (within certain constraints) can then be accessed by any standard web browser client, as well as by the proprietary Lotus Notes client. The revised strategy now positions Lotus Notes as, additionally, the standard heavy-duty web publishing environment for the school. It can also particularly serve as the underlying architecture for web-based conferencing.

The comments made here should be placed in a context of being written in early 2001, and particularly in relation to the skills available to the City University Business School at that time - an individual acting as technographer equally capable in Notes and web technologies.

8.14 Were the Educational Objectives Achieved?

Referring back to the objectives originally set:

1. **Prepare for Work in Asynchronous Teams**. In general this was met; students who did not enjoy the exercise mostly stated it was a valuable experience.

2. **Key Business Aspects *e.g.*, Social/Process.** This was partly met, but more effort needs to be given to achieve insight into the roles and phases of asynchronous work.

3. **Apply Information Management Theories.** This was achieved well overall. Students had the opportunity not only to apply methods but to discuss their use and face discussion and criticism practicalities.

4. **Creating Pressures.** This was achieved in relation to timeliness.

5. **Challenging, Enjoyable and Fun.** It was challenging and a large minority of students found it enjoyable. As a result of the logistical problems and a hard-learning experience in discussion 1, a significant minority unfortunately did not find it fun.

6. **Coursework Achievement.** The high level of collaborative learning reached was a major benefit but much greater student effort than planned for was needed to achieve this.

8.15 The Future

In 1999-2000 a statistical monitoring system was introduced, written in Javascript. This computed in real time the volume of communications by each group in recent days and weeks, so groups could see for themselves whether their groups were above or below the average volume of discussion items.

A major future addition being considered is to add a radio button panel to each discussion conference form. Completion of this panel will be mandatory. The panel will require the student to consider the conversational categorization of their particular input. The categorization methods currently under consideration are firstly, the action language perspective [28] and, secondly, a more general purpose approach such as that found in [4].

The intention here is to introduce some element of self-diagnostic for both individuals and teams. Participants will be able to view the conversational nature of their own inputs, and the teams will be able to do the same for the group as a whole. Our assumption is that if we are able to provide some kind of conversational role model for the different phases of a discussion, groups will have a way of comparing their actual overall approach with this role model. They will perhaps need to review their behavior if, for example, they are in the final phase of discussions and relatively little convergent activity has taken place.

8.16 Conclusions

In a generally critical perspective of the current application of CSCL in UK Higher Education, [19] it was concluded:

"What we need are computer tools to support educationally proven group learning techniques, based on best practice and educational research, not a programmer's (limited) imagination. Much can be done by extending existing technologies."

Our own experiences would fully endorse this conclusion.

References

1. Alpert, D. (1975) The PLATO IV system in use - A progress report, in Lecarme, O. and Lewis, R. (Eds), *Computers in Education*, North Holland, Amsterdam.

2. Cockburn, B. and Ross, A. (1978) Working Together - Group Work in Education, University of Lancaster, Lancaster.

3. Collier, K.G. (1980) Peer group learning in higher education: The development of higher order skills, in *Studies in Higher Education*, 5, 1, 55-61.

4. Crowston K., Malone, T. and Lin, F. (1988) Cognitive science and organizational design: A case study of computer conferencing, in *Human Computer Interaction*, 3(1), 59-85.

5. De Villiers, C. (1995) The integration of information technology in a co-operative learning environment, unpublished D.Com. dissertation, University of Pretoria, South Africa

6. Easton, G. (1982) Learning from Case Studies. Prentice Hall International, Englewood Cliffs, New Jersey.

7. Engelbart, D. & English, W. (1969) A research center for augmenting human intellect, in *Proceedings of FJCC*, 33(1), 395-410, AFIPS Press, Montvale, NY.

8. Goodlad, S. and Hirst, B. (1989) Peer Tutoring - A Guide to Learning by Teaching. Kogan Page, London.

9. Goodlad, S. (Ed) (1995) Students as Tutors and Mentors, Kogan Page, London, in Association with BP.

10. Hashim, S., Rathnam, S. and Whinston, A. B. (1991) CATT: An argumentation based groupware system for enhancing case discussions in business schools, in DeGross, J. *et al.* (Eds), in *Proceedings of the 12th International Conference on Information Systems*, ACM, Baltimore, MD, 371-385.

11. Hiltz, S. R. (1994) The Virtual Classroom - Learning without Limits Via Computer Networks, Ablex Publishing, Norwood, NY.

12. Hiltz, S.R. (1995) Impacts of college level courses via asynchronous learning networks - focus on students, in Sloan *Conference on Asynchronous Learning Networks*, Philadelphia, PA.

13. Hiltz, S.R. and Turoff, M. (1978) The Network Nation: Human Communication via Computer, MIT Press, Cambridge, MA

14. Holtham, C. (1993) Improving the performance of work groups through information technology, City University Business School Working Paper, City University, London.

15. Holtham, C. (1995) Integrating technologies to support action, *Interacting With Computers*, 7,1, March, 91-107

16. Mason, R., and Kaye, A. (1989) Mind Weave - Communication, Computers and Distance Education, Pergamon Press, Oxford.

17. McNair, M. D. (Ed) (1954) The Case Method at the Harvard Business School, McGraw-Hill, New York

18. Murray, F. B. (1990) Cooperative learning, in Entwistle, N. (Ed) *Handbook of Educational Ideas and Practices*, Routledge, London, 859-864.

19. Newman, D. (1994) Computer supported cooperative learning, in Lloyd, P. (ed) *Groupware for the 21st Century*, Adamantine Press, London.

20. Rich M. (1993) The Use of Electronic Mail and Conferencing Systems in Management Education, City University Business School Working Paper, City University, London.

21. Rich M. (1994) Building computer supported group work into an MBA programme, in *International Journal of Computers in Adult Education and Training*, 4 (1/2).

22. Rich M. (1995) Supporting a case study exercise on the World Wide Web, in *Proceedings of International Conference on Computers in Education*, Singapore, 1995

23. O'Shea, T. and Self, J. (1983) Learning and Teaching with Computers, Harvester Press, Brighton.

24. Stinson, J. E and Milter, R. G. (1995) The enabling impact of information technology: The case of the Ohio University DMBA, Ohio University Working Paper, Ohio.

25. Sykes, R. (1996) The IS function in new ICI, *Information Management: People, Performance and Profit Conference*, Elan Group, London.

26. Turoff, M. (1996) Teaching computer systems management in the virtual classroom environment, Report for the Sloan Foundation Virtual Classroom Project, NJIT.

27. Van Mentis, M. (1990) Active Talk - The Effective Use of Discussion in Learning, Kogan Page, London

28. Winograd, T. and Flores, F. (1985) Understanding Computers and Cognition: A New Foundation for Design, Ablex, Norwood, NJ.

Chapter 9

A Review of the Use of Asynchronous E- Seminars in Undergraduate Education

Jacqueline Taylor

This chapter will focus on the use of CMC systems to support electronic seminar (e-seminar) discussions conducted asynchronously. Although *synchronous* e-seminars offer the opportunity to teach and learn at a distance, *asynchronous* e-seminars are not constrained by time and therefore a number of further benefits can be realized. The reported benefits arising from the use of asynchronous e-seminars will be discussed. These include: (i) enhanced student interaction for traditional learners and improved communication support for remote learners; (ii) critical reflection - leading to more informed contributions from students; (iii) enhanced team and communication skills, and (iv) access to new ideas, perspectives and cultures. A review of the literature has identified a number of issues which require further research. These include: (i) academic assessment of e-seminar discussions; (ii) student motivation, and (iii) the role of individual differences regarding student attitudes and use of e-seminars. These issues will be discussed and illustrated with reference to a number of e-seminar evaluations conducted by the author who has been using e-seminars within undergraduate programmes for seven years. The chapter will conclude with a list of best practice guidelines to assist educators in the design and implementation of e-seminars.

9.1   Introduction

Although lecturers are increasingly being encouraged to use some form of web-based activity or resource in their teaching [1], so far the potential for asynchronous computer-mediated communication (CMC) systems to support teaching and learning has received less attention than other forms of computer-assisted learning. As Crook [2] notes, "little attention is given to distributed computing; and (it is) curious how slow educational practitioners have been to recognize the relevance of networking to the support of collaborative practices" (p. 197). This may be because lecturers fail to see computer networks as offering anything more than an efficient means to coordinate teaching activities and the administrative tasks associated with teaching. Others may be wary of the technical implications of setting up e-seminars or assessment issues. This chapter will review the research investigating the way e-seminars have been used to support teaching and learning. Section 9.2 will highlight the benefits arising from a more flexible and reflective learning environment. Although e-seminars are being used by more lecturers than was the case when the first edition of *The Digital University* was published [4], there is still little empirical research evaluating the effectiveness of their use in terms of students learning the required material and developing the required skills, and in terms of the way learners use and perceive e-seminars [3]. An important question arising from this review is whether all students benefit equally when traditional seminars are converted to e-seminars. Section 9.3 will discuss this question and other issues requiring further investigation, such as student motivation and assessment. The final section of this chapter (9.4) will conclude with a list of best practice guidelines. This will suggest ways for educators to realize some of the benefits highlighted in Section 9.2 and consider those factors identified in Section 9.3.

9.2   Benefits of E-Seminars

The reported benefits arising from the use of asynchronous e-seminars include: (i) enhanced student interaction for traditional learners and improved communication support for remote learners; (ii) critical reflection leading to more informed contributions from students; (iii) enhanced team and communication skills; and (iv) access to new ideas, perspectives and cultures.

9.2.1 Enhanced Student Interaction

E-seminars enable flexibility of attendance, which has become an important issue in traditional universities with many students now undertaking paid work during traditional teaching hours. As a direct result of this flexibility (seminars can be open 24 hours per day), e-seminars have been shown to lead to higher levels of participation from students within traditional course delivery. In her study, which involved students taking part in a series of five e-seminars, each of two weeks duration, Taylor [4] found that participation in 85% of the e-seminars was 100% and in only 15% was it 80%. As more students are undertaking paid employment while studying, it is also becoming increasingly difficult to maintain communication between lecturer and student. Duffy, Arnold and Henderson [5] replaced traditional face-to-face seminars with e-seminars in a music department. They found that two of the main advantages of these were that there was 100%

attendance and students perceived there to be easier access to the lecturer. Not only does increased student participation encourage communication between lecturer and student, it also encourages communication between students. E-seminars have been shown to facilitate collaborative learning [2], because students are interacting more at an academic (as well as social) level [6].

It seems that the predictions of Hiltz [7] regarding the "electronic campus" and the "virtual classroom" are now finally being realized on a large scale. CMC has helped to improve access to distance education; for example, part-time students are finding it easier to take part in Higher and Further Education [1]. As with traditional education, using e-seminars within distance education can improve communication channels between students, and between lecturers and students. Institutions like the Open University in the UK are recognizing the opportunity that computer conferencing offers to the distance learner; conferencing is being used to bring contact and interaction to the isolated learner. On a global scale, the work by Riel [8] thoroughly explores how CMC is bringing lecturers and students, working remotely, together using "learning circles".

9.2.2 Critical Reflection

Pickering [9] warns that if CMC is seen as merely a way to do what teachers do now, only quicker, an exciting opportunity will be missed. CMC has the potential not only to encourage interaction but also to improve the quality of that interaction. Because of the asynchronicity of communication in e-seminars, there is time for reflection, critical thinking and additional research to take place between communication turns. A common theme of most definitions of critical thinking is the creation of meaning from a learning experience that enables the learner to see things in a different way. A key aim of higher education is the transformation of students into "critical reflective thinkers" able to cope with a rapidly changing world [10]. Newman *et al.* [11] state that CMC can offer opportunities for reflection by using communication and collaboration to assist students to evaluate and adapt their ideas.

However, although a number of educators have cited CMC as an effective way to achieve reflection and promote these skills in students, there are very few empirical evaluations investigating the relationship between the use of e-seminars and reflection. This may be because of the difficulties associated with investigating critical thinking and reflection, possibly requiring the use of qualitative techniques, which have been less than popular in computing research. One such investigation [4] employed content analyzis to examine students' responses to an open-ended item requesting them to note the best features of e-seminars. Nearly a third of students' comments related the asynchronous nature of discussion to the further research they were able to undertake before making their next contribution to the e-seminar. Seale & Cann [14] also make use of qualitative techniques to analyze the way learning technologies were used to facilitate reflective thinking in students. One of their case studies used a web-based hyper-mail discussion list to support learning on a psychosocial science unit. Seale & Cann illustrated how a small group of students engaged with the material and through discussion were able to make links with other learning experiences or see things in different ways. They conclude that learning technologies help to facilitate reflection for some students; however, they state that the evidence is not overwhelming. They identified a number of factors which may influence the success of learning technologies. They include: (i) the way the learning technology is used (whether their use is made compulsory or optional for students); (ii) the nature of the student groups (in terms of the computer skills/attitudes and level of education); (iii) the role of the tutor; and (iv) student preferences for 'offline reflection'. Many of these factors will be discussed in Section 9.4.

9.2.3 Enhanced Team and Communication Skills

Giving seminar presentations and contributing to group discussion help students to develop many useful transferable skills; effective communication and groupworking skills are recognized as important and valuable in the workplace [13]. However, many students either fail to attend seminars or do not participate fully in them. A number of factors may be responsible for the failure of some students to contribute to seminar discussion. One factor is that vocal and more confident students can dominate the available "talk time". With CMC, confidence and loudness of voice are less important and thus CMC is able to encourage interaction by enabling all communicators an equal opportunity to communicate, without interruption. CMC research has frequently shown that there is a more balanced participation in computer-mediated group discussion, compared to face-to-face group discussion [12]. This is thought to be due to both the lack of social context cues (*e.g.*, status and gender information) and non-verbal cues (*e.g.*, eye contact) in CMC which are proposed to "equalise" participation. Observations of CMC use within educational settings provide some support for this. Hoare and Race [15] found that, when using a computer conferencing system to communicate, students felt able to address topics which they would have been reluctant to address through normal conversation or correspondence, and that "shy students were able to express themselves in a voluble manner". Similarly, when Duffy, Arnold and Henderson [5] used computer conferencing to replace traditional seminars, they found that there was more active debate because "quieter group members found it easier to contribute". They proposed that this was because lack of face-to-face cues reduced the pressure for instant communication and allowed time to phrase responses. However, neither of these reports measured students' "baseline" communication and group-working skills. Further research is clearly required to identify whether online group discussion can help to develop traditional and new communication and group-working skills. Wilson [16] has recently proposed that this is indeed the case. He proposes that experience of using CMC systems in project teams by software engineering students assisted them in acquiring skills in virtual group-work which would later be useful in their careers when required to participate in distributed software development teams.

9.2.4 Access to New Ideas, Perspectives and Cultures

One of the important pedagogical reasons for running seminars is not just for students to be able to ask questions of the lecturer, but for students to discuss their own views on a topic and to listen to other students' views [5]. In Taylor's study [4], students were encouraged to read the discussions taking place in other e-seminar groups and this (and the increased level of interaction) allowed students to be exposed to more views and different perspectives than would be possible in a traditional seminar. It was clear that the type of interaction taking place during the seminars was supporting the learning process; for example, 48% of students strongly agreed with the statement that during the seminars they discussed new material or material from a different perspective than that covered in lectures. This is also supported by comments made in response to an open-ended item asking students to cite the most enjoyable features of the e-seminars. Nearly 20% of students gave comments relating to the increase in quantity and variety of information exchanged during the e-seminars, compared to face-to-face seminars. These findings support the work conducted by Harasim [17], which highlights the benefits of online remote discussion groups made up of individuals from a wide variety of cultural and educational backgrounds.

9.3 Issues that Require Further Research

A number of factors are likely to influence students' attitudes to and use of e-seminars: three of these will be discussed here.

9.3.1 Student Motivation to Participate in E-Seminars

There have been a number of ambitious claims regarding the way CMC will change the way students learn. Pickering [9] believes that many educational establishments impose teaching and destroy learning. He proposes that CMC can help to encourage autonomous learning, while reducing the authoritative nature of teaching. However, this view assumes that all students are self-motivated and are willing to accept responsibility for their learning. Similarly, Browning and Williams [18] propose that if such a change in teaching were to be adopted "...given the responsibility for their learning rather than being continually spoon-fed...[would students]...actually be prepared to work in this way?" (p. 37). However, the evidence for this is so far unconvincing and the motivation of students to participate in e-seminars does seem to be very much dependent on a combination of factors including the context in which e-seminars are introduced (*e.g.*, assessment and group membership) and individual differences. Evaluations that have shown e-seminars to be less than successful, frequently identify a problem with students' negative perception of e-seminars as a key motivating factor affecting success. This will be discussed later (Section 9.3.3) in relation to individual differences.

The communication environment is a key contextual factor which the educator needs to consider prior to implementation. For example, group composition can play an important part in influencing student motivation to participate in e-seminars. Seale & Cann [14] proposed that students in one of their case studies, who were unknown to each other, felt uncomfortable contributing as they were unaware of the level that everyone else was operating at, and so did not want to appear unknowledgeable. While in another case study, of first year students who knew each other, Seale & Cann [14] provided reports which suggested students were not frightened of using the discussion list. Light *et al.* [6] also reported better results when online discussion was used with third year students, all studying the same subject, proposing that this was because they possessed more shared experience. However, the downside of this was that some students complained that responses were so similar that there was no "controversy". The impact of the mix of group members (in terms of level of education and level of acquaintance) on motivation to participate in e-seminars clearly requires further research.

To maximize learning and facilitate motivation in students using new technologies, it is essential that tutors discuss and negotiate with students what their goals might be and clarify expectations of use [1]. Although this is important in traditional teaching, it is more difficult to achieve when learning technologies are employed as the lecturer becomes less visible. Therefore, the lecturer may need to be more explicit in expressing the purpose and relevance of the discussion list [4]. Some ways in which lecturers can draw attention to the purpose and relevance of e-seminars are suggested in Section 9.4. The way that participation in e-seminars is assessed and how this is introduced by the lecturer are also likely to have an important influence on students' motivation and ultimately on quality (reflection) and quantity of participation; this will now be considered.

9.3.2 Assessment of E-Seminar Discussions

The nature of the assessment of learning material has an important influence on the potential of that material for encouraging reflection. For example, Seale [19] has argued that competency-based materials encourage students to focus on the knowledge they can gain and will be tested on rather than how they reframe and conceptualize the information (reflection). A major dilemma facing the e-seminar educator is whether to make the use of e-seminars compulsory or not. Lee, Dineen & McKendree [20] compared compulsory and non-compulsory discussion lists and found that for non-compulsory lists, contributions were knowledge-based, arising out of students' interest, while in compulsory lists students restricted their questions to a more shallow text-based level. In support of this, Seale [19] showed that when participation in an online discussion list was made a compulsory requirement for students, they accessed the list because they had to, and not because they wanted to, and that this may have had a negative influence on some students' learning experience. For example, she suggests that making the task compulsory masked its relevance for some students and led them to adopt very strategic approaches such as leaving it close to the deadline to post responses to the list. Another factor which needs to be considered, when assessing recorded contributions to e-seminar discussions, is that much discussion occurs offline. Many students in the study by Taylor [4] reported using the interval between contributions to discuss the material with peers and tutors in face-to-face settings. It may be that while the e-seminar did not stimulate some students to engage in online discussion, it did stimulate them to engage in offline discussion. It is possible that these students may prefer non-computer-based discussion. Students have different preferences for the way they learn and study and the way that e-seminars are used may need to reflect this; this and other student individual differences will now be considered in more detail.

9.3.3 The Role of Student Individual Differences

Although educational psychologists maintain that teachers should acknowledge and accommodate the individuality of their students [21], this has rarely amounted to more than lip service when implementing CMC systems in educational contexts. Only recently has the importance of considering individual differences begun to be recognized [16]. Individual differences studied so far within the CMC literature include age, gender, computer experience, communication skills and preferences, personality, and learning style. Such differences are likely to affect the use and perception of e-seminars and ultimately the learning outcome and therefore need to be considered prior to their widespread implementation. For example, it may be that the reduced social context and non-verbal cues in CMC may encourage participation for some students, while others may be unsettled by the lack of face-to-face interaction with lecturers and peers. The key research findings for a number of individual differences will now be briefly highlighted. A more thorough review of this area is provided by Wilson [16], whose paper is directed at answering the question, "what differences in students' use of CMC, if any, are determined by individual characteristics?".

Demographic factors
Age and sex are important demographic factors, although their association with e-seminar use is largely unexplored [23]. Older students may be less willing to learn new technologies; however, they do have more diverse knowledge and experience than younger students and may be able to apply these attributes to new situations. In their study of the use of an asynchronous collaborative learning system, Morgan & Morgan [22] found that the more mature individuals disliked online group-work and were more likely to report system-based problems.

Communication and group-working skills and preferences

There has been very little research relating face-to-face communication skills and preferences with the use and perception of CMC. CMC, through the lack of social context cues, is thought to reduce evaluation anxiety [24]. Individuals who are highly apprehensive about communicating face-to-face are fearful about being negatively evaluated by others and it has been suggested [25] that individuals with high levels of Communication Apprehension (CA) may prefer to use CMC and be more expressive using this medium. In contrast, individuals who are confident verbal communicators may feel restricted using only text-based media. To investigate these suggestions, Oxley [25] compared individuals with high, medium and low levels of CA in face-to-face and electronic seminars. The results showed that individuals with high levels of CA were significantly less anxious when communicating via CMC, compared to when they took part in face-to-face discussion, and also these individuals participated more in the e-seminar discussions. However, this study was conducted using synchronous e-seminars and in a laboratory environment and therefore it is not clear how far the findings can be generalized to "real" asynchronous e-seminars.

In an early study, Taylor [26] found that perceived fluency when speaking (compared to writing) correlated with a more negative attitude towards CMC, but frequency of use of CMC was not related to this. Following on from this, the results of an evaluation of e-seminars by Taylor [4] also showed that those students perceiving their written skills to be more effective than their spoken skills perceived e-seminars to be more stimulating than face-to-face seminars. Students who feel less eloquent when speaking may benefit more from a computer-mediated format for discussion than more confident verbal communicators. A preference for group-working was related to lower levels of satisfaction, enjoyability and involvement in e-seminars, compared to face-to-face seminars. This may be because those students who enjoy working in groups do so because they enjoy the face-to-face interaction and perhaps therefore they did not enjoy the asynchronous and isolated nature of e-seminars. Alternatively, those students normally preferring to work individually may have found the e-seminars more satisfying, more enjoyable, more stimulating and more involving as this medium allowed them an equal opportunity to participate in group discussion. Further research is needed to collect more extensive measures of communication and group-working skills and preferences.

Personality

The idea of looking at personality as a factor in Human-Computer Interaction (HCI) and teaching and learning is not new, but there appears to be little consideration of it in the CMC literature. Adrianson & Hjelmquist [24] investigated the role of extroversion in CMC and found that extroverts communicated significantly more than introverts using a CMC system, although these differences were much weaker than in normal face-to-face communication. A more recent study [22] investigated the effect of personality on the attitudes and behavior of students using computer-supported collaborative learning environments in a distance education setting. Morgan & Morgan [22] found that extroverts actively looked forward to the online group activity before their sessions, while introverts reported strong negative anticipation. The results of an evaluation of e-seminars by Taylor [4] showed a significant relationship between introversion and negative scores on scales assessing perceptions of satisfaction and enjoyability of e-seminars. The results also showed that the more self-conscious students were, the more they thought the seminars were involving. This suggests that quieter individuals may benefit the most from a computer-mediated format for discussion; similarly, more vocal students may benefit the least. Unfortunately, because questionnaires were completed anonymously, it was not possible to relate questionnaire responses to contributions made during e-seminars. It would be interesting in a future study to investigate whether quieter students contributed more to the discussions than more vocal students. In conclusion, those personality traits which promote a preference for CMC may vary substantially from those which promote face-to-face communication. If this is the case, moving traditional seminars over to e-seminars may impact student performance in many ways, which clearly requires further research.

Computer experience and perceptions of computing

Research shows that experience with computers leads to the formation of positive attitudes toward computers in general; however, the literature is unclear as to whether there is a positive association between prior CMC experience and subsequent use and positive attitude towards e-seminars. Light *et al.* [27] reported that a 'skywriting' facility was used most by a small group of computer-proficient students. Seale & Cann [14] reported that lack of technical ability prevented some learners from contributing to an online discussion forum. Dislike of computers or technophobia is not an unusual phenomenon among students and may explain the low take-up rates of e-seminars experienced by some educators. Seale & Cann [14] reported that a dislike of computers prevented some learners from enjoying or benefiting from the learning experience when online discussions took place.

Learning style

Taylor [28] investigated the relationship between students' perceptions of e-seminars and their scores on the Approaches to Study Inventory (shortened version). This inventory contains three subscales: meaning orientation, reproducing orientation and achieving orientation. She found that levels of satisfaction were negatively correlated with scores on the "reproducing orientation" subscale: such that students with high scores on this subscale did not perceive the e-seminars as satisfying. Students with higher scores on the "meaning orientation" subscale appeared to achieve the most benefit from e-seminars, in that they perceived them as more stimulating and reported more understanding of the key topics of the unit as a result of electronic discussion. There was a nearly significant correlation between high scores on the "achieving orientation" subscale and a reported increase in using literature sources to support points of view expressed during the e-seminar. In conclusion, e-seminars were perceived as a positive support to learning for students scoring high on "achieving orientation" and "meaning orientation" approaches to studying, but were perceived more negatively by those scoring high on the 'reproducing orientation' approach to studying. Further examination of the role of student learning styles on computer-assisted learning can be found in Shaw & Marlow [23].

9.4   Best Practice Guidelines

The final section of this chapter provides a list of best practice guidelines, suggesting ways for educators to realize some of the benefits highlighted in Section 9.2 and consider some of the factors identified in Section 9.3 when designing and implementing e-seminars. These guidelines draw on the experience of the author [4, 26, 28] who has been using e-seminars within undergraduate programmes for seven years.

9.4.1 Group Size and Composition

It is recommended that an ideal e-seminar group size of between four to eight members is used. A smaller group increases the pace of interaction (frequency of message-sending) and a larger group increases the granularity (length of message) - both can potentially lead to information overload and communication breakdown.

Levels of student motivation to participate in e-seminars are higher if students are given some choice regarding group membership, but this may not always be feasible (dependent on task and assessment). When groups are made up of students from similar backgrounds (*e.g.*, studying the same unit or degree) higher levels of motivation and participation were shown. However, perceived similarities between group members can lead to a more stilted and uncontentious discussion.

9.4.2 Moderation and Lecturer Presence

One of the ways in which lecturers can draw attention to the purpose and relevance of e-seminars is to take an active part in them. Lecturers can post messages to the e-seminar at strategic times and highlight the ways in which students can create meaning from the experience. This needs to be done sensitively so that students do not feel threatened by the lecturer's presence.

Experience has shown that it is preferable that each group be allocated a moderator who can be called on where necessary.

9.4.3 Requirements for Participation and Assessment

Prior to the start of the e-seminar, the educator should ensure that students are provided with: the pedagogical aims of the e-seminars (*e.g.*, to encourage reflection on the learning process at the same time as learning about the discussion topic); and the precise nature of the assessment of contributions (if any), and the requirements for participation (*e.g.*, to make at least one contribution per week or to check daily for new messages).

E-seminars are most beneficial when they allow students to present and lead discussions as well as contribute to other students' presentations. In this way they can practice their skills of facilitation, discussion and collaboration.

Enough time needs to be allowed to complete the discussion: remember it takes longer to type than to talk and time is needed between contributions to allow reflection and research to take place.

Encouragement to join other discussion groups as guest members allows students to compare the progress of other groups and to assimilate the different views.

9.4.4 Technical Issues

Training sessions on the relevant software and hardware are essential prior to implementation. A practice e-seminar should then be set up to allow students to experiment with the system and the process of e-seminar participation.

An online advice discussion should be maintained throughout the duration of the e-seminar for students experiencing technical problems.

9.4.5 Group Atmosphere

Contributors need to feel that e-seminars are a safe environment in which to contribute personal and academic contributions, therefore an element of trust needs to be fostered. Students should not feel threatened; therefore it is important that the lecturer makes every effort to encourage students to support each other. This is clearly important in traditional seminars but, because of the nature of CMC, it is even more important to consider in this situation. For example, anonymity and lack of cues in CMC can encourage individuals to "flame" or self-disclose and also the permanence of the text may inhibit some individuals from contributing.

9.5   Conclusion

In conclusion, it has been shown that asynchronous e-seminars can help to facilitate communication and learning in traditional and distance education. A major consideration when deciding whether to use e-seminars is to ensure that they provide "added value" to the learning experience. It seems that we are only just beginning to explore the potential of e-seminars to deliver improved learning experiences. As the results have shown, it is necessary to consider qualitative as well as quantitative differences when academic discussion is mediated via computer. Also, it is important to consider that the potential benefits from using e-seminars may vary according to individual differences between students. Clearly more research is required to investigate whether the same student characteristics lead to academic success using CMC as with traditional methods of teaching and learning prior to the widespread use of e-seminars. In addition, future research needs to investigate the impact of different CMC contexts (*e.g.*, group size, level of identifiability, whether asynchronous or synchronous *etc.*) on the use, perception and success of e-seminars. This will allow accurate predictions to be made as to whether e-seminars or traditional seminars would be of most benefit to the teaching and learning experience.

References

1.   Dearing, R. (1997) Higher Education in the Learning Society. The National Committee of Inquiry into Higher Education, Crown Copyright.

2.   Crook, C. (1994) Computers and the Collaborative Experience of Learning. Routledge.

3.   Mason, R. & Bacsich, P. (1998) Embedding computer conferencing into university teaching. *Computers & Education*, 30(3/4), 249-258.

4.   Taylor, J. (1998) Using asynchronous computer-conferencing to encourage interaction in seminar discussion. *The Digital University*. Hazemi, R., Hailes, S. & Wilbur, S. (Eds.), Springer, 219-232.

5.   Duffy, C., Arnold, S. and Henderson, F. (1995) NetSem - electrifying undergraduate seminars. *Active Learning*. 2, 42-48.

6.   Light, P., Nesbitt, E., Light, V. & White, S. (2000) Variety is the spice of life: Student use of CMC in the context of campus based study. *Computers & Education*, 34, 257-267.

7.   Hiltz, S. R. (1985) The Virtual Classroom: Initial Explorations of CMC Systems as an Interactive Learning Space. New Jersey Institute of Technology.

8.   Riel, M. (1993) Global education through learning circles. *Global Networks: Computers and International Communication*. Harasim, L. (Ed.), MIT Press.

9.   Pickering, J. (1995) Teaching on the Internet is learning. *Active Learning*. 2, 9-12.

10. Harvey, L. & Knight, P. (1996) Transforming Higher Education. Open University Press.

11. Newman, D. R., Johnson, C., Cochrane, C. and Webb, B. (1996) An experiment in group learning technology: Evaluating critical thinking in face-to-face and computer-supported seminars. *Interpersonal Computing and Technology*. 4, 1, 57-74.

12. Dubrovsky, V., Kiesler, S. and Sethna, B. N. (1991) The equalisation phenomenon. *Human-Computer Interaction*, 6, 119-146.

13. Newman, D. R. (1994) Computer supported co-operative learning. *Groupware in the 21st Century*, Lloyd, P. (Ed.), Adamtine Press, 211-219.

14. Seale, J. K. & Cann, A. J. (2000) Reflection on-line or off-line: The role of learning technologies in encouraging students to reflect. *Computers & Education*, 34, 309-320.

15. Hoare, R. M. and Race, W. P. (1990) Computer conferencing: A versatile new undergraduate learning process. *University Computing*, 12, 13-17.

16. Wilson E. V. (2000). Student characteristics and computer-mediated communication. *Computers & Education*, 34, 67-76.

17. Harasim, L. (1993) *Global Networks*: Computers and International Communication. MIT Press.

18. Browning, P. and Williams, J. (1995) The geology@bristol experience. *Active Learning*, 2, 34-38.

19. Seale, J. K. (1997) Developing CBL packages: A reflective practice approach in science education. In Chapman, G., *Proceedings of the 3rd International CBL in Science Conference*. Czech Republic: University of South Bohemia.

20. Lee, J., Dineen, F. & McKendree, J. (1997) Supporting student discussions. *Research on Educational Applications of Information Technologies*. Darina, D. & Stanchev, I. (Eds.), VIRTECH Ltd., 124-136.

21. Biggs, J. B. (1979) Individual differences in study processes and the quality of learning outcomes. *Higher Education*. 8, 381-394.

22. Morgan, K. & Morgan, M. (2000) The role of personality factors in the design and use of collaborative tele-learning artifacts: An overview. Paper presented at *The International Communication Association 2000 Conference*. Acapulco, Mexico, June 1-5.

23. Shaw, G. & Marlow, N. (2000) The role of student learning styles, gender, attitudes and perceptions on information and communication technology assisted learning. *Computers & Education*, 34, 223-234.

24. Adrianson, L. and Hjelmquist, E. (1988) Users' experiences of COM - A computer-mediated communication system. *Behaviour and Information Technology*. 7, 1, 79-99.

25. Oxley, J. (1995) The Effects of CMC on Communication Apprehension. Unpublished undergraduate thesis. School of DEC, Bournemouth University.

26. Taylor, J. (1995) Electronic Mail, Communication and Social Identity. Unpublished PhD thesis. Department of Psychology, University of Portsmouth.

27. Light, P., Colbourn, C. & Light, V. (1997) Computer-mediated tutorial support for conventional university courses. *Journal of Computer Assisted Learning*, 13(4), 228-235.

28. Taylor, J. (2001) Approaches to studying and the perception of e-seminar discussions. Paper to be presented at *The 6th International Learning Styles Conference (ELSIN)*, Glamorgan, Wales, June 25-27.

Chapter 10

Support for Authoring and Managing Web-Based Coursework: The TACO Project

Martina Angela Sasse, Rachada Monthienvichienchai, Christopher Harris, Ismail Ismail and Richard Wheeldon

The aim of the TACO (Teaching And Coursework Online) project was to develop a generic system for distributed authoring and management of computer-based coursework. The requirements for such a system were established in requirements capture workshops with lecturers from a range of academic departments. Lecturers can create web-based self-learning exercises and assessed coursework without knowledge of HTML or other authoring languages. A form-based user interface allows lecturers to choose from a range of question types, marking schemes and weightings, including confidence assessment. Students completing coursework receive immediate feedback in the form of marks, and comments or explanations associated with questions. Lecturers and students interact with TACO through a highly familiar user interface – a web browser. The system itself consists of a Java Web server and a commercial database; the only code written for the project is a number of Java servlets which manage the interaction between these. Lecturers from different departments at UCL used the first implementation of TACO to author sets of self-learning exercises and assessed assignments for one of their courses. The results of this pilot study - involving 4 lecturers and 500 students - were encouraging. In this chapter, we report on how lecturers use and view the system after 3 years of continuing use, and discuss issues which prevent institution-wide adoption of such a system.

10.1 Introduction

Student numbers in most UK Higher Education Institutions (HEIs) have increased considerably over the past 10 years and, in most institutions, this has not been matched by a corresponding increase in the number of teaching staff. At the same time, the perception of how teaching in HEIs should be delivered has changed. Current theories of student learning in higher education emphasize the need for regular assessment and feedback throughout a course, rather than just in end-of-year exams. Both feedback and continuous assessment can be - and is in many HEIs - provided through coursework. For coursework to provide effective feedback and assessment, it has to:

● be assessed and returned to students quickly;

● point out discrepancies between an individual student's expected and actual knowledge and skills; and

● suggest how the student can remedy shortcomings identified.

Providing such coursework on a regular basis requires considerable time and effort. This poses a problem in the current situation, where most teaching staff have *less* time per student than in the past. It is therefore not surprising that the HEIs are keen to utilize computer-assisted learning (CAL) solutions to improve the efficiency of course delivery. Most CAL applications to date, however, fall into the category of *primary courseware*: they deliver materials containing knowledge about a subject to the student [1, 2]. Laurillard [3] states that educational technology that simply "pushes" information in this one-way manner does not provide effective support for the learning process. Yet there are far fewer commercial CAL systems that provide feedback to the learner, and/or support assessment. Systems including self-testing exercises are often not adopted by HEIs because the content and assessment cannot easily be tailored to the requirements of a particular course. Plagiarism is another concern often raised in this context – a widely used standard set of questions for a particular topic would make it possible for students to identify correct answers without working through the material.

There are many examples of lecturers writing their own computer-based systems to distribute self-teaching exercises and/or assessed coursework for their particular courses and topics (*e.g.*, [4, 5]). The majority of lecturers, however, lack the expertise required to write their own systems from scratch. It is also self-evident that, from an HEI's point of view, the construction and maintenance of a myriad of systems for coursework in different subjects or courses cannot be an efficient solution. The aim of the work reported in this chapter was, therefore, to investigate whether it is possible to provide a generic platform system for authoring, distribution, marking and administration of assignments for student feedback and assessment.

The Web provides a good platform for such a system:

● Most faculty and students already use web browsers, so they are familiar with the user interface.

- Web materials can be accessed from a wide range of different hardware platforms and operating systems.

- Remote access is possible – there is an increasing requirement to support:

  - teaching staff and students working from home or residences;

  - HEIs with geographically distributed sites;

  - HEIs who collaborate and deliver joint courses;

  - HEIs who deliver courses to commercial organizations.

TACO (Teaching And Coursework Online) was created to provide a generic web-based coursework authoring and delivery system. Lecturers and students interact with the system via web browsers (see Figure 10.1).

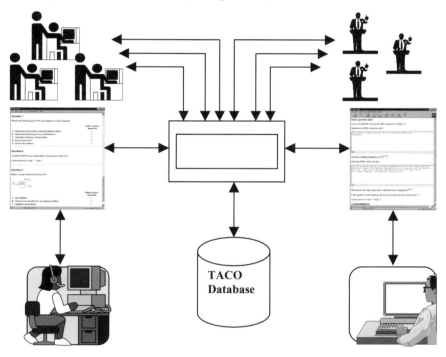

Figure 10.1. Lecturers and students interact with TACO via web browsers.

The authoring tool enables lecturers of any discipline to create learning exercises and assessed coursework without using HTML or other web programming tools. They can choose from a range of question types and marking schemes, assign weightings to different questions, and add *confidence assessments* if they wish. The need for these features had been identified during the requirements capture phase (described in more detail in Section 10.2). Apart from marks, lecturers can attach comments or explanations to any question to further students' understanding. Since an increasing number of lecturers provide course materials – authored by themselves or others – via the Web, integration of those materials with the coursework system is necessary. TACO supports this because materials are accessed via URLs, and URLs can be incorporated into comments (see Section 10.3 for a detailed description of TACO's architecture and implementation). TACO was used by 4 lecturers in UCL in autumn 1997 to author and distribute coursework to their students; Section 10.4 reports the results of the evaluation by lecturers and students. Section 10.5 discusses the continuing use of the system over the past 3 years. An overall reflection on the adoption of the system, and possible further developments, is provided in Section 10.6.

10.2 Background

As in many other HEIs, a number of systems for student feedback and assessment had been developed by individual lecturers in various departments of UCL. The Higher Education Research and Development Unit (HERDU) conducted a survey of such systems, and arranged a number of exhibitions and workshops to raise awareness amongst other teaching staff about the availability of these systems. Some systems, such as LAPT [4] (developed by Anthony Garner-Medwin in the Department of Physiology), met the requirements of lecturers teaching related subjects and have been adopted for courses in other departments – e.g., Pharmacology. A recurring concern among teaching staff, however, was the difficulty of adapting existing systems to the pedagogical and administrative requirements of other courses.

Two existing web-based systems for self-teaching exercises and assessed coursework (developed by Kevin Boone in the Department of Physiology, and by M. Angela Sasse and Chris Harris in the Department of Computer Science, respectively) created most interest during those workshops. The main reasons for the interest in web-based solutions were lecturers' and students' familiarity with web browsers, and the ability to access such systems from a wide range of systems throughout UCL and from home (see also Section 10.1).

HERDU offered three workshops for lecturers who had expressed an interest in using a web-based system to create student exercises and assessments. The aims of those workshops were:

- To provide lecturers with a detailed understanding of the functionality provided by the two existing systems.

- To give lecturers hands-on experience of authoring and completing sample assignments for their own courses using the existing systems.

- To identify requirements for a generic system for authoring and distributing coursework.

These workshops were, therefore, organized as requirements capture workshops in the tradition of *participatory design* [6, 7], a design approach that is being adopted by an increasing number of projects developing educational technology [8, 9]. Of the 25 lecturers who had expressed an interest in using a web-based system and were invited, 6 attended the workshop, and one sent a detailed wish-list by email. The workshops were moderated by Kim Issroff of HERDU, with the designers of the existing systems (Kevin Boone and M. Angela Sasse) explaining the functionality offered by existing systems, and discussing ways of implementing requirements raised by lecturers. Despite the small number of lecturers participating, the organizer felt that a sufficient range of subjects and requirements was represented (Biochemistry and Molecular Biology, Dutch, Electrical and Electronic Engineering, Greek and Latin, Mathematics, Pharmacology, Primary Care and Population Sciences). The discussions during the workshops were recorded (with lecturers' permission) and transcribed; the transcripts provided the basis for the requirements specification. The draft set of requirements was circulated for comment to the 25 lecturers on the mailing list; 3 lecturers provided detailed comments and feedback. The final set of requirements (see Section 10.2.1) formed the basis of the system specification, and the system was implemented over a period of 8 weeks.

The first implementation of TACO was then submitted to a pilot study. Four lecturers (3 who had contributed to the requirements, and one of the designers, M. Angela Sasse) used TACO to author sets of assignments for courses running in the autumn term of 1997. Almost 500 students were registered for the courses in which the sets of assignments were used (see Section 10.4 for details of the evaluation and results). The system has been in contininuing use ever since, and coursework delivered via TACO has become an integral part of about 10 courses at UCL.

10.2.1Requirements for a Web-Based Coursework System

The requirements identified in the workshop can be divided into 4 different aspects: *authoring, distribution, marking* and *administration* of coursework. A detailed list of the requirements elicited are shown in an appendix. (Requirements not addressed in the first implementation of - TACO because of limited time available before the start of the pilot - are printed in italics.)

One of the major concerns we expected to be raised in connection with the *authoring* of coursework was whether lecturers would have to use the Hypertext Markup Language (HTML) or another Web authoring tool. While some of the participants had used HTML previously, all agreed that most lecturers would not consider using a system that would require them to learn and use HTML. Other systems such as CASTLE [13] and QUASI [15] have addressed this by providing form-based user interfaces which generate the HMTL code for the assignments. These existing systems do not, however, support the range of *question types* which lecturers want to use, since they tend to focus on supporting binary and multiple choice questions (MCQs).

Like many other lecturers, the participants in this project felt that these question types can encourage the "wrong" type of student learning: students may try to guess the right answer, and - with repeated practice simply learn which answer is the "correct" one for a particular question (*"The correct answer to Questions 5 is B "*). Despite these concerns, MCQs have been used extensively over a considerable period of time, and a number of techniques have been developed to combat these problems:

1. Penalty *weightings* for incorrect answers can deter students from taking a guess when they do not know the correct answer.

2. The addition of *confidence assessment* can encourage students to assess how well they have understood topics covered in the course, and thus provide meaningful feedback [4, 10].

3. Making students *assess each answer* (instead of asking them to choose one or more answers) can encourage students to compare answers and reflect on their merits; this type of reflection leads to deeper understanding of the topics [11].

4. Creating a *pool of question variants*, and selecting variants randomly, can make learning the "correct" answer more difficult.

The merits and drawbacks of these techniques were discussed in some detail during the requirements capture phase. It emerged that individual lecturers have very strong beliefs – grounded in their own teaching experience - regarding:

●   which question types are suitable for particular topics and students; and

●   which of the techniques available will encourage the desired type of learning and behavior amongst particular students.

Consequently, any system which aims to support authoring of assignments for a large number of lecturers and academic disciplines has to offer a great deal of *flexibility*: a wide range of preferred question types has to be supported. The same is true for *marking* and *feedback*: a wide range of marking schemes, weightings and associated techniques has to be supported. All lecturers agreed that providing feedback to students is important. The form and extent of feedback lecturers want to give, however, varies widely. Some lecturers want to:

●   display the correct answer to the student - others do not;

●   provide comments or explanations as well as marks;

●   display detailed feedback irrespective of student performance - others want to direct student effort towards topics where their knowledge is weak;

●   integrate assessment with other materials, such as lecture notes, textbooks, lab exercises.

Support for *distribution* of electronic coursework is inherent in TACO's chosen architecture. Like many HEIs, UCL has a wide range of hardware platforms and operating systems, but the vast majority of computers are networked and have web browsers installed. All lecturers in the workshops had use of a suitable machine in

UCL, and a significant number had web access from home. An increasing number of students also have web access from home, and thus can access and complete assignments without taking up a machine in UCL. One group whose requirements could not be addressed in the first implementation was students who have a computer, but no internet access. It is, in principle, possible to download assignments onto disk. However, lecturers were wary of the *security* implications of allowing students to download questions - and answers - that are part of assessed coursework.

Increasing student numbers and Quality Audits are likely to be at the root of the detailed *administrative* support requirements elicited in this study. One obvious requirement is to *export* student marks in a particular format at the end of the course (*e.g.*, in lecturers' spreadsheets or an HEI's examination systems). However, lecturers also wanted to monitor individual students' effort and performance *during* the course, in order to identify those who were not practicing, or performing well enough. Statistics on assignments and questions were seen as an essential feature to weed out "bad" questions (too easy, too difficult, ambiguously phrased), and to identify topics where student performance across the board indicates lack of understanding (*e.g.*, because of the way in which the material was delivered). Dynamic query mechanisms need to be provided to allow lecturers to identify problems while a course is in progress, i.e. problems related to individual students or sections of the learning material.

A final but fundamental issue emerging from the discussion is many lecturers' perception of computer-based coursework as an efficient, but somewhat inferior, means of providing feedback and conducting assessment. Computer-based assessment is seen by many as a *necessary* means of coping with increased numbers of students and coursework, rather a *desirable* tool for supporting student learning. The distinction may be a subtle one from a system developer's point of view. However, we can infer from previous case studies of technology and change [6, 12] that this is likely to have a major impact on the rate of adoption, and quality of coursework, produced with such a system. From the evidence obtained in this study, we believe that what is required to change this perception of computer-based assessment is support for more *active* ways by which students interact with the system, *i.e.*, learning tasks in which students can enter text, numbers or drawings in response to a question requires that they understand the material they have been taught. Actively constructing an answer requires a "deeper" understanding of what is required for choosing options from a list of answers, and is an essential part of an effective learning process [3]. From the developers' point of view, the problem is that these types of questions require more elaborate technical solutions than MCQs. Active images and student submission of drawings via the Web require a Java plug-in and/or XML support. A marking facility for numerical and text submissions that can identify partially correct answers requires intelligent processing, or at least sophisticated pattern-matching.

10.3 The TACO System

The design team realized early in the project that the high degree of flexibility requested by lecturers (see Section 10.2.1) ruled out using existing systems such as CASTLE and QUASI as a basis for implementing a generic coursework authoring and management system. This section presents a summary technical description of the software and processes that constitute the TACO system. Supporting active images and submission of drawings by students via the Web can only be implemented in Java; even though the first implementation of TACO does not support these features, the platform was chosen so that they can be implemented later. Lecturers and students interact with the system via a web browser; the choice of platform means that the browser has to be Java-compatible (*e.g.*, Netscape 3 or higher).

The TACO architecture consists of a Java web server, which facilitates the interaction between student and lecturer clients, and the TACO web server and a database (Oracle[1]) [2]. These requests are made using CGI (Common Gateway Interface) requests to a number of specially designed *servlets* (described below). The reason for adopting a CGI-based design was grounded in the fact that very few machines around the University were running Java-enabled versions of the Netscape Navigator browser. Subsequently, it was decided to address this constraint by using a CGI-based interface to TACO, which works independently of Java on the client machine.

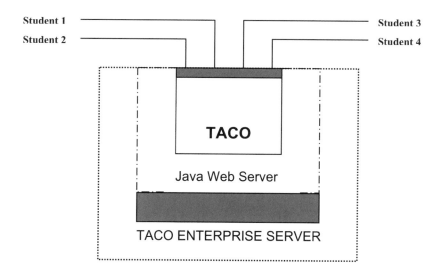

Figure 10.2. A TACO servlet with 4 threads.

---

[1] TACO uses ORACLE, but any other commercial database can be used.
[2] TACO runs on an ENTERPRISE II Server with 2X300 MHz processors, 256 megabytes of RAM and 4.2 Gb of disk space.

A Java web servlet (see Figure 10.2) is a program that responds, in this context, to requests made by student and lecturer web clients. When, for example, a student wishes to start an assignment, they submit their authentication details via a web page to the TACO system. The TACO servlet (in this case TacoQuestionSetGenerator) receives an HTTP request containing the student's user ID and password in form of a CGI stream. This stream is broken down to extract the student user ID and password; this allows the servlet to deal with the student's request. Similarly, when a student submits an assignment the appropriate servlet (TacoQuestionSetMarker) receives a CGI stream containing the answers entered by the student. Again, this stream is used to extract the relevant answers and apply the appropriate marking schema to it. The Java web server contains three servlets that handle the *lecturer authoring tool*, the *question set generator* and *the question set marker*. These servlets are briefly described below:

- *TacoDisplayFrontEnd*: allows lecturers to interact with the TACO authoring tool. Lecturer ID and passwords are validated, then a list of existing courses, courseworks, questions and variants are presented to the lecturer's client (see Figure 10.3) along with the authoring options. If there are no existing courses for a particular lecturer, the authoring options are presented on their own.

- *TacoQuestionSetGenerator*: authenticates student ID and passwords, and retrieves a random set of questions from the database, for the appropriate coursework assignment, to present to the student's client.

- *TacoQuestionSetMarker*: receives the student's answers, stores them in the database and applies the appropriate marking scheme to produce the student's results. A breakdown of the marks, on a question-by-question basis, along with relevant lecturer comments is presented to the student (with the final score).

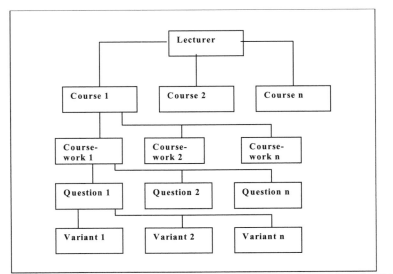

Figure 10.3. Hierachical structure of courseworks and questions in TACO.

These three servlets work in conjunction with an Oracle database. The database stores:

● lecturer and student user IDs and passwords;

● course/coursework/question/variant data (see Figure 10.3) and associated comments/feedback;

● student answers and marks.

The dialogue between these two subsystems is achieved through the use of a JDBC (Java Database Connectivity) connection. The rationale used to isolate the database and external connections from the clients is based in the growing concern for Internet security. By establishing connections with the database through an explicit set of servlets, the TACO system maintains a secure firewall between the database and the outside world.

The interactions between the various TACO system components are illustrated in Figure 10.4.

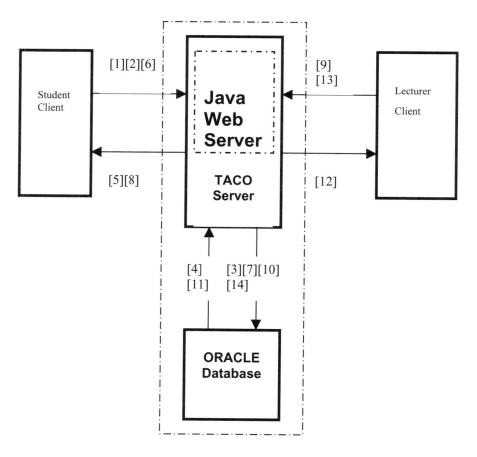

1. Log into TACO with student ID and password.

2. Request coursework assignment.

3. Authenticate student ID and password .

4. Get questions from database.

5. Issue coursework assignment to student.

6. Submit completed coursework assignment.

7. Mark coursework assignment and store student results.

8. Issue student mark and lecturer's comments.

9. Log into TACO authoring tool with lecturer ID and password.

10. Authenticate lecturer ID and password.

11. Get existing course/coursework/question/variant information.

12. Issue authoring options and present existing course/coursework/question/variant information.

13. Request creation of course/coursework/question/variant entry.

14. Store course/coursework/question/variant entry.

Figure 10.4. TACO architecture diagram.

10.3.1 The TACO Authoring Interface

As discussed in Section 10.2.1, a key requirement for any web-based coursework system is to allow lecturers to author questions and assignments without knowledge of HTML, CGI, *etc.*

In TACO, lecturers set up courses and assignments via menus and dialogue boxes. This determines the type of assignment (practice or assessed), and the way in which it is administered (question-by-question or a set of questions).

Questions (or variants) are authored or edited through forms. After selecting a question type (see Appendix), lecturers add question text, comment text and answers into the form displayed (see Figure 10.5). They can add confidence assessments and choose scoring and weighting for each individual question, and mark a question as compulsory. Default values are set for those who do not want to apply any of these options.

Access to a lecturer's assignments, questions and marks is protected (see above). Furthermore, only students registered for a particular course can complete the assignments, unless the lecturer chooses to make it an open assignment.

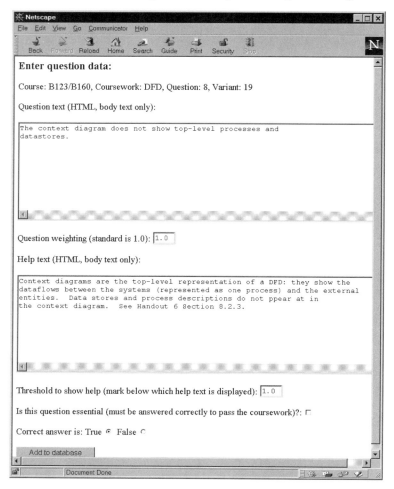

Figure 10.5. TACO question form for a binary question.

10.3.2 The TACO Student Interface

Students completing assignments via TACO only need to know how to use a web browser. After connecting to the HTTP address for a particular assignment, they have to identify themselves through a TACO username and password[3].

If more than one assignment is active, they choose the assignment they want to work on from a list. If an assignment can be completed both as practice and

---

[3] This can be set to be identical with their system login ID and password to avoid extra memory load.

assessed coursework, students have to chose between these two modes; most lecturers allow students to complete assessed coursework once.

Once an assignment has been chosen, questions are displayed to the student (see Figure 10.6 for an example).

When an individual question (or a whole assignment) is submitted by the student, it is returned to the TACO server for marking. Answers selected or entered are compared with the answers selected by lecturers. Marks are then displayed to the student; if the lecturer has added comments or explanation, and the mark achieved by the student falls below a specified level, these will be displayed as well (see Figure 10.7 for an example).

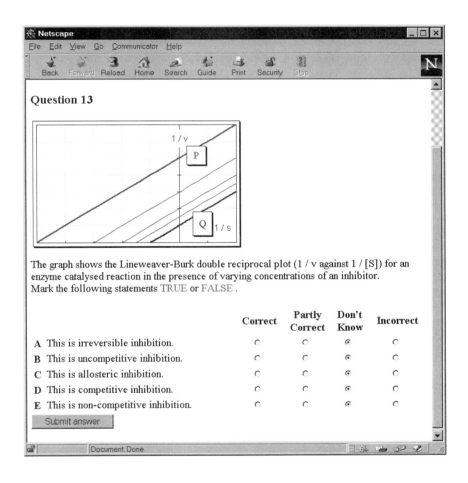

Figure 10.6. Question displayed to student (assignment on a *question-by-question* basis, question type *evaluate each answer*).

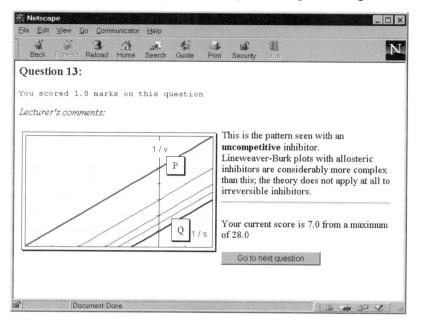

Figure 10.7. Marks and comments displayed to the student.

10.4 Results from the Pilot Study

The first implementation of TACO was evaluated through a pilot project in the Autumn term of 1997. Four lecturers from different academic departments (Biochemistry, Computer Science, Greek and Latin, Mathematics) authored sets of assignments for courses on which over 500 students were registered. We first report results from interviews with two of the lecturers. We then summarize the results from a questionnaire study with students, and some of the statistics on student use of the system.

10.4.1 Evaluation by Lecturers

Interviews with two of the pilot lecturers (from Biochemistry and Mathematics) were conducted in an unstructured manner to allow lecturers to raise any observations or criticisms. Lecturers were asked to provide a general assessment of the first implementation, to raise any problems encountered with the system, and to make suggestions for improvements.

General impressions

The first system provided adequate functionality for the purpose of authoring assignments in these two subjects. Assignments can be created speedily and easily through the structured approach which the authoring interface prescribes.

However, the lecturers felt that the "look-and-feel" of the form-based user interface for entering questions was out of date, mainly because every screen was text-based, and transitions were triggered by clicking on a piece of text. It was also somewhat "tedious" to use, because question and answer text on the current form were separated (see Figure 10.5).

Reliability of the system was the other major issue - *i.e.*, the server was down sufficiently often in the pilot phase to give students the impression that it was not reliable.

Suggested improvements

Both lectures wanted a WYSIWYG *(What You See Is What You Get)* editor, or at least a *preview* facility, when authoring questions – immediate feedback as to what the question looks like is essential to check and correct questions. Ideally, lecturers want to interact with the authoring system using *direct manipulation*, *i.e.*, moving variants, questions and assignments by *drag-and-drop*. Other amenities of a Windows interface, such as a toolbar, online documentation and help, were missing.

A simple improvement was that it should be possible to attach a label to questions to indicate what they are about (rather than just Question 1, Question 2).

10.4.2 Evaluation by Students

The student evaluation was conducted via a web-based questionnaire. Students were encouraged to participate in the anonymous questionnaire study (it was conducted by a final year student, rather than the lecturer) by raffling 3 book vouchers among those who completed the questionnaire. 40 students – *i.e.*, less than 10% of the total number of users - completed the questionnaire over a period of one week.

General impressions

The general impression was that web-based feedback and assessment was "a good idea"; the majority of students stated that web-based assignments were faster and easier to complete than paper-based coursework, and that they identified the essential concepts of the course faster than they would have otherwise. 20% of the respondents said they had used similar systems before. Reliability of the server during the pilot was an issue – half of the respondents had been unable to access coursework at some point.

Suggested improvements

The vast majority of respondents in this sample (80%) had completed their assignments using machines in UCL. Even though most of them indicated that they had no problem finding a terminal when they wanted to complete an exercise, the single most frequently suggested improvement was "to be able to take practice exercises home on disk". This may indicate that there is a substantial number of students who have computers at home, but either have no internet access, or are unwilling to use it because of the associated cost.

Students also realized that the usefulness of the system to support their learning activity very much depended on the quality of the authoring: complaints raised included:

● ambiguous phrasing of questions;

● typing errors in questions;

● "incorrect" marking (including receiving no marks at all for mis-spelt or partly correct answers on free-text or numerical answers);

● lack of integration with other material.

10.4.3 Observation on Student Behavior

Analyzis of system logs for students on one course (Computer Science) revealed something that many lecturers have suspected: students' working patterns are very much deadline-driven. On assignments announced 10-14 working days before the deadline, the vast majority of students started their first practice coursework 3 days before. Most completed 2-3 practice runs before submitting assessed coursework.

10.5 Evaluation of TACO in Continuing Use

Since the pilot trial in 1997, a dozen lecturers have used the system in over thirty courses, creating more than 140 assignments in total over the course of three academic years. However, not every lecturer who tried TACO continues to use the system for their courses, while some lecturers are using the system in almost every course they teach. A second evaluation of TACO was carried out to determine why some lecturers choose to employ TACO in their courses while others reject the system. The range of academic disciplines covered by these lecturers includes Computer Science, Biochemistry, Mechanical Engineering, Geology and Greek and Latin.

Interviews were conducted with five lecturers who are currently using TACO. Three lecturers are frequent users of the system, one will not be using the system in the next academic year, and one has stopped using the system all together. The interviews were semi-structured: each lecturer was asked the same questions, but interviews were carried out in a manner which allowed issues raised by the interviewees to be explored in depth. Another source of data used for the analyzis was the TACO system logs, which contains quantitative data on all courses that were authored using TACO (including those by lecturers who were not interviewed), such as the number of courses and assignments created by each lecturer, and how often students practiced each coursework.

The interviews revealed that the single most important factor for those who adopted TACO was its *perceived practicality*. All lecturers used TACO in response to a problem they had in delivering a particular course. The system logs showed that those lecturers who perceived TACO as being *practical* created the largest number of assignments, and made extensive use of the feedback facility (help text) for the students. The log also shows that students of these lecturers used the practice assignments more often before completing assessed coursework than students of other lecturers. In assignments where practice was allowed, 17% of assignments were practiced ten or more times, 29% five or more times, and 54% less than five times. In all assignments where practice was allowed, each student completed at least two practice runs.

The interviews also identified a number of problems which put lecturers off using the system. One lecturer who participated in the interviews decided not to continue using TACO because it took her *"as long to compose TACO assignments as setting and marking a paper-based one"*. The was not due to the lecturer's lack of skills, but the lack of support for authoring a large number of similar or related questions (*e.g.*, for lecturers who want create a large number of variants - see Section 10.2.1). Since the current system does not provide support for reuse of questions, or generates simple variants automatically (*e.g.*, by shuffling answer options), the cut-and-paste operations by which lecturers generate variants was described as *"very tedious"* – a sentiment shared by other lecturers. However, the other lecturers felt that they saved significant amounts of time in subsequent years, the three interviewees who used the system regularly said updating a TACO assignment took 10% of the time it would take to set and mark a paper-based one.

Another factor that influenced the decision to adopt TACO was the perception of system reliability. There were a number of system failures – one of the limitations of the first implementation was lack of field protection in the authoring forms, which means it that it is possible for users to enter character strings that cause the web server to crash. Lecturers who used TACO frequently felt able to cope with technical problems (or where to get help), and were not particularly upset or aggrieved. Lecturers who had used TACO during the pilot stage (when there were quite a few problems – see Section 10.4) felt that there were *"very few"* reliability problems in continuing use.

10.6 Improvements Identified During the Trials

10.6.1 User Interface

As reported in Sections 10.4.1 and 10.5, the authoring user interface to TACO requires considerable improvement. During the requirements capture phase, lecturers' main concern was that the system should have a "really simple" user interface. That was exactly what TACO provided. Once lecturers started to use the simple, form-based user interface, however, it became clear they wanted something that was simple to use, *i.e.*, that shielded them from HTML or other programming-style authoring tools. However, like many users today, they expected the look-and-feel and functionality offered by contemporary Windows interfaces: WYSIWYG, menus, icons, moving files by "drag-and-drop", search functionality, and bubble help. Absence of these features not only makes the interface look less attractive, but fails to support many aspects of the authoring process (see also Section 10.6.2). From the developers' point of view, these features are not technically difficult to implement, but they require considerable time and effort. One major problem with the user interface from the students' point of view was that pressing the return key submitted the coursework for marking. Several students accidentally submitted their coursework before they had completed all the questions; since assessed coursework can only be submitted once, lecturers had to remove the "accidental" mark from the database to allow the student to complete the assignment properly.

10.6.2 The Process of Authoring Coursework

Both lecturers and developers discovered early during the pilot that some aspects of authoring coursework had not been considered in the requirements capture phase. The process of authoring coursework was described as a top-down approach. Each lecturer is responsible for a number of courses and plans a number of assignments for a particular course. For each assignment, the lecturer writes a number of questions, and maybe a number of variants for each question. When all questions are written, the assignment is released to the students. While lecturers started to author assignments in this manner, it quickly emerged that questions - rather than assignments - are the level of granularity at which authoring is done. Lecturers were more inclined to write a number of questions and variants, and then put together an assignment by selecting a number of questions. Lecturers also discovered that they wanted to reuse questions in assignments on different courses. The model of authoring which emerged from these observations was that lecturers could create a library or pool of questions, from which they then put together assignments.

Furthermore, there is the issue of reuse or adaptation of other lecturers' questions. Some courses cover similar material, but from a different perspective. Some assignments have more than one author. This requirement became evident with one of the pilot courses, which taught mathematics to geology students. A perennial problem with such service courses is that, while it is desirable to have the subject taught by an expert mathematician, students often fail to relate the material taught to their own subject. Ideally, mathematical knowledge should be presented in the *context* of problems arising from the students' subject. Such questions could be created as a joint effort between two lecturers - the expert mathematician and an expert in the other subject. Since this requirement exists for many other subjects, the expert mathematician could create sets of questions on a range of topics, which could then be adapted for use in different subjects. Implementation of both suggestions - question libraries and joint authoring - will require modifications to the design of TACO: the current model has a virtual web server owned by each lecturer, and the hierarchical model of course, coursework and questions (see Figure 10.3).

10.6.3 Coping with Distributed System Environments in HEIs

As outlined in Section 10.1, most HEIs have a variety of hardware and operating systems. One of the main reasons for choosing a web-based system was that it could be accessed from a wide range of hardware platforms and operating systems. During the pilot, all students could access their coursework, but there were still a number of problems arising from the distributed and heterogeneous nature of the terminals:

- some of the machines were not very powerful and, as a result, scrolling through long sets of coursework was slow;

- network access from some clusters was slow;

- some machines had several versions of web browsers installed - students using very old versions found that not all features of the coursework (*e.g.*, color) were supported.

It is easy for lecturers to forget that the coursework they author may have a different look-and-feel on some students' screens. Guidelines stating "best practice" for not to be developed, and one recommendation would be that lecturers test assignments on machines which are used by their students. This will help to detect some, but not all, potential problems, since some students (and many lecturers) prefer to complete (or author) coursework from home. While this reduces the demand for machines in the HEI, we found that it can create other problems. Since telephone costs are lower outside normal working hours, most outside access to the system occurred in the evenings and at weekends. Unfortunately, there is no support available if any technical problem or query about an assignment arises during those hours. Even though students had been made aware that this was the case, they were still upset when they encountered a problem and found they had to wait until normal working hours to have it dealt with. Similarly, lecturers' planning was badly upset when a night or weekend authoring session could not be completed as planned.

10.6.4 Participatory Design in the Development of Educational Technology

Participatory design advocates the use of early prototypes: (a) to help users to envision how they will work with the system; and (b) to detect omissions in the requirements, or problems in the use of the system, at an early stage. In many projects, user interaction with prototypes takes place in a series of short lab sessions, where the designers observe users "walk through" a small number of selected tasks. This type of evaluation is, however, not sufficient to validate requirements for, and identify potential problems with, a large distributed system. It is also unlikely that a short session with simulated tasks gives users sufficient opportunity to discover all the major problems which may arise in everyday use of the system.

The evaluation of the first implementation of TACO - the prototype in this project - was therefore conducted as a field trial. In retrospect, it did yield additional requirements and helped to identify some problems that had not been anticipated by lecturers and the development team. It is difficult to imagine that the development of the type of technology which will support the digital university can be undertaken without this type of field study, where a large number of potential users evaluate a new system in the context of real courses. Developers should, however, be aware that some users find it difficult to distinguish between prototypes and fully developed systems. This poses a dilemma for any development project as to when to submit the system to a field trial: running it too early may create a negative response which kills the project; running it late may mean that fundamental omissions or problems are only discovered very late in the design process.

The pilot study with real users completing real tasks was extremely valuable, but it was also resource-intensive and occasionally straining. Many students (especially those taking Computer Science courses) did not appreciate the difference between a prototype and a fully tested and stable system. Reports of problems with, or failure of, the system early in the pilot were sometimes accompanied by derogatory comments about the technical abilities of those who had developed it. The developers were able to recognize that these comments were born out of temporary frustration, and the unique combination of arrogance and ignorance with which some first year computer science students tend to view other people's software. However, there is a danger that users may form a tainted view of a system through interaction with a prototype. It is therefore best to ensure that the system used in this context is stable before large numbers of users get involved in the trials. There have been few problems with the continuing use of TACO over the past 3 years; consequently, the feedback from students using TACO is overwhelmingly positive, to the extent that they ask why it is not used in more courses. The two positive features cited most frequently by students are: (1) that they do their coursework from home (charges for dialup access are less of an issue than at the start of the project); and (2) they receive immediate feedback, which is viewed very positive by compared to paper-based coursework.

10.7 Conclusions

At the review workshop held at the end of the pilot phase, all participants agreed that the TACO system had achieved the original aim of the project: it demonstrated that it is possible to provide a generic system to support authoring, distribution, marking and administration of computer-based coursework. Lecturers' and students' use of the system, and subsequent feedback, identified many possible changes and additions that would improve the effectiveness, efficiency and usability of TACO. The project also provided a more detailed understanding of the overall process of authoring and completing computer-based coursework in a distributed environment. The development team learnt some extremely valuable lessons about carrying out participatory design project in the context of a multi-faculty HEI such as UCL; the findings on technical and design issues have been summarized in Section 10.6. While the start of the projects was very encouraging, we have to conclude that the project never gathered sufficient momentum to push through a full-scale development and deployment of the system. This experience is not unique. Our research on adoption of educational technology has led us to conclude that this experience is not unique; while there are usually good reasons as to why educational technology should be adopted, the number of success stories is limited.

Research has identified common barriers to the implementation of innovation in educational settings, particularly when introducing information and communications technologies (ICT). There are four main factors which affect the success or failure of attempts to implement an innovation in an educational setting.

1. *Lack of clarity and practicality of the Innovation.* The lack of clarity and practicality of an innovation [18, 20, 21, 23] was the most common cause of failed implementation attempts while other factors could also play major roles in influencing the rate of success of an attempt. Staff do not invest time into getting to know a new system [23] unless the benefits and practicality are clear. Existing time pressure can also influence how practical an innovation is for lecturers. Issues that have been raised include the lack of time to use a new system [19] and the lack of opportunity to discuss the new system with colleagues [17, 20].

2. *Lack of Resources and/or Skills.* The lack of resources [18, 19, 23] and skills [21] is another major factor influencing the implementation of a new system. Lack of access to appropriate hardware and software have been mentioned as key problems. Real or perceived lack of technical and other professional

skills needed to use a new system are a major issue. Lecturers need to receive training not only on how to a particular new system, but also on how to integrate the new system in the delivery of a course.

3. *Lack of Support from Senior Staff.* The support from senior staff [19, 22, 23] can play a crucial role in ensuring the success of an innovation. Such support can help to adjust organizational arrangements that hinder the implementation of an innovation. Endorsement of, and interest in, the adoption of a new system from senior staff in the central divisions and departments of an HEI is essential to ensure successful adoption of a new system.

4. *Lack of Ownership.* The last major factor that may influence the implementation of an innovation is the feeling of ownership of a new system among its intended users. Here the emphasis is placed on the participation of users at the planning stage of a new system [17], as well as their control over the use of it. Such participation allows the users to adapt and improve innovation as appropriate during the new system's usage, rather than just adopting the innovation with no further improvements made.

Often, these factors are related to and/or dependent on each other [20], and any widescale introduction will depend on tackling them from the outset. The authors were aware of the first two problems, but ultimately failed to progress beyond the pilot stage because they did not address the last two issues.

Three years after the pilot study, the TACO prototype system is still used on a regular basis by a dozen lecturers; these regular users want to keep the system going and are very concerned to protect the investment (time and effort) they made in developing the materials. Even more, they would like to see a full implementation of the system that provides all the required functionality, and addresses the usability issues identified in Sections 10.4 and 10.6. To those users, the educational and administrative benefits are obvious. However, the authorities in charge of educational technology provision at UCL were not willing to commit the funds necessary to implement TACO. The lack of support from senior staff (see point 3 above) may be routed in the fact that the spirit of the times is very much against large-scale in-house development projects. Since the financial situation in HEIs is hardly rosy, committing significant resources to a large-scale project carries significant risk. It is therefore not surprising that such a project is unlikely to proceed unless the prospective users endorse it. The project leaders did not involve academic departments - as opposed to individual lecturers – in the process from the start (see point 4 above), and this ultimately proved to be a stumbling block. Academic departments often have prejudices against development projects run by a central IT unit. Technology-friendly departments such as Computer Science and Engineering view centrally-provided systems as not state-of-the-art, whereas at the other end of the spectrum, technology-shy departments such as arts and humanities are inclined to suspect the same system would be too advanced and expensive for them. Buying a variety of cheaper off-the-shelf products that individual departments demand spreads the risk, and distributing the longer-term cost of installation, maintenance and support means it is less visible.

Acknowledgements

TACO was a UCL-internal project, funded by the Department of Computer Science and the Education and Information Support Division (EISD). Sun Microsystems UK generously donated the Enterprise II server, Java Server and Java development kit. Dr Kevin Boone (now at the University of Middlesex) helped the development team by giving feedback on the design and implementation planning, as well as contributing to the requirements specification. Nadav Zin helped with the setting up of the Oracle Database, and writing SQL queries for retrieving results.

Dr Kim Issroff from the Higher Education Research and Development Unit (HERDU) was involved in the project from the beginning; Dr Issroff set the challenge of designing a UCL-wide authoring system and made arrangements for funding the pilot. Many UCL lecturers contributed through the requirements capture workshops, and comments on the requirements specification; others helped by evaluating the first version of TACO. The three "pilots" were Dr David Bender (Department of Biochemistry and Molecular Biology), Dr Rowena Bowles (Department of Mathematics) and Professor Bob Sharples (Department of Greek and Latin). All three made very important contributions throughout the project and developed substantial coursework sets for their students.

References

1. Mayes, J. T. and Fowler, C. (1999) Learning technology and usability: A framework for understanding courseware. *Interacting with Computers* 11 (5), 485-497.

2. Mayes, J. T. (1995) Learning technology and groundhog day *Hypermedia at Work: Practice and Theory in Higher Education*. Strang, W., Simpson V.B. and Slater D. [Eds.] University of Kent Press.

3. Laurillard, D. (1993) Rethinking University Teaching: A Framework for the Effective Use of Educational Technology. Routledge.

4. Gardner-Medwin, A.R. (1995) Confidence assessment in the teaching of basic science. *ALT-J*, 3, 80-85.

5. Cann, A. J. (1996) On-line interactive computer-assisted learning in biology and medicine. *Computers in Biology Education* (vCUBE) 96.

6. Bødker, S. (1991) Through the Interface: A Human Activity Approach to User Interface Design. Lawrence Erlbaum Associates.

7. Schuler, D. and Namioka, A. [Eds.] (1993) Participatory Design: Principles and Practices. Lawrence Erlbaum Associates.

8. Bellamy, R. (1996) Designing educational technology: Computer-mediated change. *Context and Consciousness: Activity Theory and Human-Computer Interaction*. Nardi, B. [Ed.], MIT Press.

9. Hughes, J. and Sasse, M. A. (1998) Design to instruct: Lessons for training through involving teachers in design. *Proceedings of SITE98, Annual Conference on Technology and Teacher Education.* Washington, DC, March 10-14.

10. Gardner-Medwin, A.R. and Curtin, N.A. (1996) Confidence assessment in the teaching of physiology. *Journal of Physiology*, 494:74P.

11. Paul, J. (1994) Improving education trough computer-based alternative assessment methods. *People and Computers IX: Proceedings of HCI'94*, Cockton, G. *et al.* [Eds.], Glasgow August 1994. Cambridge University Press.

12. Grudin, J. (1991) Interactive systems: Bridging the gaps between developers and users. *IEEE Computer*, April 1991, 59-69.

13. CASTLE (Computer Assisted Teaching and Learning) Project at Leicester University. URL: http://www.le.ac.uk/cc/ltg/castle/

14. LAPT (London Agreed Protocol for Teaching) Project at UCL. URL:

    http://www.ucl.ac.uk/~cusplap

15. QUASI (Question and Answer System for the Internet) by Kevin Boone – now defunct.

16. TACO (Teaching and Coursework Online) Project at University College London. URL: http://taco.cs.ucl.ac.uk:8080/taco/www/

17. Blumenfeld, G. J., Hirschbul, J. J., *et al.* (1979). Computer-based education: a case for planned culture change in the school. *British Journal of Educational Technology* (10): 186-193.

18. Cuban, L. (1986). Teachers and machines: The classroom use of technology since 1920. New York, Teachers' College Press.

19. Davis, D. (1993). Implementation and educational uses of computers. *The IEA Study of Computers in Education: Implementation of an Innovation in 21 Education Systems.* Pelgrum W. and Plomp. T., Oxford, Pergamon Press: 73-123.

20. Fullan, M. (1982). Research into educational innovation. *Management of Educational Institutions*. Gray. H. New York, McGraw-Hill: 245-261.

21. Gross, N., Giacquinta, J., *et al.* (1971). *Implementing Organisational Innovation: A Sociological Analysis of Planned Educational Change.* New York, Basic Book.

22. Nicholls, A. (1983). The human factor in innovation. *Managing Educational Innovation.* London, Allen & Unwin: 39-46.

23. Plomp, T., Pelgrum, W., *et al.* (1990). Influence of computer use on schools' curriculum: Limited integration. *Computers & Education* 14: 159-171.

Appendix A: List of Requirements for a Web-Based System

(Requirements not implemented in the first version of TACO are printed in italics)

1   Question Types

1.1 Multiple-choice questions :

- student selects one of n;

- student selects n of n ;

- student has to evaluate each answer;

1.2 Binary questions (true/false).

1.3 Numerical response (student enters value+unit);

- *accommodate acceptable range of answers.*

1.4 Text response:

- one-word responses;

- short (1 line) freeform text:

  - *approximate phrase-matching;*

  - *spell-checking and feedback of error.*

- long text answers :

  - stored for hand-marking by lecturer;

  - *automatic marking (using pattern matching).*

1.5 Image-based questions:

- displaying figures/formulas/tables;

- selecting images;

- *active images 1 (hotspots - student selects region on image);*

- *active image 2 (student annotates/edits or drawing;*

- *student draws image from scratch.*

2   Confidence Assessment

2.1 Option of adding confidence assessment to any question.

2.2 Provide range of weighting scheme for confidence assessment.

2.3 Make confidence assessment scheme transparent to students.

3   Marking Schemes

3.1 Straight count.

3.2 Questions weighted (weighting specified by lecturer).

3.3 Essential questions (assignment failed if question failed).

3.4 Dynamic scoring:

- *multiple attempts at questions allowed, scoring adjusted accordingly;*

- *recommend switching to certain levels depending on progress.*

3.5 Scaling marks:

- *scale marks to achieve normal distribution.*

4   Feedback to Student

4.1 Display score.

4.2 Display correct answer.

4.3 Display explanation (pre-stored by lecturer.

4.4 Return explanation depending on score achieved.

4.5 Feedback on whole assignments (assessed coursework).

4.6 Compilation (histogram) of scoring during testing.

5   Assignment Types

5.1 Self-learning exercises.

5.2 Assessed coursework.

5.3 Assignment display:

- sheet-based (student completes all questions before submitting);

- question-by-question (student completes and submits answer before next question is displayed).

6   Authoring Assignments

6.1 Authoring via form (no knowledge of HTML, CGI, Java required).

6.2 Choice of:

- Question types (see 1);
- Confidence assessment (see 2);
- Marking schemes (see 3);
- Feedback (see 4);
- Assignment type (see 5).

6.3 Random selection from a pool of questions.

6.4 Links to other online documents.

6.5 Automatic transfer of existing MCQ documents (*e.g.*, MS Word files).

6.6 Preview facility when authoring questions.

6.7 Spell-checking.

6.8 Basic syntax and consistency checking.

6.9 Support for Maths/Greek symbols.

7   Reports and Feedback to Lecturers

7.1 Every student interaction with system logged.

7.2 Reports on students:

- registration of student details;
- which assignment completed when (see 7.1);
- where assignment was completed from;
- assignment results;
- file results for import into spreadsheets;
- which questions attempted;
- time spent on questions;

- where assessment was completed form.

7.3 Reports on questions:

- how many attempts;
- which answers chosen;
- student comments on questions.

8   Security

8.1 No student access to questions or marks.

8.2 Time limits for completing assessed coursework.

8.3 Notification when assignment started.

Chapter 11

Using Lotus Notes for Asynchronous Collaborative Learning and Research

Susan Armitage and Mark Bryson

A touchstone of Lancaster University's learning technology strategy is the use of IT to support collaborative learning. The university has been using asynchronous computer-mediated communication to support collaboration in teaching, learning and research since 1988. Since 1993, Lotus Notes [1] has been in use at the university and was adopted as the university's centrally supported conference system in April 1995. Soon afterwards, Lotus renamed the Notes server as "Domino" to emphasise its shift to the use of internet protocols, since then we have tried to exploit its potential to support robust and secure use of the Web for collaborative activities.

This chapter describes completed work and work in progress that uses Domino as the support environment for asynchronous collaboration and information sharing. The factors that were involved in the choice of Lotus Notes as the centrally supported system are outlined, along with some of the practical support implications. Today we have almost 700 separate Domino web sites supporting a wide range of collaborative activities. The largest category by far is a hybrid discussion/noticeboard design.

11.1 Asynchronous Collaboration

This area of activity takes distinct forms where Domino is used as an integral part of an academic course of study, for research support or for support of professional networking activities. The following sections provide examples of these forms.

11.2 Academic Courses

The first two cases in this category are at the MA level of study. Each course had a common need to support distance learners in a flexible way, to fit with the students' work practices. The student body mainly comprises busy professionals who wish to pursue a course of study for professional or personal development. As such, academic programmes with constraints of time and place are unsuitable for them. There are a variety of models for CMC participation [2, 3, 4] some of which are repeated below:

Query and Response: problem centred communication, with all participants able to see the question and suggested solution(s).

Electronic Seminar: the discussion is started with a short written presentation or question relevant to the area to be discussed. Students then participate in ongoing debate about this area

Electronic Learning Sets: takes the idea of face-to-face learning sets and translates it to an electronic medium. Learners explain their own current problem or task (generally with a work-based focus). The set then acts as a resource to assist them in thinking through their course of action or understanding of the problem/task.

Case 1: Professional Development for Practicing Management Developers

The "traditional" face-to-face design of this course was examined to determine whether CMC had a *rôle* to play in increasing opportunities for participation in the programme. The traditional course has a series of week-long residential workshops that focus on different aspects of Management Education and Development. At these workshops, learning sets are formed, between 4-6 participants in size.

These sets then meet 3-5 times between the workshops, at a convenient time and place with a tutor, to discuss their coursework. As can be imagined, the difficulties of negotiating the time and place can become overwhelming as work pressures take over from commitment to the course.

Initially, a separate computer-mediated version of this course was offered. Since 1997, the computer-mediated version and the 'traditional' version have been amalgamated, leading to greater flexibility and choice for the participants [5]. Residential workshops still take place as before. However, participants can now choose whether to take part in face-to-face set meetings or Electronic Learning Sets in between the workshops. At each workshop, where new learning sets are formed, participants can again choose which method will suit their current work pattern the best.

Each set has its own discussion database, with read access for other members of the larger group being allowed by most sets. There is also a group discussion database, where whole group issues can be raised and discussed. Problems with using Lotus Notes are passed on to the Notes support staff by teaching staff, or participants can contact the administrators directly.

Previously, participants exchanged their written work using postal means, but commented on the work using the conferencing system. Now, since Notes clients allow them to attach files containing their papers, this process can also be speeded up.

Since 1995, they have also instigated a half-day workshop to familiarize participants with the use of Notes. They feel this has significantly speeded up the process of getting people online and focusing on the course content, rather than on their initial experiences with the technology.

Participants particularly appreciate the offline working capability of Notes that allows them to take their discussion spaces with them on laptops when travelling and working away from the home/office.

Case 2: A Modular Programme for the Development of Learning Technology Professionals

This programme of study [6] is based around a set of self-contained course modules. A resource pack is supplied to support the independent study period, consisting of tutor notes, readings, audio-visual material *etc*. Lotus Domino is used to support tutorial discussion and learner interaction, with different databases being created for both discussion topics and focused tasks and activities.

Online communication happens between participants and their peers, and between participants and tutors, and it is an integral part of each module. Participation in the online community is intended to become part of the participants' everyday working practices. This provides an expanding source of professionally relevant information as well as a forum for debate. Resources are developed around learner's queries and discussions, with remedial information and updates being quickly disseminated through the electronic discussion space. Learner collaboration and the exchange of knowledge and experience are central to this programme's approach [7].

Participants on these modules can either install the Lotus Notes client to access discussion spaces or access them via the web. This flexibility is a major benefit as some participants are based in higher education and so find it easier to use a web access route. Other participants are based in organizations or at home and require the offline working facility of the Notes client.

Case 3: Second Year Law Undergraduates

This course has conducted its case-based negotiations unit via web access to a Lotus Domino discussion space for the past four years. In the past, getting face-to-face inter-team meetings was problematic due to constraints of time and space.

Using a web client to access the discussion areas means that students can participate from anywhere they have internet access.

The lecturers who participated commented that, although participation was variable, in those instances where students engaged enthusiastically, the quality of the interaction and *rôle*-playing was of a significantly higher standard than they had experienced in previous years when the activities were confined to the classroom. Students also found the medium useful for general communication with tutors over both academic and administrative queries [8, 9].

11.3 Research and Professional Network Support

Domino and its predecessor at Lancaster were both initially used in distributed research projects rather than in support of taught courses. For a discussion of online distributed research issues see [10]. Recent projects are described here to illustrate what is possible.

Case 4: Student Accounts of Residence Abroad

This web site brings together accounts from students writing and talking about their experiences during their period of residence abroad. The data consists of diaries written while students were away, and interviews and focus groups conducted after their return. The accounts cover a wide variety of topics, focusing particularly, but not exclusively, on intercultural issues. Searching the site gives access to a very large number of students' real life experiences. The site can be browsed by students and there are suggested learning activities available too [11].

Domino's scripting language (a superset of Visual Basic) was used to develop a program to transfer SPSS text analyzis reports into a Domino database on the web. The process was so quick that the web site could be updated or recreated easily each time a new batch of text had been analyzed. Overall about 30 megabytes of text was incorporated into the web site.

The Domino design client was used to construct a specialized search form matched to the parameters of the SPSS text analyzis. When users find something of interest, they can choose to see it in the context of adjacent text items from the transcript, which they achieve by clicking on a link that runs another Lotus script program that builds the web page on demand from an arbitrary number of text elements. There is an associated interactive web bibliography, also hosted on Domino.

Case 5: PASOLD Database

The Pasold Research Fund was established in 1964 by Eric W. Pasold OBE, whose special interest was the history of knitting. The current Director is Dr Mary B. Rose, Senior Lecturer in Business History at Lancaster University. The Fund provides a Domino web site as a resource for historians throughout the world working on any area of textile history, in whatever period. The aim is to help historians find colleagues with similar textile related interests [12].

The Domino design client was used to design a Web site that allows easy searching of a directory of textile historians, together with simple browsing by name and by researchers' personal interests, *e.g.*, cotton, wool, England, USA. Updates are done via ODBC from a Microsoft Access database maintained by the Pasold Fund.

Case 6: Public Health Research & Development Network

The Public Health and Health Professional Development Unit at Lancaster University is a partnership between the university and the National Health Service in the North West. The Unit aims to promote professional development for public health practitioners in the north west and elsewhere. As part of this activity the Unit maintains a web site of public health expertise. The site describes the location and activities of public health professionals throughout the north west, plus occasional announcements and notices of interest to health professionals [13].

The web site is a Domino database, in which any member of the R&D network can maintain their own details by editing them directly on the Web. The site sends email alerts to members if their personal entry remains unaltered for a specified time; it also allows its administrator, a member of the unit, to create new entries and obtain data from the database for mail merges and similar activities.

Case 7: User Configurable Webs

A Domino web site is maintainable by users entering and editing information via web forms. Domino has been used to write a general-purpose site builder such that a research group or department can collaboratively maintain a web site, using nothing more than a web browser. An audit trail of site alterations is maintained automatically [14]. There is, perhaps obviously, a limit to how configurable a site can be when it is maintained entirely from a web browser.

11.4 Asynchronous Information Sharing

Lotus Domino is a Notes server *and* a web server. A Domino server will interact with a normal web client to provide access to both standard HTML files and Notes databases. Notes databases are displayed on the Web in a very similar format to the way they appear in Notes itself, with the possibility of having different views of the same information. For example, documents can be organized by author, creation date, keyword *etc*. Notes automatically generates the HTML code both for displaying documents and for the links between the documents, effectively acting as a secure, multi-platform, multi-user web authoring environment.

This approach has been particularly appropriate for information sharing, since many users are familiar with web technology, but have neither the time nor the inclination to learn how to use Notes.

Again, case studies are used to illustrate how Notes and the Web have been used.

Case 8: Teaching Developments Database

This is an ongoing project aimed at disseminating examples of good teaching practice at the university. A Domino database has been custom designed to act as a repository of the information. Since the main aim of the project is dissemination, publication of the information held in Domino onto the Web is essential to the success of the project.

Links can be made to other information accessible via the Web *e.g.*, a lecturer or department's own web page or other useful web resources.

Case 9: Scholarly Activities

A number of academic staff are taking advantage of the information sharing/organizing aspects of a Domino supported web space to share documents and information with colleagues at other institutions or in other organizations. Typically, this has been used to support submission of conference papers, production of conference proceedings, and collation and sharing of chapters for edited volumes. The ability easily to associate comments on chapters with the chapters themselves, through the use of main topic and response documents, has been cited as a major advantage.

Case 10: Lancaster University (LU) News

The design for this site was originally specified as a research project dissemination tool. In fact, as in the case of LU News, the design is also proving useful for dissemination of general information and, at the time of writing, there are several other groups trialling it for similar purposes.

Anyone can contribute articles, short news items, letters and adverts but none appear on the site until approved by the site administrators.

All users or administrators need to do is copy and paste text, plus an optional image file if they have one, into a web page. No understanding of HTML or site organization is required.

When the administrator approves the submission she also selects an "issue" and whether or not to highlight the page in the site's scrolling banner. As usual with Domino web sites, internal site links are built automatically [15].

11.5 Support Issues

Offering any centrally supported service necessarily raises issues concerning the type and level of support offered. Perhaps one of the main advantages of Domino is also a potential disadvantage; it has great flexibility but, paradoxically, this exacerbates the problem of being clear to users about the level of support offered and exactly how much web development work is justified for a particular application.

This is a major contrast with more specialized Managed Learning Environments such as Blackboard and WebCT. Our team consists of three support staff, two of whom have significant other work responsibilities. Support could legitimately be restricted to learning support activities; however, to allow users to remain ignorant of other possibilities would be a disservice to the user community. Although we use Domino for some administration and research activities, we do not run workshops or produce user documentation except for learning and teaching support.

11.5.1 Administration

User management
NT web authentication is used for members (staff and students) of Lancaster University. We use Domino's own authentication for non-members (*e.g.*, alumni, external research collaborators *etc.*). Complete integration of staff and student user accounts with management user accounts and course registration data is not fully automated and is a current priority. Creation of accounts for external users is largely delegated outside the support group.

Logins and passwords are a constant issue but use of NT authentication is very helpful because: (a) people can't access any resources without their NT login so they tend to remember it; and (b) there is a another support point for NT login and password problems anyway.

We have had to abandon using the NT Challenge/Response login mechanism supported by Internet Explorer 4 and above because people using a dialup Internet Service Provider other than Lancaster University's own had so many difficulties with it.

Licensing

Each member of the university is required to have a Domino personal "Client Access License" or CAL allocated to them. These are transferable from one user to another. A separate server license accommodates external users. Ordering licenses is easy. Maintaining records of which departments have licenses and how many are in use at any given time is not!

Application development

As people become aware of the range of web facilities available, they naturally wish to harness them to their own advantage. Where our standard designs provide the functionality and behavior required, this is a simple matter of creating a new database, giving it a suitable name and setting access controls. However, we have found that the universally suitable online learning environment is a myth and a degree of customization is often requested.

Until recently, most lecturers have not wanted more than a minor, supplementary part of their teaching on the Web (many still don't), so a full-featured and integrated online learning environment has not been needed.

Growing IT sophistication of lecturers and students together with increased web accessibility and interactivity is encouraging a demand for more web based activities and a more ambitious learning environment approach. Increased student numbers, course flexibility and overloaded support staff also necessitate greater integration of the online environment with course registration information and other central data.

Initially the Web was a (large) collection of handcrafted HTML documents. Increasingly it is becoming a collection of transaction-based applications where web pages are built and displayed dynamically and uniquely for each user from underlying data systems.

The next round of web evolution will see web applications interacting dynamically and automatically with each other. Currently Domino seems well placed to cope with these and other changes. Fundamental changes to the underlying nature of the Web have no foreseeable end-point. There are also a huge number of software tools available for the support of teaching and learning on the Web with probably just as many theories about how to use them [16].

Staff development

Staff need to be made aware of the possibilities provided by Domino-supported web spaces. More critically they need to know how, pedagogically, they should incorporate this technology into their educational provision [17, 18, 19].

They also need to think through their role and to develop skills as online, as distinct from face-to-face, tutors [20, 21]. Critical to the quality of this support is the nature of the collaboration between support and academic staff [22].

In association with the university staff development office, courses have and will continue to be offered. The courses cover best practice in the use of conference systems to support learners, using examples from UK Higher Education, not just Lancaster-based examples.

Student experiences

A JISC funded project regarding students' experiences of networked learning in higher education has just been completed at Lancaster University [23] and so a local source of theoretical and practical expertise is available.

Staff/student training

Once a member of staff has decided to incorporate a Domino application into their course in some way, there is then an additional training need for any other members of teaching staff and students. To date, the central support staff have provided about 50% of the training required for staff and students. Increasingly student training appears unnecessary for web-based applications.

11.6 Problems Encountered in Supporting Distance Learner Use of Notes

Lancaster's distance-run courses have shifted over time from predominantly using Lotus Notes clients to a preference for web clients. There are a number of reasons for this. On occasion, users have found installation and set up of dedicated Notes client software problematic because, for example, it is against their company policy to install software not specified by a local IT department or their company firewall does not permit Notes client communication.

On the other hand, many users already use Lotus Notes in their organization and are very happy to use it for their learning activities too. For the averagely IT-literate person, often enrolled on a short-term course, the overhead of installing and learning about a full Lotus Notes client is too much. This is particularly apparent now that all of them have a web browser and can easily connect to a course web site. One major virtue of the Notes client, namely the ability to work while disconnected, is becoming available to web browsers too. This is a very recent development and so far we have not made the facility available to staff or students.

Earlier problems such as unreadable floppy discs and unrecognized modem types have largely disappeared because virtually everyone now has a CD drive and working internet connection. The need for supporting documentation is also greatly reduced when using web clients instead of Notes clients, although the impact of Domino offline services (DOLS) on the documentation has yet to be assessed.

11.6.1 Replication

Perhaps one of the main difficulties distance learners experience with the Notes client is the concept of *replication*. This is where an identical copy of a database, held on the Notes server, is made on a learner's own machine. A learner can then work on the database locally, *i.e.*, without incurring any network connection charges, an important consideration for distance learners.

After this initial copy is made, the learner must regularly update the server copy (replicate with it) to register comments they have made and 'collect' any comments that have been made by others.

Since the on- and offline working environments in Notes are so similar, learners sometimes forget to replicate and wonder why things are so quiet. The importance of regular replication is stressed in the supporting documentation and demonstration and practice of the process at residential workshops reduces the problem.

Lancaster's Notes servers are available to remote Notes client users by one dedicated direct-dial modem and by the Internet. Lancaster University provides a dialup internet access service and only a few off-campus users still connect to Notes by direct dialup.

Typical remote connections average only 3 to 4 minutes. Connections are short because of Notes' built-in offline working environment and replication capability. Users can schedule replication to occur during quiet periods (typically at night) or click a button to begin an *ad hoc* replication whenever they choose. In both cases, their Notes client automatically connects to their server, exchanges changes and disconnects. People need to work online only briefly when initiating the first replication of a conference.

11.6.2 The Groupware Mindset

Another conceptual hiccup tends to be a result of the need to encourage people away from an email-centric view of the world and towards a groupware mindset. Since many users are familiar with email, they expect conferences to be an extension of that, which, of course, in some ways they are.

The main difference is to ensure people understand that everyone with access to a discussion space can read what is written, even if they are not writing anything.

There have been instances of personal messages being placed in a public discussion space because the person had forgotten that this was not private email.

11.6.3 Hardware

Notes release 5 is available as a dedicated client application for Windows NT/95/98 and Mac Power PC with OS/9. The design client is available only for Windows. There is a dedicated administration application for Windows clients and, in any case, any Domino server can be administered from a web client.

The Domino server is currently available for Windows (NT2000, NT4, 98, 95, NT Alpha), Solaris 2.6 Intel & SPARC, OS/2, Linux (Intel: Caldera, Red Hat, SuSE, Turbolinux), IBM (AIX, AS/400, S/390) and HP-UX.

The Notes release 5 Windows NT client requires a minimum recommended specification of a Pentium compatible processor, 32Mb RAM and 112Mb of disc storage. The R5 client after release 5.03 is certified for Windows 2000.

11.6.4 Development versus Stability

The very rapid evolution of HTTP-related technology and universities' inherent interest in keeping up with developments and trends means that new ways of supporting and enhancing opportunities for collaboration are appearing all the time.

On the other hand, many of the people actually collaborating online do not always appreciate alterations to their online environment or suggestions that they upgrade or change their web browser.

This can create tension; for example, development is easier if sites are written for specific browsers, while on the other hand there may be a legal requirement (as in the UK) not to discriminate against a disabled person by :

(a)   refusing to provide or deliberately not providing a service;

(b)   offering a lower standard of service;

(c)   providing a service on worse terms.

In terms of a web environment, this means ensuring that all pages are available and usable in text-only mode. Use of image-maps, Javascript and even HTML tables in web pages can make them difficult or impossible for sight-impaired people to use with screen-reading software.

Using a database-driven web system like Domino means that content can more easily be served in whatever form the user requires and that new facilities can be added to the site simply by changing the database design and without any need to alter site content.

11.7 Advantages of Using Notes to Support Learners

A touchstone of Lancaster University's learning technology strategy is the use of IT to support collaborative learning. As such the choice of a robust, flexible collaboration system is an essential element in implementing that strategy. Initially, consultation with the user-base was undertaken to form evaluation criteria to apply to the various conference systems on offer at that time (early 1995) and an extensive review of these systems was then undertaken against criteria generated by the user community consultation. Another review is currently underway, this time including an evaluation of some web-accessible Managed Learning Environments that did not exist in 1995.

The potential advantages of using Notes were identified and implementation in various scenarios has shown that these have been realized in practice (since 1995). Advantages as far as *distance learners* are concerned are the integrated support for offline working; the ability to share documents electronically; and the multiple media possibilities that Notes supports, for example, sound files, graphics, and video clips. Developments such as Domino's very effective use of the Web, have merely served to support the original decision.

Currently, in our opinion, some of the main strengths of Domino to support collaborative learning and research are:

the support it offers for offline working;

the excellent web development tools including fully integrated server-side programming, XML, Java, Javascript, C, C++, Visual Basic *etc.*;

the integration with mail systems, Domino is an SMTP server, supporting IMAP, POP3 and Notes mail clients;

the secure and fine-grained access control to web sites with support for NT and LDAP authentication;

the flexibility to support many different forms of collaboration (not just discussions);

the potential for adaptation for specific requirements, *e.g.*, in research and administration projects;

the extensibility through the API, integrated development environment and companion products;

the potential to integrate other sources of data, *e.g.*, institutional data systems and ERP systems utilization of standard backup (*e.g.*, ArcServe, Legato) and anti-virus tools (*e.g.*, Norton).

References

1.　　Lotus Corporation, URL: www.lotus.com

2. Steeples, C. (1995), Models for CMC participation, *CMC in HE Newsletter*, 2, C SALT publication, Lancaster University, UK.

3. Davies, D. (1991), Learning network design: Coordinating group interactions in formal learning environments over time and distance, in O'Malley, C. (Ed.), *Computer Supported Collaborative Learning*, NATO ASI series, Berlin, Springer-Verlag.

4. Paulsen, M. (1995), The On-line Report on Pedagogical Techniques for Computer-Mediated Communication, URL: www.nki.no/~morten

5. MA in Management Learning, URL: www.lums.lancs.ac.uk/MANLEARN/maml.htm

6. Advanced Learning Technology Programme, URL: csalt.lancs.ac.uk/alt/

7. Goodyear, P. (1994), Telematics, flexible and distance learning in postgraduate education: The MSc in Information Technology and Learning at Lancaster Universit', *The CTISS File*, 17.

8. Bloxham, S.M., (1998), Common Law I: WWW-based Negotiation Exercises, paper given at the CTI Law Seminar, Using the Internet to Teach Law, Warwick, URL: www.law.warwick.ac.uk/seminars/98-2-sb.html

9. Jones, C., Bloxham, S. & Asensio, M. (2000), Evaluating Student Experiences of an On-Campus Networked Learning Environment, presented at ALT-C 2000, Manchester, URL: www.umist.ac.uk/isd/lwt/altc/presentations/P013.rtf

10. Lewis, R. and Collis, B. (1995). Virtual mobility in distributed laboratories: Supporting collaborative research with knowledge technology. In Collis, B. and Davies, G. (Eds.), *Innovative Adult Learning with Innovative Technologies*, Amsterdam: Elsevier Science, 163-173.

11. The Interculture Project, URL: www.lancs.ac.uk/users/interculture/

12. Pasold International Directory of Textile Historians, URL: domino.lancs.ac.uk/public/pasold.nsf, maintained by The PASOLD Research fund, URL: www.lums.lancs.ac.uk/pasold/

13. Public Health Unit, URL: www.lancs.ac.uk/users/phdu/index.htm

14. Higher Education Development Centre website, Lancaster University, URL: domino.lancs.ac.uk/hedc/hedc.nsf

15. Lancaster University News, URL: domino.lancs.ac.uk/info/lunews.nsf

16. FOCUS: Learning and Teaching using the Web, URL: www.focus.ac.uk

17. Wells, R. (1993), Computer-Mediated Communication for Distance Education: An International Review of Design, Teaching and Institutional Issues, Research Monograph No. 6, American Centre for the Study of Distance Education, College of Education, The Pennsylvania State University, USA.

18. McConnell, D. (1994), Implementing Computer Supported Cooperative Learning, London, Kogan Page.

19. Hiltz, S.R. (1993), Correlates of learning in a virtual classroom. *International Journal of Man-Machine Studies,* 39, 71-98.

20. Perkins, J. (1995), E-Discourse in Education, paper presented at the World Conference on Computers in Education, Birmingham, 24-28th July, available from perkins@fhs.mcmaster.ca

21. Eastmond, D. (1992), Effective facilitation of computer conferencing. *Continuing Higher Education Review*, 56: 1-2, 23-34.

22. Bloxham, S and Armitage, S (1999), The virtual lawyer partnership, in Rothery, A. and Jenkins, M. (Eds), *Supporting Learning and Teaching Through Collaboration*, 5-10, Oxford: UCISA TLIG publication. URL: www.ucisa.ac.uk/tlig/

23. Goodyear, P. *et.al.*, (2001), Effective Networked Learning in Higher Education: Notes and Guidelines, URL: csalt.lancs.ac.uk/jisc/

Chapter 12

Quality of Use of Multimedia Learning Systems: Practical Considerations

J. Kirakowski

This is a practically-orientated chapter which outlines an approach for engineering the quality of use of multimedia learning systems, following the International Standards Organization DIS 13 407 standard. It demonstrates the applicability of the standard to multimedia learning systems and gives references to sourcebooks of information on methods and procedures for carrying this out in practice. A case study from an anonymous source is given, showing how some of these principles were effectively integrated into a product development after development had started.

12.1 Introduction

There are at least two senses in which a learning system may be evaluated: one may evaluate it for content, and the effectiveness of the application as a way of approaching the content *(learning effectiveness)*; and one may evaluate it for the ease with which it may be used *(quality of use)*. Good learning systems strive for *transparency*: that is, the learner is unaware of the application as such, and engages fully in exploration of the subject matter. For the learner, the application *is* the subject matter. Thus improving the *quality of use* will have a positive, beneficial effect on *learning effectiveness*. This chapter outlines some practical considerations for developing multimedia learning systems for which quality of use is an important end goal.

12.2 Learning Effectiveness versus Quality of Use

This chapter has little to say about the evaluation of the *learning effectiveness* of an application as this is clearly bound up with subject matter and the teaching goals of the application. Although good, conscientious teachers are used to checking routinely on the progress of their students, strangely enough, when they enter the world of multimedia, some seem to relinquish responsibility for the learning process and stop measuring student progress or even end-testing the outcomes of the process. The multimedia process becomes an end in itself. This is a state of mind that should be avoided. It is not enough to include self-tests to be carried out during the course of interaction with the system: there should also be some assessment of how well the system facilitates the learner for applying or using the knowledge gained in the real world.

All too often, when organizations report savings resulting from the introduction of multimedia training they mean savings in the cost of staff, hours lost during work, time spent in travel, and so on. The amount of learning retained should also be entered into the cost equation as should on-the-job performance if this is relevant.

Evaluating the teaching application from the point of view of *quality of use* raises a completely different set of issues and should to some extent at least be considered independently of the content and other pedagogic considerations.

Quality of use evaluation when carried out at the end of the development process is of limited use unless the developers have the intention of creating an update soon. Thus evaluation, or *user-based validation*, should be built in to all the stages of the design process, from the first prototypes till the pre-release stage. The forthcoming ISO 13 407 standard provides a framework for user-centered development activities that can be adapted to numerous development environments: from a straight *waterfall* type of development process (all too often the case when deadline pressures constrain the scope of development activities) to an iterative type of environment.

The ISO 13 407 standard as it is presented concentrates on the *process* of development. Two recently completed projects part-sponsored by the European Commission have produced sourcebooks of *methods* that can be used to implement the standard: the INUSE and RESPECT projects. These projects were concerned with gathering, testing, and promoting best practice methods for user-based evaluation, and user-based requirements elicitation and representation. Reference will be made to methods summarized and collected by these projects: Section 12.4 at the end of this chapter gives information about how these sourcebooks may be obtained.

12.3 Engineering Quality of Use Following ISO 13 407

In the past, statements about the adoption of *user centered design* tended to be strong on general philosophical orientations, but weak on guidance as to how these orientations should be implemented in the design process. This section outlines the model proposed by the draft standard in overview, adding comments and glosses in order to bring out the relevance of this model to the usability engineering of multimedia learning systems.

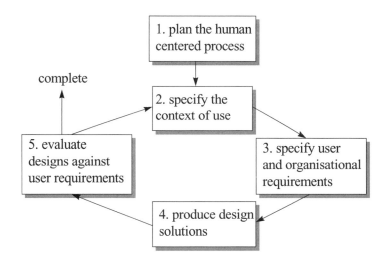

Figure 12.1. ISO 13 407 model.

The model comprises of five stages, four of which are implicitly joined in a loop. This section will examine each stage in turn. Although the process outlined above looks iterative, it need certainly not be so: it may be converted to a waterfall life cycle model if required by simply going through once only (in this case, there is simply more focus on user needs and user evaluation than one would normally expect to find in a conventional system development) or a V-type life cycle development (in which the evaluation phase is seen as signing off the specification phase). However, the true benefit of this model emerges when it is used to guide an iterative development process.

12.3.1 Plan the Human Centered Process

This first stage requires the gathering of the commitment of all concerned in the development process to the user-centered design philosophy, and to create a plan whereby there is ample time and opportunity for engaging in user requirements elicitation and testing as well as the more technical aspects of development.

The necessary side-effect of this first step should be to gain consensus among the design team that user involvement in the project is not simply at the end, that is, to "baptize" the result with "usability evaluation". A *Validation Plan* is the outcome of this first stage. Such a plan specifies how many iterations will be carried out and time-lines for each. However, this plan should also list the success criteria to be reached at each stage and the methods to be adopted to attain these criteria and to check that the criteria have been reached. The BASELINE project (see Section 12.4) proposed and tested a *User-Based Validation Assistant* which is a large pro-forma that enables an organization to manage these concerns. Although the BASELINE *User-Based Validation Assistant* was designed explicitly for use in projects involved in the Information Engineering domain of the EC's Telematics Application Programme it is orientated towards industrial usage outside of this programme, in line with the general objectives of the EC's Telematics Applications Programme as a whole.

Although the Validation Plan may appear to be outside the loop, in practice, the first draft will never be the last: it is more often a working document which is first produced in outline terms and then reviewed, maintained, extended and updated during the design and development process.

12.3.2 Specify the Context of Use

The quality of use of a system depends on understanding and planning for the characteristics of the users, tasks and the organizational and physical environment in which the system will be used. It is important to understand and identify the details of this context in order to guide early design decisions, and to provide a basis for specifying the context in which usability should be evaluated. Laboratory evaluations of the system by personnel intimately acquainted with it are likely to produce user acceptance results which are misleading when the system is later rolled out in the training room.

Where an existing system is to be upgraded or enhanced, the context may already be well understood. There may be extensive results from user feedback, help desk reports and other data which will provide a basis for prioritizing user requirements for system modifications and changes. For new products or systems, it will be necessary to gather information about its context of use through interviews and meetings with project stakeholders.

The context in which the system will be used should be identified in terms of:

- **The Characteristics of the Intended Users.** Of greatest relevance to the development of training systems is the realization that there is usually more than one type of user. The learner, or the end user, is simply one potential user among many. Consideration should also be given to the *rôle* of:

  - trainers;

  - managers of the learning process;

  - purchasers;

  - support technical staff;

  - knowledge providers;

  - evaluators.

- **The Tasks the Users will Perform.** Clearly, the major goal of the learner is to acquire knowledge with the assistance of the system. A hierarchical breakdown of this global task is likely to be similar to the map of the learning domain to be covered. However, once the other kinds of users of the system are defined, it will be seen that they may have goals quite different from learning objectives alone, and the goals of these latter groups may well be phrased in standard task-description terminology. This kind of description should include the overall goals of use of the system for this category of user, as well as the characteristics of tasks which may influence usability in typical scenarios, *e.g.*, the frequency and the duration of performance. The description should include the allocation of activities and operational steps between the human and technological resources. Tasks should not be described solely in terms of the functions or features provided by a product or system.

- **The Environment in which the Users will Use the System.** With the availability of multimedia workstations of widely differing capabilities the design team faces an unenviable task: that of designing for run-time environments which may differ radically in unpredictable ways. In addition, delivery mechanisms (the Web, LAN, CD-ROM, or a combination of all of these) make the task of settling on one kind of technical environment even more complicated. It is, nevertheless, important at this early stage to set down some markers as to what the minimal as well as the optimal system requirements should be, with the intention to user-test in these environments before release. Relevant characteristics of the physical and social environment also need to be considered. Although an office environment may well be a standard to which the design is addressed, the legislative environment (*e.g.*, laws, ordinances, directives and standards) and the social and cultural environment (*e.g.*, work practices, organizational structure and attitudes) have also to be considered. Different parts of Europe have widely-differing expectations of the style of presentation that is expected; much more so different continents (*c.f.* for instance the difference between the degree of formality expected in the USA and that expected in, say, Germany or Sweden).

There are different methods which can be used for collecting information about the context of use. In the first instance it will usually be necessary to gather together a group of *stakeholders* in the product (such as the project manager, a developer, a marketing specialist, a representative of at least some of the various types of users specified earlier and a usability expert) to discuss and agree the details of the intended context of use. Where more detailed information is required, it may be necessary to conduct a task analyzis which yields a systematic description of user activities.

The output from this activity may be summarized in a *Context of Use Description* which describes the relevant characteristics of the users, tasks and environment and identifies what aspects have an important impact on the system design. This too is unlikely to be a single document which is issued once. Some guidance on a well-tried method of context of use analyzis will be given at the end of this chapter.

12.3.3 Specify the User and Organizational Requirements

In most design processes, there is a major activity in which the functional requirements for the product or system are specified. For user centered design, it is essential to extend this to create an explicit statement of user and organizational requirements, in relation to the context of use description, in terms of:

- the quality of the human computer interface and workstation design;

- the quality and content of the tasks of the identified users (including the allocation of tasks between different categories of users for instance), should learners be responsible for configuring optimal performance of the system as is the case in many home-based applications; as well as users' comfort, safety, health and especially motivation;

- effective task performance especially in terms of the transparency of the application to the learner;

- effective cooperation and communication between different categories of users and other relevant parties;

- the required performance of the new system against operational and financial objectives.

From this, usability criteria will be derived and objectives set with appropriate trade-offs identified between the different requirements. These requirements should be stated in terms which permit subsequent testing. In particular, the following objectives should be considered for each class of user, following the ISO 9241 part 11 model:

- **Efficiency:** criteria whereby the attainment of a minimum level of effective performance may be determined (*e.g.*, if it is envisaged that the application will be set up on clients' LAN systems, it must be possible for a reasonably competent operator to set up the system on their company's LAN within a certain stated expenditure of resources).

- **Effectiveness:** criteria whereby the success or failure of task performance may be determined (*e.g.*, regardless of whether a learner has achieved the educational objectives, it must be possible to state whether a learner has completed each module of a multi-part system and not left parts of the module incomplete because it was difficult to gain access to them).

- **Satisfaction:** criteria by which the users may be judged to have interacted with the system to their internal degree of sufficiency: subjective ratings are frequently employed here, although few rating scales demonstrate enough internal consistency and validity to be of any practical use.

Usability objectives should be set for all of the major areas of user performance and acceptance. These agreed objectives should be set out in a *Specification of User and Organizational Requirements document.*

Requirements elicitation and analyzis is widely accepted as the most crucial part of software development. Indeed, the success of the user-centered approach largely depends on how well this activity is done.

12.3.4 Produce Design Solutions

The next stage is to create potential design solutions by drawing on the established state-of-the-art and the experience and knowledge of the participants. The process therefore involves:

- using existing knowledge (standards, guidelines *etc.*) to develop a proposed design solution;

- making the design solution more concrete (using simulations, paper prototypes, mock-ups *etc.*);

- showing the prototypes to users and observing them as they perform specified tasks, with or without the assistance of evaluators;

- using this feedback to improve the design;

- iterating this process until design objectives (including usability objectives) are met.

The level of fidelity of prototype and the required amount of iteration will vary depending on several factors, including the importance attached to optimizing the design. In some developments, prototyping may start with paper visualizations of screen designs and progress through several stages of iteration to interactive software demonstrations with limited real-life functionality. Later in the design, prototypes can be evaluated in a more realistic context. When trying to improve a prototype to meet design objectives such as usability, cooperative evaluation can be valuable, where an evaluator sits through a session with a user and discusses problems with the user as they occur. To obtain the maximum benefits, it is best to carry out such evaluations in several iterations with a few users, rather than fewer iterations with more users. At this stage, the emphasis is on qualitative feedback to the design. Expert-based evaluation is also useful, so long as the experts are experts in the domain of the application, rather than technical design and multimedia experts.

Even if a straight "waterfall" model is adopted (usually for reasons of time pressure) this stage simply begs for a number of small and fast iterations within the larger process. The greater the amount of confidence that user goals are being achieved with the prototypes, the more confidence there will be that the following stage of *evaluating designs against user requirements* will pass smoothly. Some guidance on user-based requirements techniques will be given at the end of this chapter.

One of the major problems in user-based work is to check the developing set of requirements against the experience and work practices of real end users. A set of technical requirements documents is not an adequate representation for most end users who will usually be unfamiliar with the methods and terminologies adopted. End users can appreciate a mock-up, paper prototype, or storyboard, and can usually give meaningful feedback in reaction to such an *instantiated* statement of requirements. This has led in some companies to an inevitable blending of the stage summarized in this section (12.2.4) with the preceeding one (summarized in Section 12.2.3). The degree to which this is desirable or possible depends on two factors: firstly, the work practices of the organization carrying out the development, and secondly, the size and scope of the project. Small, relatively informal projects can blend these two stages to advantage; a large project in a formal development environment will, of necessity, see these stages as separate processes.

12.3.5 Evaluate Designs Against User Requirements

Evaluation is an essential activity in user-centered design. Evaluation can be used in at least two ways:

- **Formative:** to provide feedback which can be used to improve design.

- **Summative:** to assess whether user and organizational objectives have been achieved.

Whatever kind of evaluation is used, it is important to understand that evaluation results are only as meaningful as the context in which the system has been tested. If the system is tested only in unrealistic environments, with access to fast machines for instance, by users for whom tasks are specified 'by rote' in cookbook style, then the results are likely to be highly misleading when compared to realistic usage. In general, the following concept should be carefully considered:

$$\text{context of evaluation} \cong \text{context of use}$$

If an iterative process is used, then early in design the emphasis will be on obtaining feedback (typically consisting of a list of usability defects) which can be used to improve the design, while later, when a realistic prototype is available, it will be possible to measure whether user and organizational objectives have been achieved.

The benefits of an iterative process are that in the early stages of the development and design process, changes are relatively inexpensive. The longer the process has progressed and the more fully the system is defined, the more expensive the introduction of changes will be. Bringing user evaluation in at the end of the process may be prohibitively expensive, and ignoring the results of user trials earlier in the process is just a waste of effort.

Evaluation techniques will vary in their degree of formality, rigor, and amount of involvement from designers and users, depending on the environment in which the evaluation is conducted. The choice will be determined by financial and time constraints, the stage of the development life cycle and the nature of the system under development as well as the degree of maturity of the organization with user-centered design. Thus organizations starting on the process maturity path may well wish to use evaluation tools and techniques which do not require a massive expenditure in time spent and expertise required. In fact, for such organizations, "cheap and cheerful" methods of evaluation are strongly recommended (see Section 12.4).

All evaluations at this stage should be summarized in a *Usability Evaluation Report* which gives the reader progressively more detail as it progresses, from *"design recommendations and summary"* at the front of the report, to statistically analyzed data on which the recommendations are based at the back. All such reports should include a detailed *context of use* as well as a *context of evaluation* as appendices.

12.4 A Case Study in Quality of Use

In this section a case study will be presented. This is a fictional account based on recent experiences with two companies in Europe who sought HCI help at a fairly late stage in the process of designing a multimedia learning application. They have been merged to form a composite which we will call "Company X". However, each incident related below really did happen in one or other of the clients.

Company X had decided to produce a multimedia training package for a market which they had identified as a niche. The company is well known for its effective training courses in this market and has a good reputation for producing quality multimedia products for other niche international markets. The current project was the first time in which these two strands of the company's expertise had been drawn together.

By the time the HCI expert had been called in, the company had produced a machine prototype in which some of the modules were finished to a high degree of detail, while others were present mainly as place markers. The overall system structure was well defined and implemented, and some parts, especially the opening screen sequences, looked very impressive. The system at this stage seemed to run fairly well without falling over so long as the end user stayed within the modules that were complete.

The company asked for help with a user-based evaluation. A series of tasks was drawn up, and a set of target learner users was recruited from a relevant postgraduate programme leading to a professional qualification in a nearby university. Users took approximately 30 minutes to carry out the required tasks, and they evaluated the software for satisfaction with the aid of a standardized user-perceived quality questionnaire, which was deemed suitable as it yielded not only a quantitative score but also opportunity for more specific user comments (satisfaction measure and user-elicited diagnoses). Some reservations were expressed that the version that would be user-tested was a prototype, and that it would be implicitly compared against completed market products in the standardisation database of the questionnaire. A record was also made of the number of steps in each task which had been achieved to pre-set criteria (effectiveness measure).

The results came as somewhat of a surprise for Company X who until then had felt fairly optimistic about progress and results. Overall satisfaction ratings were extremely low, and some tasks could not be finished without the explicit intervention of the evaluators. However, as the evaluation was starting up, company stakeholders had been drawn together in a context of use meeting, and it transpired from this meeting that a number of important issues about focusing the application development had been completely ignored: for instance, the optimal hardware platform; what users within the niche market were to be the primary targets (*e.g.*, trainers or learners); and the size of company at which the application was addressed, since there was a considerable difference in emphasis between small-SMEs and medium-SMEs in the way the issues should be covered.

In setting up the criteria for the successful completion of tasks, it also became clear that some sequences in the application were seemingly without a place in the overall structure of system objectives: they had been included because it was felt that they were a good idea and there was technological support for implementing them in the authoring package.

During the *post-mortem* after the evaluation, it was decided that perhaps too much time had been spent on trivial components of the system, such as graphics and animation sequences, and too little time had been devoted to the overall system focus and concepts.

At this stage, all the technical personnel associated with the product were put to work on another project for the meantime, and a month was spent on doing a "concept wall", a paper prototype, and later a series of storyboards.

When the low-level prototypes had been developed sufficiently to demonstrate an overall system concept and an effective coherence, the technical staff were put back in the project. A lot of low level code was reusable, and experience gained in the authoring package was invaluable. However, the appearance of the total system was radically changed, and work to the next prototype proceeded rapidly.

The moment at which the HCI evaluator had been called in, although late, was sufficiently timely to enable revision without a critical loss of development effort. The slippage in schedule was nevertheless considerable, and could have been avoided had the company decided to adopt a more user-centric design philosophy from the start.

12.5 A Guide to Available Tools and Methods

The BASELINE project IE 2013 is most easily accessed through the project web site at http://www.ucc.ie/hfrg/baseline. Several public-domain collections of documents are present on this web site in a form suitable for downloading via FTP, including the user-based validation assistant mentioned in Section 12.2.

A description of the context analyzis process is contained in *"Usability Context Analyzis: A Practical Guide"*, available from the National Physical Laboratory Usability Services, National Physical Laboratory, Teddington, Middlesex, TW11 0LW, England. This guide is particularly useful in that it has stood the test of numerous applications in commercial software environments.

The *"Handbook of User-Centered Design"* (current version 1.1 as of July, 1997) was produced by members of the European Usability Support Centers network, as part of the EC-funded INUSE Project IE 2016, and is also available from the above address at the National Physical Laboratory. This handbook gives sources and some commentary on a wide variety of usability evaluation techniques, all of which have satisfied the criterion of evidence of successful use in commercial environments. See the INUSE project web site at http://www.npl.co.uk/inuse.

A particular technique mentioned in this chapter is the *"Software Usability Measurement Inventory"* which is, at the time of writing, the only internationally standardised and validated usability questionnaire, available in a variety of languages and supported by an extensive normative database. It has been used to evaluate a number of learning systems for user perceived quality of use. It is available from the Human Factors Research Group, University College Cork, Cork, Ireland, and details can be found at:

> http://www.ucc.ie/hfrg/questionnaires/sumi.

The reader may also wish to look at other questionnaires produced by this group of relevance to the present chapter pointed to by the "questionnaires" web page.

The *"RESPECT User-Requirements Framework Handbook"* (preliminary version 2.2 for feedback, as of April, 1997) was produced by members of the European

Usability Support Centers network, as part of the EC-funded RESPECT Project TE 2010. It presents a framework for user requirements engineering within a user-centered design methodology such as that suggested by ISO 13 407, and it references a number of user requirements and prototyping techniques which have been well validated in industrial use. The handbook is available from the HUSAT Research Institute, The Elms, Elms Grove, Loughborough, Leicester LE11 1RG, England. Documents from this project are available from the project web site at http://www.npl.co.uk/respect. A collection of methods for user-based requirements engineering is publicly available at:

>   http://www.ucc.ie/hfrg/projects/respect/urmethods.

Published standards and Draft International Standards (DIS) can be obtained from the Inernational Standards Organization in Geneva, Switzerland. Committee Drafts (CD) circulated for national vote are difficult to obtain. Until this situation changes, copies for review purposes may be obtained from your national ISO contact point: for more information, contact the National Physical Laboratory at the address given above.

References

Mention has been made in this chapter of two ISO/DIS standards. They are:

ISO/DIS 9241-11: Guidance on Usability (ISO, 1997)

ISO/DIS 13 407: Human-Centered Design Processes for Interactive Systems (ISO, 1997).

Chapter 13

Design for Motivation

Kristina Edström

Motivation is maybe the most important factor for learning. When we manage to connect to students' motivation, their energy will work with the learning, instead of against it. In flexible courses, where students study more independently than in traditional courses, we need to give extra attention to how to stimulate and keep students' motivation.

So how can we create motivation in flexible courses? Think of motivation as the yeast in the dough. It has to be inherent, built into the structure of the course already when it is designed. Giving a sermon on the first meeting about why this subject is important - always in some distant future - can be as meaningless as throwing a cake of yeast into the oven when the bread is already baking.

In this chapter we present a checklist that we use with respect to considering student motivation during the design or analyzis phases of course preparation and delivery.

13.1 Are Objectives Clear and Meaningful?

What are the objectives of the course? Clear course objectives are a way to establish a firm foundation, to ourselves, to the course team and to the students. They will also help us describe the course to prospective students, to university management and to other colleagues. The success of a course depends on all these parties. Your chances of success will increase if you make it easy for all the involved parties to understand exactly what you intend to achieve.

Clear objectives will help us create a situation where students

a.   understand the objectives;

b.   see how the work in this course will help them reach the objectives;

c.   see how the assessment will show if the objectives have been attained;

d.   envision in what ways the course will increase their competence;

e.   know how this course is relevant to their overall career.

When this has been established, students will be motivated by knowing that the work in the course is worthwhile.

It takes some practice to write good objectives. First of all, it is important to think in terms of students' learning. We often see objectives formulated in terms of teaching activities: "The objective of the course is to present an ASIC design methodology…", but the problem is that teachers can achieve this objective even if students don't learn a thing from it. It is the wrong focus. Teaching is not our end product, learning is.

Formulate objectives as the intended learning outcomes, *what students are able to perform as a result of the learning experience* [1]. When we concentrate on the outcomes, it becomes much easier to assess whether students have fulfilled the objectives. State what performance you are willing to accept as evidence that the student has reached the objectives. Be realistic and concrete, because you will discuss the objectives many times.

If we have the advantageous situation that programme-level objectives have been formulated, we break these down to course level. Include both content specific and generic capabilities, such as teamworking and communication skills.

Map your course objectives against a taxonomy of learning objectives, such as Bloom's, or whichever taxonomy you prefer, *e.g.*, [2].

Learning as…

a.   …increasing your knowledge;

b.   …memorizing and reproducing;

c.   …applying;

d.   …understanding;

e.   …viewing things differently;

f.   …changing as a person.

Is there a sound balance between the different levels of objectives in the course, or do they belong mostly in the lower levels?

The objectives may not be perfect the first time you write them, but be prepared to develop and adjust the objectives over the lifetime of the course.

13.2 Is Assessment Relevant?

Objectives and assessment must be in harmony with each other. Make sure that assessment measures the student's fulfillment of the objectives, and only that. We need to analyze our courses and weed out any inconsistencies because what happens when we examine things other than the objectives? We know that assessment is the overriding interpretation of the objectives [3]. So if we measure things other than the objectives, the result is that *we don't allow students to work towards the objectives.*

It is a common mistake to over-emphasize assessment of lower level knowledge, such as recall of factual knowledge, at the expense of more complex learning outcomes. Why do we do this? Because we prefer assignments that are easy and economic to handle, instead of those which would truly show if the student has reached the objectives. We measure mostly lower level objectives, because it is easier to judge and mark reproduction than analyzis, synthesis, and evaluation. Sometimes we oversimplify because we are constrained by computer systems for assessment but since assessment is the most important instrument we have to influence students' behavior, we must give it the attention and resources it deserves.

Use the fact that students act rationally and prioritize the exam, by designing assessments that will drive them in exactly the right direction.

Assessment is often, purely out of habit, regarded as a control function, and as such a private matter between the individual student and the teacher. Instead, bring assessment into the light and make it a valuable learning experience in its own right.

Assessment can create motivation in itself, especially when it's done continually throughout the course. Think in terms of authentic assessment, having to perform something "for real". Give them opportunities to use the theories rather than memorizing and repeating them. Let them generate authentic deliverables, expert reports, newspaper articles, prototypes, business plans, video clips, poster presentations, answers to referrals, *etc*. Tell students upfront how deliverables will be judged. What qualities in the deliverables are you prepared to accept as evidence that the students have reached the objectives?

Most students know that deliverables go straight into the waste-paper basket after a course is finished; they know that the most important outcome is what they learn on the way but they are still excited about their task, sometimes to the point of getting carried away. It is just like the magic that grips you when you are running after a ball in an exciting game, instead of just running. Try to design assessment formats that excite the students - give them balls to chase.

13.3 Are Learning Activities Student-Centered?

The main outcome of a learning activity is what happens inside the learner, not the performance given by the teacher. Thus being a good teacher means designing learning activities which result in students reaching the intended learning outcomes [4]. Think of designing learning activities not as singing yourself, but rather as arranging a sing-song. Why? Remember that the main outcome is not the quality of the performance, but what happens inside the audience, and sing-song will excite the audience better than (most) performances do.

Shifting the focus away from yourself doesn't mean to shirk responsibility to structure meaningful activities, in the sense that they help students reach the intended learning outcomes.

Focusing on how students spend their time and energy in the course is also productive, because the students spend much more time working in the course than the teacher does. Do a simple calculation of the total sum of student hours that will be spent in the course. This is the time and energy you have in your hand. Your challenge is to design the structure in which all these hours will be used effectively.

It is especially important to take a student-centered approach in distance courses. Very much of what is being done online today actually attempts to package or industrialize a teaching (broadcast) model, according to which the teacher knows everything and teaches it by telling the students. "Since it is not a dialogue anyway, we might as well film the lectures and broadcast them." But just dumping materials onto the students is not efficient, either online or in classrooms.

Inventing student-centered learning activities in flexible courses requires some imagination. Give them meaningful tasks that feel natural to do. Often distance students need extra help to structure their studies and to overcome their natural resistance to get going. They need clear instructions about what to do, and a schedule with regular deadlines.

13.4 Do We Form a Learning Community?

There are several reasons for creating a learning community in flexible courses. One is because people will achieve better when they feel that others are present [5]. When we ask students to publish their assignments on the course homepage for everyone to read and comment on, they will be of a higher quality than if the papers were just to be emailed to the professor. An unexpected advantage with public publishing was that the assignments were delivered on time.

Social networks enable students to fulfill social needs among themselves. Especially in distance courses, the feeling of loneliness is a threat to learning. We run the risk of creating a situation where all students turn to the teacher for acknowledgement, sympathy and friendship. To the teacher, this can be like a nest full of young birds with open beaks, incessantly screaming for more. This is not an efficient way to use the teacher's time and energy, but an easy way to burn out teachers. Instead, make sure that students will take care of the basic social community among themselves.

We want to encourage peer learning. When one student learns from another, that student is helped, and the student who did the teaching learned even more from having to externalize his or her knowledge. Especially in continuing education, we have designed courses that are really built on course participants' collected knowledge and experience. Our challenge was to create a course interesting enough to attract the right course participants, who then create much value among themselves in their community through the structure of the course.

A well functioning learning community can take some of the workload off the teacher. One example is feedback on assignments. Much of the need for feedback stems from a need to be seen. Arrange for students to comment on each other's assignments before the teacher adds what is necessary.

I also think that deep learning requires much personal interaction – online and in real life. This enables students to reach the highest of the learning objectives, those that contain elements of developing a professional competence. Students need to be exposed to the ideas and to try them on, in interaction with teachers and peers.

So how can we form a learning community in a distance course, where social networks do not form spontaneously? Let all students introduce themselves on the course homepage, including images. This makes it easy to check classmates' names, background and interests. Include meetings with small group activities and plenty of breaks with room for coffee or meals. Arrange collaborative learning activities with lots of contacts between students.

Here are some of the ways in which meetings can strengthen the distance part of a course:

a. Students get to see that teacher and peers are "real" people. The online presence and the person converge, and are not regarded as different identities.

b. They help break the ice and form social networks.

c. They establish the culture; strike the tone of the course.

d. The teacher explains how the course will work, to get rid of any doubts or uncertainty.

e. Regular meetings will help set the pace of the course.

13.5 Do Online and Real-Life Activities Interplay?

Make use of the interplay between online and real-life activities. As we just saw, meetings will strengthen the online community but online activities will strengthen meetings too.

Example of a two-step learning activity:

1. Online: students study some materials and post input (such as formulate three questions, solve a problem, record their own reflections *etc.*). Input will often be better if students can read each other's postings. If you fear too much input, make them submit it as the result of a group discussion.

2. The meeting is then partially formed by the input you received.

This cycle should be repeated several times during the course, so that everyone gets used to it and can take full advantage.

What are the advantages?

a. The preparation work will help trigger students' questions, create curiosity and expectations, and set a tone for the upcoming meeting.

b. Student s' input will provide us with valuable clues to their motivation.

c. Knowing about their level of understanding makes it easier to shape the meeting to fit the students.

d. Students will come to the meeting with a higher level of understanding because they have been exposed to the topic beforehand.

However, please note that the main role of the input should *not* be to ensure that they have done the required reading.

There are more arguments for mixing online with reallife. Variation during learning prepares students for applying their knowledge in different situations. Using more than one arena for learning will allow more students to excel - at least some of the time - because the design of the discussion arena will influence who is the strongest.

We will affect the "pecking order" in the class by choosing what strengths we allow to be the ones that matter. Reallife or online? Spoken or written? Asynchronous or synchronous? Do we show images or not? A person who dominates seminars completely could be very awkward in an electronic discussion. When you change the arena, be prepared to explain your rationale to those students who feel that the change was to their disadvantage.

13.6 Is Students' Motivation Directly Addressed?

Find out about what motivates the students. Ask them. We ask participants to introduce themselves on the course web site. Some of the questions on the online form can be:

- What questions do you bring to the course?

- What do you want to be able to do after the course?

- What topics do you plan to bring up in the online discussion?

- What knowledge, experience are you prepared to share in the course?

Formulating answers to these inconspicuous questions is intended to sow a seed in the back of people's heads, and to help them identify with the task they are about to undertake.

What they really do is write and sign a personal study plan. The declarations are intended to create a culture of peer learning and to emphasize students' own responsibility for their learning. People who can make choices about what to do, will feel more committed to act according to their choices than if they had no choice. Declaring their choice in writing, and in public, creates a strong commitment to act accordingly [5]. Use the answers as clues to their motivation. We will also use the information for careful prodding of individual students when they need to be reminded.

I have already mentioned how meetings can be prepared with online input. Make sure to address the issues that motivate the students. Show students that you have listened to them and shaped the course according to their input.

13.7 Are Teachers Motivated?

One of the most important tasks for the teacher is to be a role model. It is necessary for the student to see how experts interact with the subject, how they attack problems, how they handle questions in realtime, how they discern what is relevant to an issue, *etc*. But to show contagious enthusiasm, you yourself have to be motivated as well, and it has to be real.

Courses should be designed in such a way that they are interesting to the teacher too. They should not wear teachers out, but be sustainable over many years to come. A good way to increase teachers' motivation is to work in teaching teams. Include teaching assistants, learning technology "techies", a teaching and learning expert, the course administrator, external experts, whomever you need.

Arrange for peer review of your course. Simply invite a colleague to analyze and criticize your course design, then do the same for your colleagues.

It is also stimulating to form a network with experts who are invited to do guest appearances in the course. We have often filmed interviews with experts and used short highlights in web-based course materials. This way we can tap this source repeatedly, and add one or two real-life meetings every time the course is run. We try to choose experts that make both the teacher and the students interested.

In continuing education, the teacher can enjoy learning from course participants' industrial experience, provided that the learning activities are designed for this. Another trick is to connect the course with teachers' academic research in different ways.

13.8 Are Learning Technologies Wisely Used?

Take away difficulties that come from improper use of learning technologies [6]. Do not let technology get in the way. Always keep in mind that learning technologies are a means to an end – as are indeed staff and universities. We are here to facilitate students' learning.

Learning activities should feel natural and be user-friendly, in the sense that they are designed in a way that makes it easy to do the right thing. Use what we know about human behavior. At least do not work against these forces.

Be careful with what you demand in terms of hardware, software, installing plug-ins *etc*. If you use overly complicated technology, you risk excluding students who have older computers, are behind firewalls, or are just not "high-techies". Choose the simplest technology that fulfills the task. Test it and master it, before you use it in a course.

We often hear metaphors such as "online classroom", "online lecture", or "online tutorial" but beware of packaging traditional teaching activities and putting them online. First of all, canned lectures are not the same as real lectures. Some of the strengths with lectures are weakened or completely lost. You cannot start a dialogue with a video clip. The lecture setting forces you to allocate the next two hours to the course, while watching a filmed lecture easily allows your mind to wander. We may not even know about all the advantages we loose if we build an artificial world – like the whispering in the benches or the chatting in the aisles and in the cafeteria, how somebody frowning makes the teacher explain again from a different angle, the sense of community in a classroom, *etc*.

Using an old metaphor can restrain us from taking full advantage of learning technologies but maybe the worst disadvantage is that we bring with us the limitations from the old world into the new medium. Old world limitations are such as these: teaching is deemed to consist of one expert talking for twenty hours; lecture halls are designed for one-way communication; we can only book two-hour slots; we do not have fifty group rooms near-by, *etc*. Why take these limitations with us into a new setting that has none of these limitations built into it? Learning technologies have other inherent limitations that we have to consider carefully, but not these.

13.9 Are Challenges Big Enough and Worthwhile?

When our task is too easy, we are bored; when it is too difficult, we give up. There has to be a balance between the challenge and our competence for meeting the challenge. Challenge the students in ways that give students the opportunity to use their full capacity. Let them feel the satisfaction of growing an inch to meet the demands of the task.

"Optimal experience usually occurs when a person's body or mind is stretched to its limits in a voluntary effort to accomplish something difficult and worthwhile. Such experiences are not necessarily pleasant at the time they occur." [7]

Give students a tough ride, but make sure that difficulties are meaningful and worthwhile. Don't "save" students from relevant hardship. The really deep learning experiences are often those that are especially tough in some way, even painful. Swedish actress Lena Endre experienced this when working with Ingmar Bergman:

"What really puts demands on you, things you have to fight for - they're all worthwhile afterwards. Even if it's hell at the time. Whereas you can barely remember something that comes to you easily." [8]

It is natural that students may need to complain about their hardship. Stay calm, and listen to them with empathy. Remind them how the challenge is relevant to the objectives. Explain that their pain is a normal symptom which occurs when they leave their comfort zone, in order to learn new things. At the end of the course, remind them about this stage. Let them tell each other how they overcame the resistance. Next time when their minds are stretched to the limit, their fear of fear itself can be reduced.

Prepare students for the real world, where there isn't always an answer, or there are many answers. Most students are used to the teacher knowing all the answers to every task they are given. When you don't have the right answers, tell students upfront. A project that does not solve the task is excellent, provided they have good arguments that there was no solution that met the demands.

Do not prevent students making mistakes, but create an allowing culture where people can learn from failure. There is much to be learned from failure, not just whatever the specific mistake illustrates, but also the generic capability to survive and learn from their experiences. A project group whose cooperation comes to a total meltdown can be a useful experience for the whole class. It can even save some from having to perform the meltdown exercise on their first job.

References

1.   Gronlund, N. E. (1999), How to Write and Use Instructional Objectives, Prentice Hall.

2.   Marton, F., Booth, S. (1997), Learning and Awareness, Lawrence Erlbaum Associates.

3.   Trowald, N. (1997), Råd och idéer för examinationen inom högskolan, Högskoleverket, National Agency for Higher Education, 1997:14 R.

4.   Barr, R. B. and Tagg, J. (1995), From teaching to learning – A new paradigm for undergraduate education, *Change*, 27(6), 13-25.

5.   Cialdini, R. B. (1993), Influence: The Psychology of Persuation, Quill.

6.   Burge, E. J. (1999), Using learning technologies: Ideas for keeping one's balance, *Educational Technology*, 39(6), 45-49.

7.   Csikszentmihalyi, M. (1991), Flow: The Psychology of Optimal Experience, Harper Perennial.

8.   Lena Endre was interviewed by Christer Olsson in Cosmorama (Scandinavian Airlines Magazine) April 2000 issue.

Chapter 14

Educational Metadata: Friendly Fire?

Rachada Monthienvichienchai, Martina Angela Sasse and Richard Wheeldon

In this chapter, we investigate the usability of educational metadata schemas with respect to the case of the MALTED (Multimedia Authoring for Language Teachers and Educational Developers) project at University College London (UCL). The aim of the project is to facilitate language learning by allowing teachers to share multimedia material for language teaching and to provide a user interface that will efficiently support retrieval and usage of this material when authoring courses or exercises. We conclude that there are serious incompatibilities between the current educational metadata schema, as promoted by the Learning Object Metadata (LOM) working group of the IEEE Learning Technologies Standardization Committee, and the way language teachers actually go about authoring teaching material. This chapter highlights such incompatibilities encountered by the project, especially those that could only be found through adopting a participatory design approach during the development of the MALTED system.

14.1 Introduction

14.1.1 Metadata

The concept of metadata was introduced to facilitate searching for items not only via the items' technical attributes but also via additional information about the items. Unlike technical information of an item, metadata is created with the aim of supporting certain user groups or tasks. For example, online bookshops often provide additional metadata on books in the form of "Customer Comments" in order to help their customers decide whether to buy the book or not. Consequently, rich metadata schema can allow sophisticated or very specific search requests to be carried out.

14.1.2 Education and Metadata

The idea of searching for educational material from external resources and reusing them is not new. Education professionals regularly use and reuse material from outside their classrooms as part of their teaching material, for example, newspapers, videos, posters and other props. Educational metadata schemata, such as that specified by the LOM working group of the IEEE Learning Technologies Standardization Committee [6], aim to help teachers find multimedia material that suits their pedagogic needs by facilitating sharing of that material among education professionals. LOM objectives go so far as to enable exercises to be generated automatically by computer agents that are given certain specific criteria. Consequently, the LOM metadata schema is extensive, with over sixty fields organized into nine categories. The schema archives a wide range of information concerning the material, ranging from the description of the material to the kind of student interactions for which the material is authored. This not only enables teachers to search for material by subject or course but also by age of student, level of competence or by the kind of interaction the teacher would like the multimedia material to use.

Other related metadata projects aim to deal with the practical problems of the scale of the LOM schema either by creating a subset schema that is compatible with the more extensive LOM schema (*e.g.*, ARIADNE [4]) or by creating an alternative lightweight schema (*e.g.*, Dublin Core Metadata Initiative [5]).

14.1.3 The MALTED Project

MALTED is a European Commission-funded project led by University College London (UCL). The aim of the project is to facilitate authoring of multimedia material for language learning. Computer-based multimedia exercises can enrich the self-study part of language learning, which requires a certain amount of drill-style practice, for several reasons:

1. By utilizing sound, video and animation, a wider range of language skills can be exercised than through paper-based exercises.

2. Computer-based exercises provide immediate feedback to the learner.

3. Well-designed multimedia material appeals to many learners and thus increases the amount of self-study.

For these reasons, many language teachers would like to utilize multimedia exercises.

Authoring effective and attractive multimedia material is, however, time-consuming and requires a level of computer skill that many teachers neither possess nor have time to acquire. Building a time-telling exercise with an animated clock and sound clips, for example, can take many hours. MALTED aims to reduce the effort required to produce effective and attractive material by allowing teachers to share multimedia material for language teaching, and offering a comparatively intuitive interface for retrieving material and composing exercises and courses from them. Video/audio clips, animations and other items are stored in a repository for reuse by other teachers. Each stored item is tagged to allow teachers to identify suitable material for a particular exercise. Without tagging, identifying suitable material would require tedious and time-consuming scanning of long lists of the repository contents. Since effective and efficient reuse of educational material is at the core of MALTED, it offered a case study of educational metadata in action.

While we will outline the technical implementation of the MALTED system (Section 14.2), the focus of this chapter will be on issues concerning usability of metadata from the point of view of language teachers at UCL who are using the MALTED system to author teaching material for their courses (Section 14.3). In particular, we will highlight serious incompatibility between the metadata schema advocated by LOM and the processes that language teachers actually employ to author teaching material (Section 14.4.1).

14.2 The MALTED System

14.2.1 System Architecture of MALTED

The MALTED system consists of three main parts: MALTED clients, MALTED assetbase and the database backend. Figure 14.1 presents a simplified system diagram of the whole MALTED system.

The client applications provide interfaces through which teachers can access and manage material or "assets" and their metadata via the MALTED assetbase, allowing them to perform tasks such as searching for and adding new assets to the backend database. Other facilities provided by the client applications include asset authoring and management. It is solely through these client applications that teachers interact with the MALTED assetbase.

The assetbase performs the standardization of metadata between the client and the database. This is accomplished by converting a database query or update requested by the client in eXtensible Markup Language (XML) into the appropriate Structured Query Language (SQL) query or update for the database and *vice versa*. A custom data dictionary – containing a mapping of XML attributes to database tables or views, with associated typing – is used together with a Document Type Definition (DTD) to enable the assetbase to store the assets and their metadata in the appropriate place on the database. This gives the advantage of flexibility as different subsets can be used for different asset types. For example, technical information such as frame rate and codec are appropriate for a video, but meaningless for a text file. The same data dictionary is used to create the XML files to return to the client following a query by extracting and combining data from multiple tables, where each XML file represents the metadata associated with a single asset.

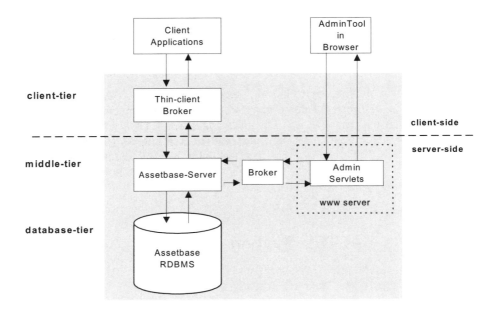

Figure 14.8. The MALTED System

A database is used to store assets and their metadata in order to optimize the speed of access for queries and to enable complex queries, which may be inefficient if carried out via XML, to be performed. While it is possible to use other database packages, the MALTED system uses Oracle, which communicates with the assetbase via JDBC (the assetbase is written in Java).

14.3 Handling Metadata in Malted

It is possible to achieve a number of LOM objectives directly through the use of metadata to tag educational material with relevant information on the material. The following LOM objectives [3] are particularly relevant when designing a system to handle metadata:

- to enable learners or instructors to search, evaluate, acquire, and utilize Learning Objects;

- to enable the sharing and exchange of Learning Objects across any technology-supported learning systems;

- to enable the development of Learning Objects in units that can be combined and decomposed in meaningful ways.

Teachers using MALTED first encounter metadata when searching for assets on assetbases and then while contributing new assets to assetbases. The MALTED project has encountered some significant usability issues concerning metadata while implementing facilities to support these two tasks. The following issues were raised during both formal and informal interviews and focus groups with users of the MALTED system.

In this section, the term "user(s)" will refer to language teacher(s) at UCL, unless explicitly stated otherwise.

14.3.1 Searching via Metadata

From the user's point of view, metadata is first encountered when searching for material on an assetbase. To support this task, MALTED provides a search dialogue in which the user specifies what to search for and in which metadata field. At this stage, a large number of fields in the metadata schema is very useful to the user as a large number of fields allows the user to specify search criteria very precisely. For example, the user can search for assets for French language teaching at first year undergraduate level with multiple-choice questions as the interaction type for students whose mother tongue is not French. Even fields that have little or no pedagogic value can be of some use for the user – the fields for file size and format can be of use if the user is concerned with download time or compatibility issues.

After a search request has been submitted, the search result is then displayed to the user showing information about the assets structured by the metadata schema. Again, the fields in the metadata schema are useful for the user as the schema gives structure to the information on the material. However, if too many fields are displayed to the user at the same time, some of the information given may be irrelevant and, if there are a large number of irrelevant fields, the user may experience information overload.

14.3.2 Tagging Material with Metadata

The rich and extensive metadata schema that helps the user search for and view asset information causes significant overhead for the user when he or she is adding new material to an assetbase. There are a significant number of usability problems concerning metadata that arise when the user performs this task.

Too many fields

The problem experienced by the user, at this particular stage, is not so much information overload, but information "over-demand". Although almost all of the fields are applicable (*i.e.*, the material does have attributes that can be categorized by the field), they may not be important. Users feel that it is not necessary to identify all possible characteristics of the material they are submitting to the assetbase, just the "relevant" or "important" ones. We found that such overhead imposed on the user could deter the user from using the system because it takes too much effort to share material. Previous research [1, 2] on the factors influencing implementation of educational technology strongly suggests that the user's perceived practicality of the system is one of the main factors affecting whether the system will be used or not. In the case of MALTED, the user was spending a lot of time filling in each field and also working out the most appropriate content of each field. MALTED users feel that this process takes far too much effort and time.

Ambiguous field names

Often the user is presented with two or more fields that, in their opinion, refer to the same attribute of the material they are trying to add. For example, users often consider the fields "Content" and "Description" to be the same. Consequently, the user finds it difficult to fill in some fields as it is felt that the information has already been entered in a previous field. As in the previous problem, the user feels that more work than necessary is being demanded of them by the system.

Irrelevant fields

Users often do not categorize their material in terms of the fields offered. This is particularly the case with users who teache modern languages. For example, if the user wants to add a picture of a cat to the assetbase, the user must specify for which language and level of competency the material should be used. While such information on an asset may be appropriate for a whole course, these fields are clearly not relevant for low-level material such as pictures. Furthermore, such material can be useful for authoring lessons or exercises for a wide range of subjects which the user did not have in mind, from modern languages to art and even physics! Consequently some fields demand information which is too specific for certain material. Ironically, highly specific tags may sometimes prevent material from being widely used, contradicting the notion that metadata was introduced to allow greater sharing and reuse of material.

14.3.3 MALTED Metadata Interface

Usability problems reported in the previous section indicate that there are some design issues that need to be addressed; particularly of concern is the design of dialogues dealing with metadata in MALTED. Some of the main issues are:

1. How to present a large number of fields without overwhelming the user?

2. How to get the user to complete the fields as quickly and accurately as possible?

3. How to reduce the number of fields to be filled in by the user?

4. How to determine which fields are relevant for certain material?

Automatic field completion

There are a number of fields that can be completed automatically by the system. These contain information that can be derived from the file system, such as file size, file format and other technical information. MALTED automatically fills these fields in for the user when the material is submitted. Additionally, if the user is adding a course to the assetbase, all the assets in that course inherit the tagging from that course.

Reduction of the number of fields

MALTED reduces the number of fields for a given piece of material by displaying only the fields that are relevant to the type of material being added. Taking an earlier example, MALTED will not prompt the user for information concerning "Frame rate" if the user is adding a text or an audio file to the assetbase. This helps to reduce the problem of having too many and/or irrelevant fields. Additionally, MALTED differentiates between mandatory fields and optional fields by hiding optional fields from the user unless the user explicitly asks to fill in those fields. Currently, the following fields are presented to the user via the search dialogue:

Quick search	Refined	Advanced
Media type	Language	File name
Asset topic	Language level	File extension
	Publisher	File size
	Word count	ID
		Color depth
		Width
		Height

Determining field relevancy

A possible counter-argument against reducing the number of fields can emerge from what has already been discussed in Section 14.3.1. Large number of fields allows the user to define a search very specifically. There will always be a case where a user might want to search for material under an obscure field, such as the "Semantic Density" or the "TaxonPath" of a material (LOM schema). These fields add to the amount of information demanded from all users while satisfying the requirements for only a minority of users. By attempting to satisfy every possible use of metadata, metadata schemas such as LOM may have made themselves unusable to small-scale or individual users.

Every usability issue so far has been dealt with by improving the design of the dialogues within the MALTED system. However, the question of determining which fields are relevant or irrelevant is not just concerned with optimizing MALTED dialogues. In order to find out which metadata are required by the user, it is vitally important to find out what the users actually want to do with the material and what they expect from a metadata schema. This is discussed in greater detail in the next section.

14.4 Discussion

While the MALTED project has not been able to solve all the usability problems concerning metadata that it has encountered, it has managed to highlight issues that require further debate and enquiry. From a broader perspective, during the development of MALTED, knowledge about what functionalities are required by language teachers when authoring electronic multimedia material has been acquired. Such insight into how teachers actually go about authoring their teaching material would not have been possible if a participatory design approach had not been adopted by the project.

This, in turn, has raised the issue of the appropriateness of educational metadata schema in relation to how language teachers actually go about creating teaching material.

14.4.1 Material Usage and Metadata

Problems discussed in Section 14.3, such as over-demand and overload of both relevant and irrelevant information about material, raise the possibility that sharing and reuse of educational material between users happens at a much lower level of granularity. In the case of MALTED, users just want to pick out elements of a course or just find a single diagram that they can use in their own question. The LOM metadata schema suggests that users would want to reuse other people's whole exercises or even courses. This raises a fundamental question concerning how teachers and lecturers go about authoring their teaching material and what kind of computer support they actually require.

Syllabus and instructional goals

The current view of the teacher's task of authoring multimedia teaching material is one of adapting an existing course created by someone else to suit an area of the syllabus that he/she is trying to cover. The LOM metadata schema codifies the course in terms of the syllabus that the course is covering. This assumes that what the teacher is trying to accomplish in class – instructional goals – is very similar to the syllabus, or at least derivable from the syllabus. Figure 14.2 shows the task diagram of the authoring task as implied by this line of thinking.

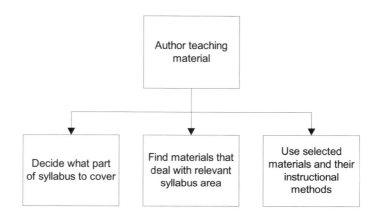

Figure 14.2. Task model as implied by LOM metadata schema.

However, in the case of language teachers (users of MALTED), the task they engage in is a very different one. Instead of finding a course or exercise that deals with a certain part of the syllabus and adapting their instructional goals to suit the course/exercise, language teachers approach material authoring from the opposite end. That is, they first form a set of instructional goals and then find material – such as pictures, audio or a particular element of an exercise (*e.g.*, time-telling elements of an exercise) but not a whole exercise or course – that can fulfil or be adapted for each individual instructional goal. The main reason for this "reversed" approach is that language teachers feel they need to know the students' abilities first before writing instructional goals that would be the road map for those students to accomplish what the syllabus has set out.

Figure 14.3 shows the task model for MALTED users when they author their teaching material. While the goal of creating teaching material by reusing previously authored material is the same in both cases, the subgoals, or how the main goal is achieved, are very different. Teachers are not looking for "ready-made" courses or exercises to use. Users of MALTED feel that it is their responsibility as teachers to identify the instructional goals for their students. Moreover, other people's exercises may cover the right part of the syllabus but not necessarily via the most appropriate instructional goals. Supporting the task model where the instructional goals are set by someone else would be a critical failure to support the correct subgoals.

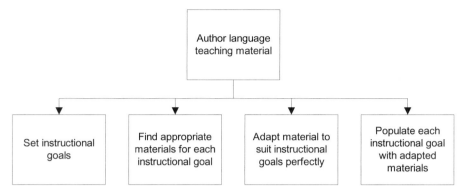

Figure 14.3 Task model for MALTED users

14.5 Conclusion

14.5.1 Technical Implementation

In the most general sense, MALTED had to tackle two main technical issues. While XML allows client applications to communicate with backend databases via the assetbase, its lack of strong typing meant that validation of certain field entries could not be achieved within XML. The second technical issue to address was concerned with using a relational database to store assets and their associated metadata, instead of storing everything in XML. The main reasons for this were: to increase the speed of access to metadata; and to allow complex queries to be performed on the metadata.

14.5.2 Metadata Schema

While it was very important to solve technical problems encountered during the implementation of MALTED, the issues of the usability of metadata management facilities in MALTED are very significant factors in determining whether the system will be used or not by the teaching profession.

While extensive metadata schema for educational material facilitates very accurate search queries, the schema has serious usability problems from the enduser's (teacher/lecturer) point of view when contributing new material to an archive. In order to use the extensive LOM metadata schema, a professional archive manager is needed to perform the tagging as the process is too time consuming for the teachers to undertake themselves.

A significant finding during the MALTED project is that language teachers reuse material at a much lower level of granularity than LOM metadata schema would suggest. Language teachers write instructional goals based on the abilities of their students, then find material that would satisfy the pedagogic needs of those instructional goals. Separate assets of a course or exercise, such as pictures or audios, are individually picked out by the teachers and are used to author a new course or exercise. Consequently, the user requires authoring support at a much lower level of granularity. While the highest possible level of granularity of reuse is using a whole pre-authored course, language teachers rarely reuse whole courses through adaptation. They reuse smaller components of courses that are appropriate for instructional goals that have been set by the teachers themselves. This model of usage may also be applicable to other cases where teachers reuse multimedia material from resources other than their own. It may also be applicable to other subject areas and other levels of education.

14.5.3 Future Work

Future work scheduled for the MALTED project involves increasing the level of functionality and fine-tuning to the system. In the immediate future, this involves implementing facilities to allow media to be streamed, multi-lingual support for metadata on the server side and import and export facilities for transferring multiple assets between assetbases. Technical fine tunings include creating enhanced shutdown routines for the assetbase, improving security by enabling Secure Sockets Layer (SSL), automatic updating of the client applications and a more user-friendly installation routine. However, such improvements will only be useful if the metadata schema adopted by the system efficiently supports what teachers really want to do in their classrooms – teach.

References

1. Davis, D. (1993). Implementation and educational uses of computers. In: Pelgrum, W. and Plomp, T. (Eds), *The IEA Study of Computers in Education: Implementation of an Innovation in 21 Education Systems*. Pergamon Press, Oxford, 73-123.

2. Fullan, M. (1982). Research into educational innovation. In: Gray, H. (Ed) *Management of Educational Institutions*. McGraw-Hill, New York, pp 245-261.

3. LOM (2000). Learning Object Metadata Working Draft (WD4) http://ltsc.ieee.org/wg12/index.html

4. ARIADNE (Alliance of Remote Instructional Authoring and Distribution Networks for Europe), http://ariadne.unil.ch/

5. Dublin Core Metadata Initiative, http://purl.oclc.org/dc/index.htm

6. IEEE Learning Technology Standards Committee (LTSC) Learning Object Model (LOM) Working Group, http://ltsc.ieee.org/wg12/index.html

7. MALTED (Multimedia Authoring for Language Teachers and Educational Developers) Project at University College London, http://malted.cs.ucl.ac.uk/uk/

Chapter 15

Learning Activities in a Virtual Campus

Claude Viéville

The international standardization process has already resulted in the production of a draft about Learning Object Metadata (LOM), which provides a means to describe learning resources. This effort makes retrieval of learning resources easier and encourages interoperability and reusability of educational components. The work presented in this chapter has been done in an industrial context in which the interoperability with other online training platforms was a major issue. An implementation of this emerging standard has been successfully conducted. Several weak points of this standard are explained after a global presentation of the services offered by the platform. Nevertheless, the most attractive points of this online training platform are not restricted to the pedagogical resource delivery or management but are more centered on the learning activities support. In previous educational projects, the system designed at Trigone Laboratory mainly encouraged a collaborative way of learning using asynchronous communication channels; this system strongly structured the conversation to help the users co-ordinate their actions. In systems we are currently working on, this "on-the-fly co-ordination" is balanced by offering a structured context of work in terms of scheduling learning activities. This chapter shows the complementary aspects offered by structuring learning objects on one hand and by structuring the organization of the user's work on the other hand.

15.1 Context of the work

The work presented in this chapter is one of the results of a long-term internal project conducted at Trigone laboratory since 1992. This long-term project was successively supported under different European projects (Co-Learn [6], Modem [9], Demos [8]). As a consequence, a platform has emerged [1], which has been used in several French universities [2]. Finally an industrial transfer in collaboration with a private company was conducted in 1999. During this last step it was decided to make an effort to provide interoperability with other existing platforms. So, investigation on international standardization forced us to take into account emerging results from the major parties. Ariadne and IMS have contributed to the development of the LOM specification published by the IEEE LTSC P1484.12 working group [5]. Although there are other working groups at the IEEE that wish to standardize all the aspects of computer implementations of education [3], training components and systems, effort has been concentrated on LOM. This is intended to facilitate exchanges of learning resources between different editors independently of the platform.

The commercial name of the platform presented in Section 8.2 of this chapter is "Le Campus Virtuel"™. It is followed by a short presentation of the delivery service which implements a draft release of LOM (Working Draft 4). Section 15.4 explains how the system supports learning activities, collaborative or not. The last section, the conclusion, discusses the importance to work, in the future, on the learning activity metadata.

15.2 Platform Services

"Le Campus Virtuel"™ is a teleservice platform to which access is gained through the Internet via a web browser. It relies on four major services that are articulated around a virtual desktop, which is a kind of personal entry point for the users:

- the enrolment service;

- the workgroup service;

- the work organization service;

- the delivery service.

The delivery service and a subpart of the work organization service (the workflow engine) are presented in detail in Sections 15.3 and 15.4 as they are both central to the discussion pointed out in this chapter. Figure 15.1 represents these services and their relations.

15.2.1 The Virtual Desktop

The virtual desktop organizes and controls access to the four other services and facilitates interrelation between each of them. The users are able to organize their personal workspaces and store their preferences. The virtual desktop is a multi-windowing operating system controlled by a web application. It controls user authentication and allows the assignment of access rights, but its main task is to present a personalized environment. As in any multi-windowing system, the user is able to control the windows' size, color and relative position on the screen.

Likewise, the virtual desktop provides a configuration mechanism allowing users to compose menus, select applications, and define their language. Moreover, the users can select the information they want automatically to appear on their desktop from among various sources. Agents belonging to the platform continuously collect the information on the Web and distribute it to the user's desktop if there is a valid subscription. This behavior is close to that of a web portal.

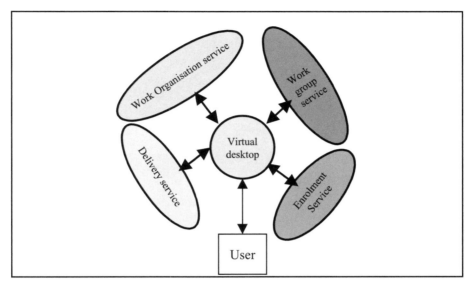

Figure 15.1. Global view of "Le Campus Virtuel"™

15.2.2 The Enrolment Service

This service is mainly based on the notion of a "course unit". To use the platform services, people must be registered. They receive a login and a password and become users. At this stage they are limited to visit "Le Campus Virtuel"™: they can read the public information and they can obtain a virtual desktop. The registration procedure attributes a role to each user (learner, tutor, teacher, administrative staff, *etc.*) and gives them the appropriate access rights. In order to make full use of the services, the users must be registered in at least one course unit. If they belong to a course unit, the users can participate in the learning activities defined by that course unit. The course unit defines a set of pre-defined learning activities (task definitions) that are scheduled by a workflow engine. Each activity uses a given set of learning resources. The course unit also defines a default "learning path" that is currently run by a set of learning groups or by individual learners. A tutor is responsible for one learning group that is the concrete entity designed to activate a course unit; however, several groups related to a same course unit can be instantiated. The tutor can adapt, for each group, the default learning path, which is nothing more than a definition of a sequence of learning activities, as well as the scheduled time of each activity. The learning path is managed by the tutor in two different ways. The first case represents individualized learning, a self-training mode. The second represents a more social approach to learning where people are members of a group. Each member may or may not share the same learning path.

The workflow model, as well as the default learning path, are presented in more detail in Section 15.4 as they are both subcomponents of the work organization service.

15.2.3 The Workgroup Service

The workgroup service is based on three subprocesses:

- an interpersonal asynchronous communication system (an email service);
- an asynchronous group conferencing system (a news service);
- a workgroup file manager service.

The first two items are part of the communication system implemented in the platform. They can be used as a classical email or news server from a browser. However, they both manage message attachments in a consistent way: a relationship between themselves and the workgroup file manager ensures that documents are stored in a dedicated folder of the user file system.

Normal use of email is to support informal exchanges between users. For example, a tutor can encourage a learner by writing an email. However, the email service can also be used by a tutor to direct their learners. In an email message they can tell the learners to work on a document they have attached to the message. Or, they can tell the learners to work on a document they refer to in the body of the message. This reference can also be a learning resource provided by the delivery service (see Section 15.3). It is a very flexible way to organize the work of the learners as there is no need to prepare this pedagogical activity before group instantiation.

Experimentation shows that organization of the work in the conversation space, even if it is very flexible, is not the more efficient way of working [1, 9]. As a result of the informal aspect of the communication, the system cannot help directly in organizing the work and cannot help the users to keep track of work in progress. For this reason, structuring the conversation is an important feature. This is achieved through the use of semi-structured forms [7]. The computer is able to interpret a set of fields that are useful in tracking the progress of the learning activities. This is what we call "on-the-fly co-ordination" between users inside a workgroup [10]. This feature introduces a feedback loop in conjunction with informal exchanges between humans. It has a positive impact on the organization but it needs to be complemented by features that allow the users to see a longer timescale and a more global vision of what they must do – the learners as well as the tutors need to know how all the learning activities of a course unit are scheduled. This service is flexible but is limited to currently running activities.

The file manager service is the most important part of the information space of the platform. As has been outlined above, it stores the documents attached to messages in dedicated folders. The users of "Le Campus Virtuel"™ own personal folders to manage their documents. Moreover, each learning group also has a folder accessible by all its members. This is the basic area used to allow people to work together. The user of the service can completely manage each folder in the normal way. However, since a quota is given to each user and to each group, the user can ask the service to compress the data in the folder in order to save disk space. In this case, the document is automatically decompressed when it is downloaded.

The teacher will use these folders to post a document destined to a particular learner or to a group of learners. Homework can be given using this service. If the teachers have built a learning resource which is not yet available in the learning resource database, they can drop it in a folder and then post a message using the interpersonal or group communication service to notify the learners.

In conclusion, the workgroup service is a collection of functions that is useful for working together but provides only a short term vision. The work organization service complements it in a useful way.

15.2.4 The Work Organization Service

The work organization service supports users in planning their work and helps the teachers to track the learners' activities. It can be viewed as the structured layer of "Le Campus Virtuel"™. It adds value to the services presented in the previous sections. This service relies on two subcomponents:

- a personal and group organizer;

- a workflow engine.

The personal and group organizers offer the possibility for each user to manage events manually by defining them in a calendar. The users own their personal calendar of events but can access a calendar related to each learning group to which they belong. An event in a personal calendar can also be automatically inserted in the calendar of a group, in which case members of the group can be notified of this insertion. The service will also send notifications to users at given dates in order to remind them that a particular event has occurred.

In addition to this notion of events, there is the notion of tasks. The tasks are personal or can be defined for a learning group. A task is manually defined by giving a starting date, a deadline and a priority. A notification to remind users of an approaching deadline can be defined.

This personal and group organizer is a useful component that completes the communication services. The tutor has the ability to schedule a live talk at a given date or to give homework by defining a task for the group. The learners can combine all these constraints and put them into their personal agendas in order to self organize.

15.2.5 The Delivery Service

This service is composed of a database storing the learning resources and all the information about them on one hand and a server on the other hand. It is detailed in Section 15.3.

Figure 15.2 shows a more complete view of "Le Campus Virtuel"™, in which the entities are defined more precisely.

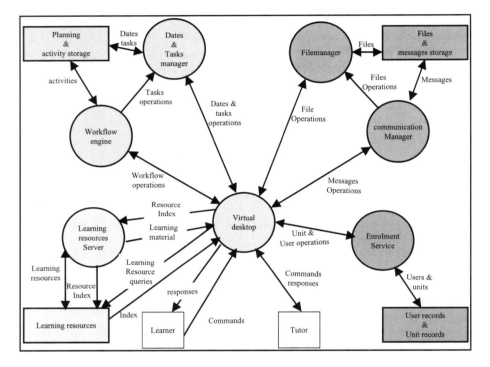

Figure 15.2. Complete view of "Le Campus Virtuel"™

15.3 Delivery Service

15.3.1 Describing the Learning Resource

In order to be easily retrievable in a database that stores numerous elements, metadata are useful to describe the learning resources. This leads us to design a new kind of structured document attached to each resource: the notice. This notice is implemented in XML technology using a Document Type Definition (DTD) based on the draft of LOM specification. A typical usage of this notice is to help an instructor to build a learning path for a particular learner or for a group of learners from the resources stored in several databases. What the instructor should initially know is the execution environment of the learners, the learners' needs, the users' profile and the pedagogical objectives and prerequisites. Then, the system provides the tools to retrieve the most appropriate learning resources.

In the previous release of the platform, before this industrial process, the notice of an educational resource was limited to a title, a set of authors, a creation or modification date, a set of keywords, a rigid classification mechanism with three levels (discipline, theme, subtheme), the size and the URL of the resource itself. This simple way of designing a notice limits the description to the content of the resource which is not sufficient for the instructor. Moreover, it is impossible to imagine that all the editors will classify their resources with the same taxonomy.

In the final implementation of "Le Campus Virtuel"™, LOM specification has been extended with several elements as detailed in the following section.

15.3.2 LOM as the Basis of Notice Design

LOM was used as the basis to define the notice for the learning resource. The delivery service was designed around two major components: a database containing all the learning resources as well as their metadata, and a server that returns the learning object and the metadata with a strict verification of the user's access rights.

According to IEEE 1484.12 working draft 4 recommendations [5], each learning resource (a learning object in the LOM terminology) is inserted into the database with a set of metadata which gives information along the following lines:

- general information;
- information about the metadata itself;
- the technical aspect of the resource;
- the pedagogical usage;
- the life cycle;
- intellectual property rights;
- relationship with other resources;
- comments on the educational use of the resource;
- the location of this resource in different classification systems.

This information about the learning resource allows a very fine-grained search in a huge database; queries on the database operate on the notice attributes. As a consequence, it encourages reusability of pedagogical material.

As anticipated during the specification work, it was necessary to extend the LOM definition with a classification part. From the eleven items that describe the purpose of LOM, the analyzis that has been conducted mainly retains the following points:

"To enable learners or instructors to search, evaluate, acquire, and use learning objects,

To enable sharing and exchanging of learning objects across any technology-supported learning system,

To enable documenting and recognizing the completion of existing or new learning and performance objectives associated with learning objects,

To enable education, training and learning organizations, including government, public and private, to express education content and performance standards in a standardised format that is independent of the content itself." [5]

To a lesser extent, the following points are also interesting in our current work:

"To enable a strong and growing economy for learning objects that supports and sustains all forms of distribution; non-profit, not-for-profit and for profit,

To provide researchers with standards that support collecting and sharing comparable data concerning the applicability and effectiveness of learning objects

To support necessary security and authentication for the distribution and use of Learning Objects". [5]

The automatic and dynamic composition of a personalized lesson for an individual learner by a computer agent has been excluded. In "Le Campus Virtuel"™ , this task is devoted to a human agent. The final choice for the design of the learning resource notice has been made, taking into account the searching process. Criteria that are set in a searching grid help the course unit designers to select the metadata. The second step of the searching process is refinement, where the user defines other criteria to obtain a list of learning resources of reasonable size. Finally, the last step is based on the user, who has to read the complete notice, which presents informal information such as appreciation from other previous users.

The following table represents our analyzis of the LOM metadata according to the main identified needs for designing the notice.

The notice that has been implemented contains a subset of LOM metadata, those which were considered useful in one of the three columns of Table 15.1. However, the designers of the notice added other metadata:

● to indicate if the resource is usable without help of a tutor;

● to indicate the kinds of learning activities that can be proposed to the learner with a given resource (exam, self-assessment, experiment, exercise, get information, discuss, argument, etc.).

Table 15.1. Usefulness of the LOM metadata

LOM category	LOM subcategory	For retrieving	For refinement	For selecting	Remarks
General					
	Title			Y	
	Catalogue	Y			Allow interoperability between editors and platforms
	Language		Y	Y	
	Description			Y	
	Keywords	Y			
	Coverage			Y	Not always applicable
	Structure		Y	Y	
	Aggregation Level	Y		Y	
Life cycle					Mainly useful for designers of learning objects
Meta Data				Y	Useful to qualify the notice information source
Technical		Y	Y	Y	Very important
Educational					
	Interactivity type		Y	Y	
	Learning resource type	Y			
	Interactivity level			Y	Suggestive
	Semantic density			Y	Suggestive
	Intended end user role	Y			
	Context	Y			
	Typical age range				Redundant with context
	Difficulty				Too suggestive
	Typical learning time			Y	
	Description			Y	
	Language		Y		
Rights				Y	Important
Relation				Y	Important to build a consistent learning path
Annotation				Y	To share experience among teachers
Classification		Y		Y	To extend LOM but problem of interoperability
	Purpose	Y			
	Taxon Path	Y			
	Description			Y	
	Keywords	Y			

The platform provides a specialized editor to allow construction of the notices, as well as specialised search grids which are proposed to the users in order to retrieve the most appropriate set of learning resources according to the pedagogical objectives (see Figure 15.3). The document server extracts the document referenced by the notice and can send the content with the appropriate representation to the user.

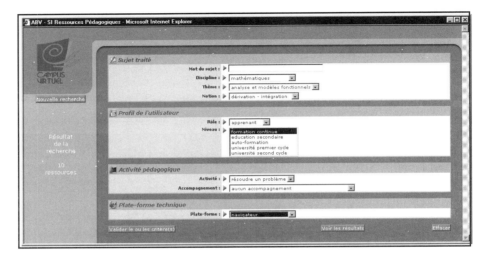

Figure 15.3. Searching a learning resource.

15.4 Supporting the Learning Activities

The platform provides a workflow engine to allow definition of the scheduling of the learning activities and to maintain the activity states. The designers of the platform encourage the teachers who set up a course unit to define a sequence of activities that could be used as a default learning path when a user starts working inside this course unit. From the internal point of view, this sequence of learning activities is a model, a static definition of the activities and the possible transitions between them. Most of these models define simple transitions in a sequence, though more complex transitions are possible. However, end users currently find these latter transitions very difficult to model.

The default model represents the organization of the work within the group, together with whatever coordination is forecasted. When tutors create a new group attached to a course unit, they must define the parameters of this new instance: the participants, the dates, the group folders, and the group discussion spaces. They could also modify the default behavior by editing the workflow model. All of these parameters are grouped in a work plan document that is personalized and distributed to all the participants of the group. This document provides an interaction space where both learners and tutors can retrieve information about:

- the learning path from a content point of view;

- the learning path from a temporal scheduling point of view;

- the current work to do;

- the work already done;

- the important dates (face to face meetings, work deadlines, *etc.*);

- direct access to discussion groups;

- access to the group folders where all the documents created on-the-fly by both learners and tutors are stored (group information space).

The tutors can read the work plan of each student who belongs to a group for which they are responsible. This document allows the learners to organize their work more effectively, since they can obtain a long-term perspective as well as a short-term perspective by using the conversation space service (email and structured conversation). This workflow engine is also coupled to the personal user organizer: it fills in their organizer with tasks the users must do.

15.5 Conclusion

Even though the platform is currently commercially available, its designers believe that there are still open questions.

In the current notice implementation, as well as in the LOM working draft, the sharing of learning resource usage is done through an annotation document which is nothing more than an informal document. A more efficient way of sharing experience could be done through sharing how the learning resource has been really used within a group. In the implementation of "Le Campus Virtuel"™ the object that contains the usage is the workflow model relative to a course unit: it is precisely the learning path defined by the tutor. So it is easily shareable but only inside the platform or between identical systems. To allow a larger form of sharing, between different kinds of platforms, the description of the learning path should also be standardized. The designers of "Le Campus Virtuel"™ are looking towards the WorkFlow Management Coalition (WfMC) [4] to determine more on interoperability between workflow systems. This is the subject of the work around Interface 1 in WfMC [11] and the expected outcome is that users will be able to rely on a standard that says how to define the workflow model independently of the workflow engine which runs the model.

The learning path is not necessarily public as it contains the know-how of an organization. As such, it is an added-value component that could be marketed. Then, the question becomes: "How should one describe the learning path as a kind of learning resource?" Technically speaking, it means that this resource is a workflow model which describes the learning path and so it should be conform to a standard defined by Interface 1 of the WfMC [11]. This description is complex and unreadable by typical end users. It would be more useful to describe this model with metadata whose vocabulary can be finely selected.

Considering the current working draft 4 of LOM [5], the aggregation level should be extended to learning activity and the type of resource should make a distinction between different collaborative learning activities. The metadata must provide a vocabulary to describe the coordination between members, the feed-back characteristics and the type of tools used in order to help tutors or instructors to select or not select a course unit. This can best be achieved not only by allowing the specification of most of the characteristics of the content, as in the LOM draft, but also by allowing specification of the learning activities and how they are articulated along the learning path. This new feature should be very attractive as these kinds of metadata are more "learning service" oriented than "learning resource" oriented. This work is currently in progress at Trigone laboratory.

Acknowledgements

This work has been mostly funded by a French institution: ANVAR. The design of the delivery service of "Le Campus Virtuel"™ has been conducted in relation with Alain Derycke, Manager of Trigone laboratory, Stéphane Réthoré and Bruno Vanhille, both staff of USTL, and Eric Ruyffelaere, Manager of Archimed Company.

DiViLab, a European project of the Information Societies Technology Programme, has partially contributed to the funding of this work.

I also want to thank Yvan Peter who contributed to improving the quality of this chapter.

"Le Campus Virtuel"™ is a TradeMark of Archimed Company.

References

1. Derycke, A., Viéville, C. (1994) Real time multimedia conferencing system and collaborative learning. In *Collaborative Dialogue Technologies in Distance Education*. Verdejo, F., Cerri, S. (Eds), NATO ASI Series, Berlin, Springer-Verlag, 236-257.

2. Derycke, A., Hoogstoël, F., Viéville, C. (1997) Campus virtuel et apprentissages coopératifs, Actes des 5emes journées EIAO de Cachan, Environnements Interactifs d'Apprentissage avec Ordinateur, Ecole Normale Supérieure de Cachan, Baron, M., Mendelsohn, P., Nicaud, J-F. (Coordonnateurs), 11-24.

3.   Farance, F., Tonkel, J. (1999) IEEE 1484.1, LTSA Specification, Learning Technology Systems Architecture, Draft 5.

4.   Hollingsworth, D.,(1995) Workflow Management Coalition: The workflow reference model.

5.   IEEE P1484.12, (2000) Draft Standard 4 for Learning Object Metadata.

6.   Kaye, A. (1995) Final Evaluation Report, Synthesis of Co-Learn Trials and Experimentation, Deliverable 33 of Co-Learn d2005, 1995

7.   Malone, T. (1987) Semi-Structured messages are surprisingly useful for Computer-Supported Collaboration, *ACM Transactions On Office Information Systems*, 5, 115-131

8.   Viéville, C., Derycke, A. (1997) Self organised group activities supported by asynchronous structured conversations, *Proceedings of the 1997 IFIP TC3/ WG3.3&3.6, Join working conference, The Virtual Campus: Trends for Higher Education and Training*, Madrid, Spain, 27-29 November, 1997, Verdejo, F. and Davies, G. (Eds), Chapman & Hall, 175-188.

9.   Viéville, C. (1998) An asynchronous collaborative learning system on the web, *The Digital University - reinventing the Academy*, Hazami, R., Hailes, S. and Wilbur, S. (Eds), Springer, 99-113.

10.   Vieville, C. (1995) Structuring conversation in asynchronous communication systems to support collaborative learning at a distance. In *Proceedings of ED-MEDIA 95*, Graz, Austria, 816-817.

11.   WorkFlow Management Coalition Interface 1: Process Definition Interchange Process Model V1.1 Document number WfMC TC-1016-P Final 0ctober 29, 1999.

Chapter 16

The Relevance and Impact of Collaborative Working for Management in a Digital University

Brian R. Mitchell

This chapter seeks to explore the impact and relevance of formal collaborative working on the management of universities. As a result of increased competition for students, staff and funds, HE institutions are being subjected to pressures for continuous improvements in academic and financial performance. The thesis of this chapter is that a formal development of collaborative working practices, supported by appropriate technology, can make a substantial contribution to the effective running of a modern university. The chapter also attempts to place current university management practices in the broader context of commercial management practice in the twentieth century.

One critical point of principle: there is NO assumption that the human relationship between teacher and student should be replaced in whole or in part by electronic means of communication. For some institutions, an increase in electronic communication in teaching and learning may be desirable and appropriate, but the perceptive use of collaborative working for *management processes*, supported by technology, has a contribution to make to academic activities by releasing academic staff time for person-to-person contact with students and colleagues. Technology has now created the opportunity for HE institutions to choose how their management processes are to be managed. By "management" we mean all those administrative processes which provide the resources and facilities to support academic staff in teaching and research, and support students in the process of learning.

16.1 Management Issues

On 7th September 1997, the headline in The *Independent on Sunday*, read "A farewell to form-filling as the State goes electronic." The article defined Ministers' objectives:

"They plan a technological revolution to cut down form-filling and eventually to enable people to collect government allowances and benefits 24 hours a day from cash-point machines. The technology will allow people to file tax returns, pay vehicle duty or apply for licenses at the touch of a button."

David Clark, the Chancellor of the Duchy of Lancaster, who is in charge of the project, told the newspaper:

"This will be a massive reform of the system of government, started by looking at things from the citizen's point of view. When people think of government, they think of forms and queues. We must put an end to that."

Those sentiments could be the manifesto for a programme to create a Digital university which could be defined as:

- To look at the institution's management processes primarily from the point of view of those teaching, learning and researching.

- To put an end to - or at least significantly reduce - the management and administrative workload of academic staff, by reducing form-filling and delays.

- To enable the institution to be seen, in appropriate areas, as a whole rather than as an assembly of separate units.

This aim can only be achieved in a large institution by means of an appropriate technological infrastructure - networks, desktop facilities, coherent information - and a cultural shift towards a willingness to share information. This will involve a trade-off to some degree of personal and departmental independence and self-determination in the interests of easier sharing of information and a reduction in the duplication and reconciliation of data. The underlying cultural change is to move towards more "collaborative" or "asynchronous" working.

From the outset, it must be made clear that the views expressed here do not derive from any formal research. They are the considerations of an experienced IS manager, recently recruited from industry, who is required to manage the continuous delivery of administrative systems to a large college within the University of London and, more specifically, to manage practical and effective systems projects.

16.2 A View on the Development of Management Thinking

16.2.1 The Balance of Power Between Competition and Cooperation

The view that collaboration is a normal or desirable method of working is not universally held. Throughout history, indeed throughout the whole process of evolution, there has been conflict between the forces of collaboration and co-operation and the forces of competition.

The truth of the matter is that there is no absolute: in some situations a competitive response is appropriate, in others a collaborative response is likely to be more effective. Individuals operate in both modes without much difficulty. They cooperate with members of their own family or club or country (in times of war) as the most effective strategy for Life, Liberty and the pursuit of Happiness. The same individuals will compete vigorously against an anti-social neighbor, an opposing team or the enemy.

The history of management presents a specific and more localized case of the same diversity of opinion. Generally, the prevailing philosophy of commerce is that of competition. Most managers would hold the view that what is good for their own organization must be bad for other organizations with which they are in competition. This is clearly not an absolute: trade associations are living examples of structures set up to exploit the benefits of cooperation with the very institutions with which they compete in other arenas. Universities compete to attract the best students, best staff and most research funding, but they still find overall benefit when cooperating in their dealings with government.

The process of management shows a similar dichotomy. Some - many - managers see themselves as being in competition with their colleagues and staff as well as other divisions in the same enterprise. This type of manager sees commercial life as nasty, brutish and short, and acts accordingly but there are other types of manager: the work of W. Edwards Deming, for example, has shown that collaboration with one's colleagues, suppliers, customers, local communities and even with other suppliers in the same industry is actually more effective than competition. Given his success in the development of the Japanese electronic and motor industries since the war, such views are very compelling. Maybe the recent cold winds blowing through the Pacific tiger economies might have been less traumatic had Deming also been invited to apply his philosophies to the property and financial sectors.

What is certainly true is that the maturing of electronic communication has introduced a new dimension into the collaboration/competition equation that we ignore at our peril. At first sight, this could look like a war-winning weapon for the forces of competition but electronic communication, effectively used, can profoundly improve the effectiveness of the collaborative approach. My two key hypotheses are:

1. That it is possible to manage even large enterprises which exploit the benefits of size but without creating a bureaucratic monster, subject to the development of a cooperative culture, and supported by a suitable means of inter-personal communication. In any large organization, this must mean electronic communication.

2. That universities could particularly profit from this concept. HE institutions must resolve two conflicting cultural pressures: to maintain their traditional liberal role as teachers and employers, while at the same time responding to governmental demands for tighter cost control, more accountability expressed in statistical terms and more responsiveness to the "market".

16.3 Demands on Universities

16.3.1 The Problems of Managing HE in the Late 20th Century

This is not the place to describe the pressures on the management of HE; enough has already been written. However, the increase in the size of institutions from both organic growth and mergers, reduced unit funding, additional government involvement, student expectations, litigation and funded research has created major problems to which formal management responses are needed.

It is here that the parallel between HE and commercial organizations can be instructive. Until recently, most UK universities could have been usefully described as operating in the "proprietorial" phase of development: individual members of academic staff operated rather as proprietors of particular courses or leaders of unique research teams. It is this highly organic relationship between staff and students that characterizes much of HE in the UK but universities then began to suffer the same kind of pressures from growing scale and complexity that the commercial proprietors saw, but the commercial solutions did not fit Universities well, at least in the UK.

There are good reasons why this should be so:

● UK universities do not operate in a free market: the role of the funding councils makes universities feel much more like nationalized institutions.

● Universities are very complex organisms. They do not have the clear definitions of products, shareholders, directors, managers, and customers that even large commercial organizations have.

● The notion of "management authority" lies much less easily in HE than in commerce. There tends to be a far higher percentage of inquiring and questioning staff in universities than in commerce. Indeed, many commercial organizations find difficulty in "managing" knowledge workers - such employers as stockbrokers, investment houses and the media go to extreme lengths in salaries and bonuses to retain and direct key knowledge workers.

16.3.2 Asynchronous Working Requires a Culture Shift in Management Thinking

The development of electronic information systems has both caused and facilitated dramatic changes to the way in which institutions - commercial, industrial and public as well as educational - operate. By facilitating the rapid creation and communication of information, and its interlinking with administrative processes, it has created the opportunity for a revolution in management thinking. The benefits could be especially relevant in HE, which is fundamentally knowledge-based and needs to achieve a fine balance between academic freedom and administrative efficiency. Unfortunately, collaborative working has not so far been a readily adopted concept among the Western population at large, and especially not as a management approach.

The creation of a digital university will not be an easy, or cheap, exercise, but in the increasingly commercial culture in which universities operate, the degree of collaboration which it permits should improve both the effectiveness and efficiency of the institution while improving the quality of life which it provides for its students and staff. The need to move in this direction has been recognized by Sir Ron Dearing, whose recommendations include the exploitation of Communication and Information Technology, and the development of a new Institute for Teaching and Learning, covering among other things the "management of teaching and learning".

Electronic, collaborative working may provide the answer to a whole family of problems - those related to personal relationships within an enterprise - which a host of management philosophies (or fashions) have sought to resolve by non-technological means. Collaborative working, based on electronic communication, could cause a ground shift in management, organizational and motivational theory.

From this point, this chapter follows three threads:

1. An outline of the way in which *collaborative working might impact a university*.

2. A description of the *process for developing collaborative working* using electronic information systems.

3. A short perusal of where *previous management theories* might be absorbed within the broader concept of collaborative working.

16.4 The Way in which Collaborative Working might Impact a University

16.4.1 Features of a "Collaborative University"

There are situations for which the collaborative approach is particularly appropriate:

- **Knowledge Workers**. The collaborative approach works especially well where the deliverable is intangible, as it is more difficult to specify in advance the nature, time and cost of the result of the work.

- **Research**. Development work with an external requirement for a specific outcome at a specific time may need more mechanistic management. However, the exploratory stages of projects of this type can be ideal for a collaborative approach.

- **Distance Working**. The costs of the traditional structured meeting (*i.e.*, of getting everyone together in one place at one time) are becoming widely recognized. Eliminating such meetings appears to be in opposition to the concept of collaborative working; however, once the dimension of full electronic communication has been built into the management style from the beginning, arms-length operation becomes the norm.

Under all the above criteria, universities seem an ideal ground for exploiting the opportunities offered by collaboration based on electronics. Assuming that a university has decided to adopt the collaborative model, it will demonstrate a number of features:

- A set of shared values that permeate the whole institution. These values will inevitably and desirably differ between institutions. Each will settle on its own balance between research and teaching; between covering all faculties and academic specializations; between high technology and human chemistry as the main teaching techniques; between metropolitan and remote campus site; between centralized and department structures; between fixed courses and flexible inter-disciplinary programmes; between traditional formality and inventive anarchy. It may of course be of value not to have a single value, but to encourage cultural diversity. However, a university will experience problems if its academics are designing inter-disciplinary programmes of study, but its administrators are unable to provide staff and students with the means to generate, publicize, present and examine such courses.

- The purposeful blurring of the established distinction between "administrative" and "academic" roles. All administrative procedures, whether undertaken by academic members of staff or not, must support the teaching, learning and research activities which the university undertakes. This is easier said than done: the university has legal obligations which cannot be evaded but which do not obviously support academic endeavor.

- Widely distributed decision-making at the point closest to the activity. Only major decisions are routed to, or initiated by, the senior management. Responsibility for financial decisions are delegated as far as possible to departmental level and beyond, but using electronic communication to monitor compliance with budgeting authority and the institution-wide situation. Collaborative structures therefore tend to be wide rather than deep. There have the least number of organizational levels.

- Very good lines of communication particularly across, as opposed to up and down, the institution. Communication is a two-way process, not just broadcasting.

- Elimination of fear: individuals are expected to contribute their views even if these are against the prevailing preference, and to do this requires widely disseminated information. The concept of information on a "need-to-know" basis is not collaborative, as it is not possible to predict when an item of information will be useful or by whom it will be used. A collaborative institution will establish a policy of open communication, up to the point where further communication would jeopardize personal or institutional confidentiality. Hidden agendas are seen as damaging and are exposed by peer pressure. Uncertainty is seen not as a weakness but as part of a genuine seeking for good solutions. Errors and mistakes are seen as stimuli to identify the causes and to do better next time: exploration and experimentation are encouraged and supported.

- The structure is dynamic and flexible: new groupings of individuals are created for new problems. Interfunctional steering groups, working groups, quality circles and workshops are established where each is the optimum solution to a problem. Such groupings have clear, although different, life cycles. They are created, developed, maintained and then terminated once their objectives have been met.

- There is the minimum of social stratification: individuals are valued and used because of their potential contribution and not because of their seniority or status.

- Quality is seen as something which is built into any procedure and sought by all those involved: it is not a subsequent phase of inspection and rejection of below-standard examples. Quality is a process of continuous improvement based upon an objective review of variation and not as deviation from a fixed set of norms.

16.5 Characteristics of a Digital University

A collaborative university showing the above characteristics is not an easy thing to create, and without electronic communication it would be impossible. I suggest that the following type of electronic information infrastructure is going to be a necessary prerequisite to such an institution.

16.5.1 Information must be Accurate, Appropriate and Available

There are countless examples in commerce as well as HE where information is not adequate for the task of supporting a collaborative institution. The information may be flawed in many respects:

- It may be just plain wrong - from being invalid or not up to date.

- It may be inappropriate - it may be designed for one purpose but used for another.

- It may be at the wrong level of detail and either swamp the receiver with masses of detail without summary features, or it may give bland generalizations without the ability to drill down to locate the really significant detail.

- It may be unreliable - it may be available for a period but then cease, when the individual champion who created the system moved on or got bored. It may have been written to inadequate design standards. This has become a particular problem with do-it-yourself database software. Conversely, systems for the creation and distribution of information may have been quoted by the IS professional which are so expensive or which will take so long to deliver that there would not be a hope of approval for such a project.

- A system which works fine for one or two users may fail as the number of users increases beyond the capability of the initiating enthusiast - systems should be designed for appropriate scalability.

- It may not be consistent - different definitions of critical items of information may prevent consolidation into useful higher-order reports. This may cause an associated problem: that the information cannot be shared.

- The medium may be inappropriate - a screen-based view does not help the receiver trying to work on the train home or at a research site. It may be too structured - only possible to locate the required data if the full 34-character ID code is known and so that it is entered flawlessly every time. It may be too unstructured - a long sequence of helpful menu items to home in on a record that the receiver could have identified by a simple known code.

- It may be inconvenient - it may be protected by so many levels of security that only Houdini or an enthusiastic hacker is likely to use it. It may take an inordinate length of time to retrieve the data.

- It may be inflexible – such that it would take months to create a related report for even a slightly different purpose.

16.5.2 Contribution of the Internet

No discussion of collaborative working would be complete without a few views on the Internet. The role of the Internet is so obvious that it can be taken for granted:

- It is virtually universal, relatively free of constraining technical monopolies or standards, and the subject of rapid growth and acceptance.

- It is already accessible to the overwhelming majority of those likely to be involved in HE collaborative projects. It can be accessed on-campus and anywhere a telephone line exists.

- It is the subject of great development effort. Organizations from the size of the Microsoft and Oracle Corporations down are investing large sums of money in enabling technologies.

Notwithstanding the above eulogies, I have some concerns, even though there may be no alternative:

- The nature of information exchange can be misunderstood; simply "putting up information" on the Web, may be of little help. If the resulting portfolio is a random mixture of personalized views, not presented and edited for wide consumption, the results can be downright confusing to those seeking to share the data.

- Information exchange is not sufficiently secure. Although both commercial and free security products are available, their use is not particularly widespread and is often viewed as psychologically unacceptable. Furthermore, to provide good security requires more than the simplistic application of boxed solutions, as the banking and military communities can attest from experience.

16.5.3 Example of a Process Based on Collaborative Working: No. 1 Staff Recruitment

Staff recruitment is an example of a process of something that should be very simple: all organizations, from all commercial and public sectors, undertake such processes and it would have been thought that there were no special contributions that collaborative working could make. However, there are some particular problems which universities face:

- Universities are relatively large organizations but their staff cannot be mass-produced. The contribution of an individual to a research team can be unique. This requires a recruitment process which can deal with large numbers of potential recruits, but with many unique jobs.

- Individual employment contracts may be relatively short - especially for research posts: in some cases there is one unique candidate. The recruitment process must set up effective milestones to ensure that the progress of every post must be monitored very closely and efficiently.

- Universities, in the UK at least, are running under tight budgets: there is usually no room for lavish recruitment procedures involving external agencies. On the other hand, the system has to be very effective as there may be competition with other institutions to attract and retain key individuals. Every post has to be checked against available funds, provided by funding council, research sponsors and so on.

What is required is a system that provides rapid and effective communication between all the parties involved: the employing department, the personnel function, and the budgeting function. It must also involve numerous supporting agencies: the advertising media; the interview team; pensions; health and safety; providers of references; estates and providers of accommodation and office or laboratory facilities; security; telephones; computing services... the list is extensive. If each of these agencies must be involved serially, the recruitment process will take so long that the best candidates will be long gone by the time an offer can be assembled.

It is critical here that all possible actions are undertaken in parallel, and each step that is serially dependent on another is triggered automatically as soon as the preceding step is complete. Paper-based systems cannot be that responsive: the only effective approach is electronic communication, with all parties able to access and, in appropriate cases update, a coherent pool of information.

Note that there is no distinction between "administrative" and "academic" activities here. Academic and administrative skills are needed to interact seamlessly if the whole process is going to appear efficient and sympathetic to the new member of staff.

16.5.4 Example of a Process Based on Collaborative Working: No. 2 Course Development

The development of courses may sound initially like a purely academic process; however, this is an over-simplification. There are a variety of skills to be involved, and again here, collaborative working is needed. The process is likely to involve the following steps:

- Identification of the need or opportunity for a new course, by responding to demand from students, or by identifying a gap in the market. The idea will need to be discussed with academic colleagues and a concept developed. The review process may involve a number of colleagues, in one or more departments or institutions, and may need to incorporate existing modules. This will involve communication with academic colleagues.

- The idea will need to be assessed for costs, for materials, equipment and so on, and departmental or institutional budgets earmarked. This will require communication with departmental and financial staff, usually requiring the interchange of financial models and their progressive refinement.

● The content will be developed and refined and drafts prepared. Information will need to be presented in a variety of formats - text, graphics, plans, physical and conceptual models, reference material, slides, programmes, brochures, *etc.* - and all formats should be able to be exchanged and refined in collaboration with colleagues in a variety of locations.

● The course will no doubt require institutional approval, based on a demonstrated opportunity in the market, on accurately predicted costs and potential income. It must then be added to the institution's portfolio of courses. This too requires the exchange of information across space and between individuals with special contributions to make.

● Potential students will need to be given information about the course, and details added to the registration and examination processes.

With the advent of Sir Ron Dearing's proposals, the process could be more complex still: a pricing structure may need to be created for individual courses or modules, for different types of student, at different times. Attempting to navigate through this process without electronic communication and shared local and institutional data would seem to be a hopelessly slow and tortuous task.

16.5.5 Example of a Process Based on Collaborative Working: No. 3 Research Management

Research is one of those university processes which show up most clearly the apparent conflict between administrative and academic processes. However, for many universities, the effective management of all aspects of research is critical to their ability to flourish, or even simply to survive. The problems are legion:

● Research is a process which is fundamentally collaborative. However, there are contradictory aspects: at the simplest level, there are needs for confidentiality and also for publicity. The very existence of a research project may be considered confidential, but to be first with published results has been a key objective for researchers since time immemorial. As research is based upon the interchange of results between team members, secure but convenient methods of exchange are necessary. This applies to the process of seeking funding as well as undertaking the research itself.

● Establishing a research project requires acquiring and funding of some or all of the following: staff; office or laboratory accommodation; access to information; authority and licenses. It also requires control procedures to be in place to handle some or all of: costing and budgeting; the flow of funds; meeting research deadlines; monitoring the activities of each member of the team; preparing results for publish in a variety of formats for in-house and external use; developing a product and its marketing; copyright; patents; and so on.

This process requires rapid communication between the research team and almost every administrative service in the institution. Electronic communication can achieve rapidity and reliability of information flow that would make a contribution to all but the smallest research projects.

16.6 The Process for Developing Collaborative Working Using Electronic Information Systems

16.6.1 How to Build Information Structures for Collaborative Institutions

It could be argued that collaborative working cannot be "built", that it is fundamentally an organic, cultural process, and that any attempt to implement it would be a contradiction in terms. I have heard it argued that it should emerge rather as did the Internet itself. I am not persuaded by that argument: were that case to be valid there would be more cases of fully-fledged collaborative working in operation, and fewer instances of staff asking for the facilities to work collaboratively.

- Given that it requires at least some degree of pump-priming, if not fully managed implementation, the starting point is an institutional policy to develop a culture of collaborative working: this will require supporting strategies in a number of areas:

  - A commitment from the Vice-Chancellor supported by the most senior individuals and departments.

  - An organization - steering group - to direct the development process, and to argue for appropriate levels of investment.

  - Clear objectives and recognition of the benefits - and costs. Costs will be both in financial terms and in the extent to which individuals and departments will need to relinquish some degree of freedom of choice.

  - A formal plan with details of phases of work, responsibilities and schedules.

  - The group steering the development of collaborative working must be privy to the innermost plans of the institution. Systems take time to develop, and it is highly wasteful for work to be progressing into areas which are incompatible with the institution's plans.

- An educational and communication plan, which must be based on wide, if not universal, participation by all major units in the institution, in developing and accepting the plans. A vision imposed by a few enthusiasts may act as a starting point but must develop to achieve widespread ownership by the institution's staff.

- All future systems must conform to the concept that critical information must derive as by-products from properly structured administrative processes. Institution-level information about, say, staff should be captured at source throughout the recruitment *process* and then be made available to relevant departments. The supporting system should permit information of more local use to be added. It is a sign of very unhealthy systems if users of information have to create their own pools of localized data simply to compensate for inadequacies in the institutional data. Such local pools are convenient in the short term, but effectively prevent such information being shared. This inability to share can severely damage collaborative processes.

- The institution requires a high-level data model to achieve consistent definitions of the key data entities. A single definition of such an entity as "department" should be applied across all potential uses, including financial, student, personnel, estates and course administration. This high-level model should start at the level of a simple process/information matrix. It is then available as a top-level information and process model.

16.6.2 Technical Infrastructure for Collaborative Management

Collaborative working requires a core infrastructure of common technology. Even quite simple commonality would help: one only has to consider the problems of routing text documents widely across a diversity of mail systems to be aware of the problems of technical diversity.

Very few institutions will be in a position to start from a green field in terms of technology. It is very likely that there will be a variety of hardware, operating systems, application software and development methods in place. It will rarely be possible to replace all the infrastructure at a stroke, but a progressive move towards conformity in some areas will be crucial. There are a number of strategies by which this may be achieved:

- A series of policy statements on the future direction of the institution, such that each unit will convert to products within the standard portfolio at the next major upgrade. This will be much helped by central funding and site-licensing agreements, central technical support during the conversion process, wide consultation before the standards are established, and the selection of stable, high quality, widely available products.

- The establishment of a limited number of ideal solutions among champions of the preferred standards. The message of the benefits of conformity should then be encouraged to permeate organically across the user population.

- The definition, not of standard products, but of standard interfaces between a number of feasible products.

The following elements are required:

- A high-performance, high-reliability network, right up to the socket in the wall. This should be all-pervasive, cover data, telephones and video and be the responsibility of a single coordinating function. This same function must have the right to certify all networking equipment and protocols downstream of the socket. This must be the physical link to all external networks.

- An institution-wide provision of the hardware and operating system to support all the institutional databases, including backup.

- An institution-wide standard for desktop facilities to be used by any member of staff who participates in the collaborative process with other members of staff. This must be managed at the institution-level such that all client software can be delivered concurrently to all users. This standard may be expressed as specific products or as industry standards, as appropriate. With time the nature of such a standard is becoming less onerous; as the Web interface matures it will no doubt provide the level of universality, platform independence, security and functionality that will provide the required degree of interoperability.

- The adoption of a limited range of application software: this must cover all desktop and database applications:

  - word processing and text management;

  - spreadsheet and numerical management;

  - graphics and presentation products;

  - web and email development and access tools;

  - network access tools, for on-site, at-home and mobile communication;

  - database software for use on institutional databases;

  - desktop database software, able to interface with the institutional database, and permit the development of local applications;

  - screen and report generation products, for use by development professionals, and by users. The range should be sufficient to cater for the needs for power and functionality by systems professionals and sufficiently user-friendly for users;

- systems development methodologies used for creating all the institutional systems. These may be simply standard procedures, or specific development products, CASE for example.

- A well-equipped and staffed support center, offering a helpdesk, training and consultancy. This unit must be staffed to carry out both routine support of line-of-business, as well as research into pertinent developments in the market and trials of promising products. This research and development function must not be squeezed out of the odd spare moments in the work of routine support.

- The technology must support some critical facilities:

  - reliable and recoverable file stores;

  - sound security standards to provide a known level of protection against hacking, and unauthorized use of the institution's facilities.

16.7 Where Previous Management Theories Might be Absorbed within the Broader Concept of Collaborative Working

The last fifty years or so have seen a plethora of management philosophies or methodologies which have, in their various ways, sought to deal with the problems of how best to create coordination between individuals to achieve consolidated institutional direction. Management thinking in the first half of the twentieth century could be characterized as an initial move towards the adoption of the practices of industry to management and to knowledge working. The work of a number of key management thinkers developed and refined the concept that management could be explained in objective, scientific terms:

- Frederick Taylor (who defined management in scientific time-and-motion-study terms in *Scientific Management*, 1947, Harper and Row).

- Max Weber (who applauded the role of charismatic authority in *The Theory of Social and Economic Organisation, 1947*, The Free Press).

- Peter Drucker (who is credited by Tom Peters with the creation of the discipline of management) represented management as a "hard science" in such works as *The Practice of Management*, 1954, Harper & Row).

These works predated the opportunities for degrees of distributed operation and joint participation offered by electronic communication. The following section provides the merest hint of the theories of more recent writers and suggests ways in which their philosophies can contribute to the development of a model for collaborative working.

16.7.1 Relationship with Representative Management Philosophies

Business process reengineering (Reengineering the Corporation, Michael Hammer and James Champy, 1993, Harper Collins)

Hammer and Champy demonstrate the value of seeing tasks as being performed by identifiable and continuous processes. These processes should be simplified and rationalized, or preferably eliminated entirely, with resulting savings in cost and time. One key contributor to this improvement is electronic communication which enables barriers between organizational functions to be broken down to the point where clients are provided with a single point of contact and where tasks are performed as a coherent process and not as a series of disjointed sequential steps. They outline examples where tasks have been restructured: serial tasks each performed by an expert in that task - as would be the case before the advent of robotics in vehicle mass-production - are replaced with single individuals performing all tasks related to a single process but with access to a limited number of specialists to provide collaborative advice on complex individual cases.

Empowerment (Men and Women of the Corporation, Rosabeth Moss Kanter, 1997, Basic Books)

Rosabeth Moss Kanter describes the "post-entrepreneurial enterprise" by empowering all staff with the ability to make decisions without the constant need for control from their seniors. This concept is encapsulated in the acronym PAL: *Pool* resources, *Ally* to exploit an opportunity and *Link* systems in partnerships. This could be a definition of asynchronous collaborative working, in which the most admired characteristics of management move from outdated "predictability" to the ability to take executive decisions based on an understanding of corporate policies as well as local situations.

Hierarchy of needs (Motivation and Personality, Abraham Maslow, 1970, Harper & Row)

Maslow provided the academic justification that individuals come to work for more than just the need to earn money and gain security. He was an optimist who noted the role of personal satisfaction and fulfilment of ambition as a major (if not the sole) source of motivation. This philosophy is widely recognized and practiced among most staff in universities, if not in many commercial enterprizes. Maslow provides the justification for the willingness to trust staff and share responsibility for collaborative endeavors.

Lateral thinking (The Use of Lateral Thinking, Edward De Bono, 1967, McGraw Hill)

Edward de Bono's concept of thinking differentiates lateral thinking from vertical thinking - *i.e.*, from traditional sequential thinking. Vertical thinking is a step-by-step process; lateral thinking operates by innovative leaps into uncharted waters. This disparity between thinking styles mirrors the difference between traditional hierarchical organizations, and inter-functional *ad hoc* collaborative groups.

Theory X versus theory Y (The Human Side of Enterprise, Douglas McGregor, 1960, McGraw-Hill)

McGregor formalized the distinction between authoritarian and participative (*i.e.*, collaborative) management into Theory X and Theory Y. Theory X is based on the assumption that staff are all lazy and antipathetic to work: only the stick can motivate them. Theory Y assumes that people need to work and that they actively seek responsibility and the satisfaction that comes from achievement. Theory Y has been refined in more recent years as experiments have shown that even individuals inclined to a Theory Y approach, still value some structure and predictability in the workplace. Theory Y is facilitated by collaborative approaches.

The prototyping or rapid application development (RAD) concept

The IT industry itself has explored the problems of developing systems to time, cost and functionality. Since the mid 1950s many practitioners (Martin, Jackson, Yourdon, Gane and Sarson) have sought to tackle the problem of delivering systems effectively. Particularly in the early years, they mostly involved a structured, engineered approach. This was appropriate where vast teams of specialists were required before the days of development tools with high functionality. The RAD concept not only exploits the capabilities of new software tools, it also exploits the concept of collaborative working between small teams.

Management Teams (Management Teams, Meredith Belbin, R. 1981, Butterworth-Heinemann)

Belbin extends the concept of multi-discipline teams. He identifies multi-personality teams where the personal and cultural styles of participants are also balanced to form a coherent whole. His view would be that a team with all the right technical skills can fail if everyone wants to be boss, or if internal personality conflicts emerge. This is a crucial consideration for collaborative ventures: a team comprising all egomaniacs or all subservient servants is not likely to achieve. [1]

---

[1] I can recommend a slim volume which has routed me to becoming acquainted with some of the major writers on management thinking: Kennedy, Carol (1991), *Guide to the Management Gurus*, Business Books Limited.

16.8 Conclusions

The purpose of this chapter has been to explore the impact and relevance of formal collaborative working on the management of universities, especially in an increasingly commerce-like environment. It is my conclusion that formal collaborative working could have a major role to play in making HE institutions more efficient without imposing draconian controls over financial administration, enforcing robotic management processes or impinging upon academic freedom on teaching and research.

However, there are some critical messages:

- Implementation: some formal planning and management of the development of collaborative working is required. A solely organic approach to development is unlikely to produce the required results in the time or to the quality needed.

- Culture: a greater willingness genuinely to share information and trust teamwork is required. This may be an Elysian ambition; it would be totally unrealistic to C. P. Snow but such defensive strategies - hidden agendas and so on - are inimical to the collaborative approach.

- Management: a greater willingness to accept formal management thinking is required. I have found formal management training and practice very helpful in actually getting things done. There is too great a willingness in universities to condemn all formal management thinking as pretentious self-indulgence. There are some very attractive babies in with the bathwater.

- Technology: this must be seen as the infrastructure upon which the new types of cultural relationships can be built. However seductive some of the technology is, it is a means not an end. The Web is a case in point. For all the potential, and many valuable contributions by the Web to genuine collaboration, I can see it also as a hindrance. Far too often self-proclaimed exponents of collaborative working respond to accusations that they have not actually shared anything with "but it's on the Web." The Web can be a defence against the need to collaborate.

While some degree of collaborative working has emerged in UK universities, there remain many unexploited opportunities for improving the management processes. This will need a formal institutional will, acceptance of cultural change and a major management project to develop and fund it. The continued competitiveness and effectiveness of the UK HE sector requires such a commitment.

Acronyms

ANVAR	Agence Nationale de Valorisation de la Recherche
ARIADNE	Alliance of Remote Instructional Authoring and Distribution Networks for Europe
CA	Communication Apprehension
CAL	Computer Aided Learning
CATT	Computerized Argumentation based Teaching Tool
CMC	Computer-Mediated Communication
CSCL	Computer Supported Collaborative Learning
CSCW	Computer Supported Collaborative Work
DOLS	Domino Off-Line Services, http://www.lotus.com/dols
DTD	Document Type Definition
E-seminar	Electronic seminar
ESL/EFL	English as a Second Language or as a Foreign Language
FAQ	Frequently Asked Questions
FCE	Future Computing Environments
FTP	File Transfer Protocol
GIF	Graphics Interchange Format
GUI	Graphical User Interface
GVU	Graphics, Visualization, and Usability
HCI	Human Computer Interaction
HEI	Higher Education Institution
HERDU	Higher Education Research and Development Unit
HTML	Hypertext Markup Language
HTTP	Hypertext Transfer Protocol
IEEE	The Institute of Electrical and Electronics Engineers

IMS	Instructional Management Systems
JCIEL	JISC Committee for Integrated Environments for Learners
JDBC	Java Database Connectivity
JISC	Joint Information Systems Committee, http://www.jisc.ac.uk/
JPEG	Joint Photographic Experts Group
LAN	Local Area Network
LOM	Learning Object Metadata
LTSC	Learning Technology Standards Committee
MALTED	Multimedia Authoring for Language Teachers and Educational Developers
MBA	Master of Business Administration
MD	Managing Director
MOO	MUD, Object Oriented
MUD	Multi-User Domain
NJIT	New Jersey Institute of Technology
OHP	Overhead Projection
PBS	Public Broadcasting Service
PHP	Hypertext Preprocessor
PSOL	Program on Social and Organizational Learning
RL	Real life
SQL	Structured Query Language
SSL	Secure Sockets Layer
TACO	Teaching And Coursework Online
TIES	The Institute for Educational Studies
UCL	University College London
URL	Universal Resource Locator
VLE	Virtual Learning Environments
VUW	The Virtual campus at the University of Waterloo
WfMC	Workflow Management Coalition
WWW	World Wide Web
XML	eXtensible Markup Language

Index

LB 2395.7 .D54 2002

The digital university